COGNITION AND SOCIAL BEHAVIOR

List of Contributors

ROBERT P. ABELSON, *Yale University*

JANET BERL, *Carnegie–Mellon University*

EUGENE BORGIDA, *University of Michigan*

JOHN S. CARROLL, *Carnegie–Mellon University*

RICK CRANDALL, *University of Illinois*

ROBYN M. DAWES, *University of Oregon* and *Oregon Research Institute*

BARUCH FISCHHOFF, *Oregon Research Institute*

IRENE HANSON FRIEZE, *University of Pittsburgh*

DAVID GREENE, *Carnegie–Mellon University*

DAVID L. HAMILTON, *Yale University*

DAVID KLAHR, *Carnegie–Mellon University*

GORDON LEWIS, *Carnegie–Mellon University*

SARAH LICHTENSTEIN, *Oregon Research Institute*

REBECCA SUE MORRISON, *Carnegie–Mellon University*

GERALDINE NAGY, *Kansas State University*

RICHARD E. NISBETT, *University of Michigan*

JOHN W. PAYNE, *Carnegie–Mellon University*

HARVEY REED, *University of Michigan*

CHARLES F. SCHMIDT, *Rutgers University*

RICHARD SCHULZ, *Carnegie–Mellon University*

JAMES SHANTEAU, *Kansas State University*

HERBERT A. SIMON, *Carnegie–Mellon University*

PAUL SLOVIC, *Oregon Research Institute*

RICHARD STAELIN, *Carnegie–Mellon University*

SHELLEY E. TAYLOR, *Harvard University*

COGNITION AND SOCIAL BEHAVIOR

Edited by

JOHN S. CARROLL
JOHN W. PAYNE

CARNEGIE-MELLON UNIVERSITY

LAWRENCE ERLBAUM ASSOCIATES, PUBLISHERS
1976   Hillsdale, New Jersey

DISTRIBUTED BY THE HALSTED PRESS DIVISION OF
JOHN WILEY & SONS
New York   Toronto   London   Sydney

Lawrence Erlbaum Associates, Inc., Publishers
62 Maria Drive
Hillsdale, New Jersey 07642

Distributed solely by Halsted Press Division
John Wiley & Sons, Inc., New York

Library of Congress Cataloging in Publication Data

Symposium on Cognition, 11th, Carnegie-Mellon
    University, 1975.
    Cognition and social behavior.

    "Collected papers of the eleventh annual
Symposium on Cognition, held at Carnegie-Mellon
University in April, 1975."
    Includes bibliographical references and index.
    1. Cognition—Congresses. 2. Social
psychology—Congresses. I. Carroll, John S.,
1948– II. Payne, John W. III. Carnegie-Mellon
University. IV. Title.
BF311.S83   1975   153.4   76-48939
ISBN 0-470-99007-4 (Halsted)

Printed in the United States of America

Contents

Preface

This volume presents the collected papers of the Eleventh Annual Symposium on Cognition, held at Carnegie–Mellon University in April, 1975. These papers are unique in the history of these symposia for their orientation toward the study of social behavior. This symposium brings together the two fields of social psychology and cognitive psychology in response to a growing desire among many social psychologists to seek out or develop a more systematic body of theory, and a corresponding desire among many cognitive psychologists to study the everyday affairs of people outside the laboratory.

The initial idea for this symposium grew out of the mutual interests of the editors. Our collaboration, as one social psychologist and one cognitive psychologist, on the parole decision-making project (Chapter 2) seemed to us so natural and synergistic that we were led to examine our work as a model of an approach. We began to discover parallels between issues and research in social psychology and their counterparts in cognitive psychology. The integration of our separate backgrounds served functions that seemed widely applicable, and we felt that the symposium could bring this into sharper focus.

Participants for the symposium were initially chosen because they were doing work that bridged social psychology, cognitive psychology, and real-world problems. However, this loose structure coalesced during the paper writing, presentations, and meetings of the symposium. Instead of a diverse collection of papers needing extensive introduction, explanation, and summation, what emerged were several themes and concrete examples of the fruits of this joint approach. In particular, the four discussion papers at the symposium, by Taylor (Chapter 5), Greene (Chapter 10), Klahr (Chapter 15), and Simon (Chapter 16), served so well to tie the papers together that the idea of an introductory chapter became superfluous. Instead, we will briefly state the themes brought out in these papers. These themes cut across the organization of the book, which is primarily by content area, and so provide a different way to read the papers. A suggestion especially relevant for the theme-oriented reader is to begin with Simon (Chapter 16), who deals with themes and the symposium as a whole.

Cognitive Limitations

Nearly all the chapters embody the principle that people are limited information processors. Operating in a complex world, people necessarily develop coding schemes and strategies to reduce complex tasks to manageable proportions. Because people are adaptive to situational demands, their responses at times resemble the output from optimal statistical decision rules. However, the processes that people use to generate responses may be quite diverse and may differ markedly from optimal decision procedures.

Dawes (Chapter 1) illustrates this by showing how predictions of human potential, such as response to clinical treatment or academic success, typically rest on the strong but false belief that intuitive judgments are better than actuarial predictions. Dawes labels this "cognitive conceit"—an inflated belief in our judgmental abilities. This cognitive conceit has an important corollary, in that errors in judgment are attributed to the intrusion of motivational needs instead of inherent limitations of judgment. Dawes examines this idea in the context of the Viet Nam War, where prowar and antiwar groups have viewed their own opinions as correct and the opinion of the other side as motivated by inner needs ("imperialists" or "nervous nellies"). A more reasonable view would have ascribed these differences to the different information utilized by each side.

Hamilton (Chapter 6) brings an exciting new approach to research on stereotypes. He shows how the processes of categorization and attention deployment inherent in social situations are sufficient to produce group stereotypes apparent in both evaluation and behavior. This is a strong counterpoint to the theory that stereotypes necessarily have a motivational or factual basis.

Nisbett, Borgida, Crandall, and Reed (Chapter 8) demonstrate that attempts to alleviate depressive emotions by informing the person that other people also have problems may have failed because people do not utilize abstract information about "other people." Instead, people are strongly affected by concrete information about specific people, a fact that has broad implications for theories of behavior and behavior change.

Slovic, Fischhoff, and Lichtenstein (Chapter 11) provide new insights into the problems of policy making about important and risky social decisions, such as flood insurance and nuclear power plants. They point out that cognitive limitations are equally apparent in expert decision makers and laymen when they are assessing the potentials of low-frequency disasters. Without extensive previous experience from which to draw statistical predictions, policy makers must recognize the effects of cognitive limitations on their own and the public's judgments of risk.

Concern with Process

Along with the principle of cognitive limitations, most chapters exhibit a concern with process. Not content to compare peoples' behavior to optimal decision rules, the authors seek to discover what processes occur in the various situations considered, what people actually do. For example, several contributors explore the strategies or rules of inference used by people in such situations as parole applications (Carroll & Payne, Chapter 2), consumer purchases (Staelin & Payne, Chapter 12), college selection (Berl, Lewis, & Morrison, Chapter 13), and dating preferences (Shanteau & Nagy, Chapter 14).

Accompanying the concern with process is the introduction of a new methodology drawn from information-processing psychology. Taylor (Chapter 5), Klahr (Chapter 15), and Simon (Chapter 16) point out that this transmission of theory and method across disciplines has made only initial progress. However, Carroll and Payne (Chapter 2), Frieze (Chapter 7), and Staelin and Payne (Chapter 12) introduce methodological innovations to their respective areas of interest. Schmidt (Chapter 4) makes the most serious use of information-processing techniques by developing a formal model of the way people determine the causes of social events, the attribution process, through computer simulation. Given background information and a description of an event, this model "recognizes" the motives and plans of people and can respond to such questions as "Why did this event occur?"

Two contributors present a more broadly theoretical discussion of the processes used by people in social situations. Abelson (Chapter 3) offers a general model of attitudes and behaviors based on the concept of "scripts," which are expected sequences of events of varying abstractness used to evaluate, predict, and generate specific instances. Greene (Chapter 10) suggests that social behavior can be conceptualized in terms of more or less ill-structured problems, in which individual differences contribute to the definition as well as the solution of such problems.

Causal Attributions

A great deal of recent work in social psychology has been concerned with the proposition that people engage in a process of making causal attributions—trying to determine the causes of events. From this perspective, people are seen as desiring to know the causes of events in order to understand, predict, and control their social world. A person's beliefs about the causes of an event mediates the person's response to that event. This mediation is exemplified by the concepts of responsibility, intention, and disposition, which pervade our legal, moral, and social institutions, as well as our personal lives.

Carroll and Payne (Chapter 2) examine the parole decision as an instance of attributional judgments. The parole board, and other parts of the criminal justice system, are concerned not only with the severity of a crime, but also with an evaluation of the criminal—his responsibility, the reasons for the crime, and the risk involved in release. Attributional concepts therefore provide several insights into the parole decision-making process.

Frieze (Chapter 7) outlines the importance of attributions in academic settings where achievement tasks continually provide success and failure experiences that can be interpreted in many ways. She demonstrates that attributional judgments may be based on a very selective examination of information instead of an assessment of all the relevant factors.

Schulz (Chapter 9) investigates the more general issue of feelings of control over situations. He demonstrates that a decisive feature of the institutionalization of the elderly is the deprivation of control experiences. The experimental reintroduction of control to the elderly results in enhanced psychological and physical well-being.

Natural Situations

Finally, the chapters evidence the joint desire of cognitive and social psychologists to investigate complex natural situations and social problems. This desire is manifested in the use of broad and diverse populations of subjects, bringing a balanced approach to research that has often dealt only with laboratory situations and college students. These real-world issues include political ideology (Dawes, Chapter 1); crime (Carroll & Payne, Chapter 2); group prejudice (Hamilton, Chapter 6); scholastic achievement (Frieze, Chapter 7); the emotional state of depression (Nisbett *et al.,* Chapter 8); old age (Schulz, Chapter 9); public policy, including flood control and nuclear power plants (Slovic *et al.,* Chapter 11); consumer purchases (Staelin & Payne, Chapter 12); choice of college (Berl *et al.,* Chapter 13); and interpersonal attraction (Shanteau & Nagy, Chapter 14).

Simon (Chapter 16) concludes with the argument that cognitive psychology and social psychology are fundamentally the same, so that serious efforts to merge the ideas and concerns of the two disciplines can be important and fruitful. His paper therefore provides philosophical and theoretical grounds in support of the approach taken in this book.

We would like to express our sincere gratitude to Betty Boal and Lou Beckstrom for their assistance at innumerable times with the symposium and the preparation of the book. We would also like to thank Helaine Carroll, who let these manuscripts share the family vacation on Cape Cod, and kept John Payne fueled with brownies. The 1975 symposium was supported in part by Public Health Service Research Grant MH-07722 from the National Institute of Mental Health, and in part by the Psychology Department at Carnegie-Mellon University. Editorial preparation of this book was supported by Grant DAHC19-75-G-0011 from the United States Army Research Institute for the Behavioral and Social Sciences. The views expressed herein are the authors' own and do not necessarily reflect those of the Department of the Army.

Part I

DEVELOPING A COGNITIVE
SOCIAL PSYCHOLOGY

The chapters in this section present viewpoints of a theoretical or paradigmatic nature outlining possible approaches to a cognitive social psychology—the study of social behavior based solidly on knowledge of the processes of human thinking.

Dawes (Chapter 1) examines how judgments about people rest on our inflated belief in our cognitive abilities and the accompanying belief that errors are motivational in origin and demonstrates this in diverse areas, including graduate student admissions and attitudes toward the Viet Nam War.

Carroll and Payne (Chapter 2) utilize the parole decision as a setting in which to apply recent theoretical formulations in social psychology and information-processing psychology.

Abelson (Chapter 3) presents a broad new theory of attitudes and behaviors based on the concept of "scripts," which are expected sequences of events of varying abstractness used to evaluate, predict, and generate specific instances.

Schmidt (Chapter 4) develops a formal model of the way people determine the causes of social events, the attribution process, through computer simulation.

Taylor (Chapter 5) contrasts the paradigms of social psychology and cognitive psychology and examines the problems and prospects of a cognitive social psychology.

1
Shallow Psychology

Robyn M. Dawes

University of Oregon
and
Oregon Research Institute

PHILOSOPHICAL BACKGROUND

Although the overall philosophies of Plato (1942), Aristotle (1934), and Freud (1952) were different in many ways, they had at least one view in common: the human soul—or psyche—or mind—was viewed hierarchically; the bottom levels of this hierarchy corresponded to "lower" or vegetative or animal functions, whereas the highest level corresponded to the uniquely human reasoning capacity—or conscious part of the ego. For Plato, the levels were animal, spirited, and rational. For Aristotle, the levels were vegetative, animal, and rational. And for Freud they were the id (wholly unconscious), the unconscious parts of the superego and ego, and the conscious part of the superego and ego.

For all three philosophers, inter- and intrapersonal dysfunction was to be explained in terms of the "interference" of a lower level with the functioning of a higher level. For Plato, for example, cowardice in battle resulted from interference of the animal function of survival with the spirited function of conflict, whereas stupid decisions among philosopher–kings might result from spirited ambition interfering with rationality (hence they could not own property). For the Catholic Church (heavily influenced by Aristotle), dysfunction resulted from the basic "desires of the flesh" interfering with higher spirituality and reason (St. Augustine, 1953). Freud, whom some Christian theologians have regarded as something of an anti-Christ, has reinforced this viewpoint; the whole concept of "depth" psychology is that something comes from deep within the id or nearby—either an unconscious need or equally unconscious defense mechanisms against it—to mess up our ordinary pursuit of life, liberty, and happiness.

The recent "cognitive revolution" (Littman, 1969) has challenged the assumption that cognitive dysfunction is necessarily due to interference from noncognitive sources. People's cognitive capacities are limited (Fitts & Posner, 1967; Slovic, 1974); rationality is "bounded" (Simon, 1957); just as the psychoanalytic theorists have talked about nonoptimal functioning arising from "psychic economics," it is now legitimate to talk about such malfunctioning arising from "mental economics" (Abelson, 1974).

Perhaps the greatest contribution of "information theory" to psychology was not that it presented a precise quantitative measure of "information"—which never led to much (Coombs, Dawes, & Tversky, 1970)—but that it allowed psychologists to think in terms of quantity of thought in a behavioristic *zeitgeist* in which such concepts as "mental effort" were derogated. Indeed, some of those who first discuss "information" as a technical concept now talk about "simple representation" or "*Pragnanz*" in broader terms (Attneave, 1959, 1974), whereas the early findings that people are "limited information processors" in a technical sense (Miller, 1956) have led to the general conclusion that we are "limited." These limitations do not, however, come from deep within the id—but from the "mind of man" (Slovic, 1974). In retrospect, it is somewhat surprising that we psychologists have not emphasized such limitations earlier— because so many of our disappointing students crump out or flunk out partly because they are unable or unwilling to put forth the mental effort to understand our not too difficult field. (For years, however, we have eschewed the idea of cognitive limitations by sending such people to psychotherapists or counselors, on the grounds that although their "heads" have needed examining, the real source of the problem has lain elsewhere. Cognitive incapacity was assumed to result from mental illness, which was emotional, not mental.)

I believe that it is not necessary for me to recount for this audience the many cognitive limitations that have been catalogued and investigated in the past several years. These range from an inability to integrate information (Einhorn, 1972; Hoffman, Slovic, & Rorer, 1968) to systematic biases in estimating probability (Tversky & Kahneman, 1974). In fact, there is some evidence that people cannot even keep two distinct "analyzable" dimensions in mind at the same time (Shepard, 1964), especially if they are asked to make judgments in which information about one of these dimensions may be missing (Slovic & MacPhillamy, 1974).

What I should like to do instead is to discuss two areas in which the belief that human cognition is sacrosanct and that dysfunction must be explained in noncognitive (i.e., motivational) terms *may* have led to an important misunderstanding and counterproductive, "irrational," behavior. I emphasize the term "may" because I am talking about my own observations about these areas and not about any systematic, hypothesis-based experiments.

THE ASSESSMENT OF HUMAN POTENTIAL

One of the first areas to be investigated by clinical psychologists, as the profession grew rapidly after World War II, was the degree to which human judgment could be used in the prediction of such variables as patient responses to treatment, recidivism, or academic success (Sarbin, 1943). What could such judgment add to predictions that could be made on a purely statistical basis by, for example, developing linear regression equations?

In the early 1950s, Meehl (1954) reviewed approximately 20 studies in which actuarial methods were pitted against the judgments of the clinician; in all cases the actuarial method won the contest or the two methods tied. Since the publication of Meehl's book, there has been a plethora of additional studies directed toward the question of whether clinical judgment is inferior to statistical prediction (Sawyer, 1966) and some of these studies have been quite extensive (Goldberg, 1965). Meehl (1965) was able to conclude, however, some 10 years after his book was published, that there was only a single example in the literature showing clinical judgment to be superior, and this conclusion was immediately disputed by Goldberg (1968) on the grounds that even that example did not show such superiority. I know of no subsequent examples, following the customary rules of the game, that have purported to show the superiority of clinical judgment.

The first of these rules is that the validity of the statistical prediction versus the clinical judgment both be evaluated by correlations between predicted and obtained scores on some measurable criteria. Although the nature of such criteria has come under attack (Holt, 1970), there is no reason to believe clinical intuition to be superior at predicting some unmeasurable criterion (usually "long range"), or that a correlation coefficient is not a reasonable, although flawed, measure of predictive accuracy. The second rule is that both the clinical prediction and those of the statistical model be made on the basis of the same codable input. But while the clinician may have access to variables that cannot be coded without his or her presence—for example, feelings of liking or disliking a patient or potential graduate student—there is no reason to believe that such variables cannot be coded. For a fuller discussion of the findings and the limitations, see Dawes and Corrigan (1974, pp. 97 and 98).

What effect did all this research have on the actual practice of clinical psychology? Almost zilch. Clinicians continue to give Rorschachs and TATs, to interpret statistically unreliable differences on subtests of the WAIS with abandon, and to attempt clinical integration of the data. The belief that clinicians somehow can do better than a statistical model, can integrate the information from such diverse sources into a reasonable picture of their clients, persists despite lack of supporting evidence.

More recently it has turned out that optimal statistical models are not the only ones that outperformed clinical intuition. In a business context Bowman (1963) and in psychological judgment contexts Goldberg (1970), Dawes (1971), and Wiggins and Kohen (1971) have suggested that models based on the clinicians' judgment could outperform the clinician. That is, if a "paramorphic" (Hoffman, 1960, 1968) model of an expert judge can be built, there is the "intriguing possibility" (Yntema & Torgenson, 1961) that this model may in fact outperform the judge on whom it has been based. Empirical research overwhelmingly supported this "bootstrapping" idea. It was thought that bootstrapping worked because the model abstracted the implicit weighting of the clinician while doing away with the unreliability of the particular judgments. But Dawes and Corrigan (1974; see also Dawes, 1975b) pointed out that the superiority of such "bootstrapped" models over the clinical judge involved only one of two possible comparisons—that of the judge with his or her model. The other possible comparison involved that of the judge with any reasonable statistical models. Dawes and Corrigan formed *random linear, models,* in which the coefficients were chosen in the right direction but otherwise randomly. Such models also outperformed expert human judges in a wide variety of contexts. Once the predictor variables were scaled in such a way that higher values were related statistically to higher criterion values, the weights associated with these variables were not very important. Unit weights did even better than random weights, as follows from a simple mathematical inequality (Ghiselli, 1964; Dawes, 1970). As Dawes and Corrigan concluded (1974, p. 105), "The whole trick is to decide what variables to look at and then to know how to add."

This conclusion does not say a great deal for the human capability of intuitively integrating information from various sources to reach an accurate conclusion. But then the experimental work referenced earlier should have led us to expect that conclusion. Wilks, as far back as the late 1930s (Wilks, 1938) showed that various linear composites with weights in the same direction would correlate highly with each other. It follows that if linear composites with optimal—i.e., "proper"—weights outperform human intuition by a wide margin, then so many linear models with nonoptimal—i.e., "improper"—weights, provided they are in the appropriate direction. Recent work by Wainer (1976) and Einhorn and Hogarth (1975) has supported this conclusion. Dawes (1974) has maintained that the expertise of good judges lies not in integrating information but in knowing how to code the important variables, a conclusion reached earlier in the area of medical expertise (Einhorn, 1972, 1974) and chess expertise (deGroot, 1965; Simon & Chase, 1973).

What effects have these new findings had? I cannot be sure, but let me give you some anecdotes from the area in which I am very involved—that of admitting students to graduate school. Some four universities that I know of are now using linear composites, at least as an initial screening device. Many people concerned with graduate admissions express outrage over such a "dehumanizing" device. As one dean wrote, "the correlation of the linear composite with future faculty ratings is only .4, whereas that of the admissions committees' judgment correlates .2. Twice nothing is nothing." In response, I can only point out that 16% of the variance is better than 4% of the variance. To me, however, the fascinating part of this argument is the implicit assumption that that other 84% of the variance is predictable and that we can somehow predict it.

Now what are we dealing with? We are dealing with personality and intellectual characteristics of people who are about 20 years old, and what we are hoping to predict is some vague future criterion of professional success or self-actualization that could not be meaningfully assessed until at least 10 or 15 years later. Why are we so convinced that this prediction can be made at all? Surely, it is not necessary to read *Ecclesiastes* every night to understand the role of chance; nor is it necessary to reread *Julius Caesar* to understand that there is a tide in our affairs that must be taken at the crest or its momentum lost. Moreover, there are clearly positive feedback effects in professional development that exaggerate threshold phenomena. For example, once people are considered sufficiently "outstanding" that they are invited to outstanding institutions, they have outstanding colleagues with whom to interact—and excellence is exacerbated. This same problem occurs for those who do not quite reach such a threshold level. Not only do all these factors mitigate against successful long-range prediction, but studies of the success of such prediction are necessarily limited to those people accepted, with the incumbent problems of restriction of range and a negative covariance structure between predictors (Dawes, 1975a).

Consider now the variance that is predictable. What makes us think that we can do a better job of selection by spending 15 minutes looking at applicants' transcripts and reading their letters of recommendation, or by interviewing them for a half hour, than we can by adding together relevant (standardized) variables, such as undergraduate GPA, GRE score, and perhaps ratings of letters of recommendation. The most reasonable explanation to me lies in our overevaluation of our cognitive capacity. And it is really cognitive conceit. Consider, for example, what goes into a GPA. Because for most graduate applicants it is based on at least $3\frac{1}{2}$ years of undergraduate study, it is a composite measure arising from a minimum of 28 courses and possibly, with the popularity of the quarter system, as many as 50. The evaluations in these courses are at least quasi-independent. For whereas some students of small colleges may bring their reputations with them, professors do not generally check on previous GPA before assigning a grade in a course (even though a good Bayesian may someday suggest such a procedure). Surely, not all these evaluations are systematically biased against independence and creativity. Yet you and I, looking at a folder or interviewing someone for a half hour, are supposed to be able to form a better impression than one based on $3\frac{1}{2}$ years of the cumulative evaluations of 20–40 different professors. Moreover, as pointed out by Rorer (1972), what you and I are doing implies an ability to assess applicant characteristics that will predict future behavior differently from past behavior; otherwise, why not just use past behavior as the predictor? Those who decry the "dehumanization" of admitting people on the basis of past record are clearly implying such an ability. Finally, if we do wish to ignore GPA, it appears that the only reason for doing so is believing that the candidate is particularly brilliant even though his or her record may not show it. What better evidence for such brilliance can we have than a score on a carefully devised aptitude test? Do we really think we are better equipped to assess such aptitude than is the Educational Testing Service, whatever its faults (Brill, 1974; Dawes & Hyman, 1971)?

I am not saying that there are no important variables that are often left unassessed by GPA and GRE. What I am saying is that we are unable to assess them on the basis of the data typically present in application folders, or on the basis of interviews. As Goldberg (1968) has pointed out, the answer to the problem is research designed to assess the relevant dimensions (which should be combined in a mechanical form). I am therefore entirely in sympathy with Dalrymple's recent plea that new criteria for admissions to medical school be used "so that those students can be admitted whom one can safely predict will be able to learn and use the intellectual tools that an excellent physician must possess . . ." (Dalrymple, 1974, p. 186). The question is, how can one "safely predict" such use? My answer is to orient our efforts toward isolating and evaluating the personality dimensions that involve such use—not to continue kidding ourselves that we can do so intuitively, in a burst of cognitive insight or by abandoning reasonable criteria simply because they are flawed—e.g., ignoring GPA because some students with a 3.3 are better than are some with a 3.9. How are we to tell which?

Yet another argument I have encountered against the use of linear composites for admitting graduate students is that it is not fair to minority groups. Is vague judgment better? I agree with Darlington (1971) that the best way to make decisions about how to favor members of minority groups is to do so explicitly, by making group membership a factor in the linear composite. Such a feature has a clear disadvantage of susceptability to lawsuits from majority group members, but it has the advantage of making the admissions committee face the question of minority group applications squarely and explicitly. Attempts to define "fairness" without building in such an explicit (biased) procedure have not been very successful (Cleary, 1968; Cole, 1973; Einhorn & Bass, 1971; Schmidt & Hunter, 1974; Thorndike, 1971).

Of course, admissions committee members may wish to use clinical judgment in deciding how various variables should be weighted and so may object to an actuarial formula with weights that have been determined a priori. The point is, however, that the variables themselves are better evaluated by past behavior or specialized test than by intuition, and the combining of the variables—whatever weighting scheme is desirable—is better done explicitly than implicitly.

We seem to believe that we are much better processors of information than we actually are, however, and as a result we continue unjustifiable clinical practices involving important decisions about other people's lives.

CONFLICT ABOUT THE VIET NAM WAR

Here, I am on even less solid ground. Let me just give you a few impressions, based primarily on my own activities in the (Eugene) "McCarthy movement." My analysis concerns the controversy in the United States about continuing the war.

Briefly, I would like to suggest that each side viewed the controversy mainly in motivational terms rather than cognitive ones—which resulted in a tragic inability to communicate about the problem. The antiwar people were perceived to be "nervous nellies," whereas those in favor of continuing were judged to be "imperialists" who were primarily motivated by some sort of greed for offshore oil, or something or other. Various chants ("Hey, hey, LBJ, how many kids did you kill today!") suggested that those in favor of the war enjoyed killing, whereas those opposed to the war were often regarded as cowards. The result was that each side attempted to justify its own position by pleading its own moral goodness and courage—which, of course, were irrelevant—and each side merely became enraged when the other accused it of turpitude.

An alternative explanation of the conflict is that it was caused primarily by different cognitive beliefs about what was going on in Viet Nam—differences resulting in large part from relying on different information sources. The hawks tended to rely on official government pronouncements, and the government in turn tended to rely on information coming "through channels" rather than directly from the field (Halberstam, 1972). In contrast, the doves obtained much of their information from writings and television appearances of field reporters, such as Sheehan and Halberstam.

But it is not easy to conceptualize two different people looking at the same reality and coming to different conclusions because their information sources are differently biased. It is easier to think of conflict in terms of differences in goals—as those of two football teams each wishing to win. The "mental economics" of the situation led to an impasse, with the result that the problem stayed, and stayed, and stayed.

That two different people looking at the same reality can, however, come up with completely different conclusions is well illustrated in an anecdote from Halberstam (1972):

> Westmoreland had demanded the briefing and the young American had been uneasy about giving it, apologizing for being so frank with a reporter present, but finally it had come pouring out: the ARVN soldiers were cowards, they refused to fight, they abused the population, in their most recent battle they had all fled, all but one man. That one man had stood and fought and almost single-handedly staved off a Vietcong attack. When the officer had finished his briefing, still apologizing for being so candid, Westmoreland turned to McGinniss and said, "Now you see how distorted the press image of this war is. This is a perfect example—a great act of bravery and not a single mention of it in the *New York Times*" [p. 581].

(Of course, there may be motivational as well as cognitive components in this example.)

One of the minor ironies of the controversy was that the single American politician who had enough insight into his limited intellectual capacity to understand that he had been "brainwashed" (Romney) immediately eliminated himself from presidential contention, on the grounds that such an admission was *prima facie* evidence of stupidity—not insight. So it goes (Vonnegut, 1969).

In sum, the present analysis of the Viet Nam controversy follows very much the philosophical viewpoint enumerated by Hammond (1974), who writes:

> ... the explanatory value of motivation has been exaggerated in any event, and ... more of our energies should be directed toward the analysis of the cognitive difficulties inherent in policy formation, rather than continuing to perpetuate the belief that all our difficulties follow from self-serving judgments [p. 1].

Further,

> The conventional explanation of barriers to social problem-solving implicitly suggest that man's cognitive capacities *would* be adequate—were it not for self-seeking motives which distort and degrade such capacities. The cognitive explanation to be offered here, however, suggests that man's cognitive capacities are *not* adequate for the tasks which confront him [p. 4].

CONCLUSION

In these two examples, I have hoped to show that our cognitive limitations are greater than we believe them to be, that we insist in the face of contradictory evidence that we can do more than we do, and that we tend to ascribe conflicts that can be explained on cognitive terms to motivational variables. Why? Again, the answer can be found in our cognitive limitations. First, confidence in our view of reality may be a function not so much of the accuracy of this view as of its simplicity. Dawes (1964) showed that when people remembered hypothetical, complex, political situations incorrectly as simple, they were more confident than when they remembered them correctly as complex. Kahneman and Tversky (1973) have shown that redundant personality profiles engender greater confidence in prediction than do nonredundant ones— even though the latter contain more information. Manis and Platt (1975) have shown that people choose and have more confidence in redundant messages meant to specify a target than in nonredundant messages, again even though the latter contain more information and specify the target more accurately. The view that we would all function well cognitively were it not for motivational biases and "depth" factors is indeed a simple one, hence one engendering confidence.

Finally, our own cognitive limitations may lead us to confuse the cumulative technological advances of our society with the power of a single human mind. The fact that a lot of us with the aid of a printing press, telephone, and verbal communication can create an H bomb does not mean that any of us singly can think very straight.

Not only may dysfunction and conflict arise from cognitive limitations, therefore, but our inability to grasp the role of such limitations may itself result from our limited cognitive capacity.

Although I have taken my examples from social psychology, I should like to conclude from a book on human performance, because the author seems to arrive at very much the same conclusions as I have. In discussing conscious thought, Posner (1972) writes:

> The studies discussed so far give rise to the view that human judgments involve a greatly simplified view of reality. . . . [In contrast], pattern recognition occurs effortlessly and with much less conscious involvement than the simple judgments discussed above. This suggests that more complex judgments may be made when appropriate memory structures evolved from past experience allow the judgment to bypass highly conscious processing. Memory structures which can be accessed effortlessly may be involved, for example, in the development of skills achieved by chess masters, or experts within any field [p. 83].

and later:

> It is difficult to maintain in consciousness a single cource of stimulation or a single subject matter for any length of time. The mind tends to wander. The difficulty of maintaining accurate attention is a prime problem in thinking [p. 128].

To paraphrase: conscious judgment—as opposed to automatic processing based on vast experience—is feeble. Yet it is precisely this sort of feeble conscious processing on which most people rely when attempting to solve most interpersonal and intrapersonal problems. This feebleness alone—without the help of motivational factors—may account for many of our disasters.

ACKNOWLEDGMENTS

This research was supported by the National Science Foundation, Grant No. SOC-7103827.

2

The Psychology
of the Parole Decision Process:
A Joint Application
of Attribution Theory
and Information-Processing
Psychology

John S. Carroll
John W. Payne

Carnegie–Mellon University

In this chapter we bring together two historically distinct areas within psychology as they bear on a "real-world" problem. Our purpose is to explore how theoretical and empirical work arising from laboratory studies of causal attribution and information processing in judgment can be examined, extended, applied, and unified in the context of the parole decision.

We have chosen to focus on the decision to grant parole as an initial place to examine recent theoretical formulations in psychology for several reasons. First, the issue of deviancy is of fundamental importance to the functioning of human society. Crime is perhaps the most important form of deviancy and currently is the top concern of residents in cities of all sizes (Gallup, 1975). Although the causes of deviancy are complex, many sociological theorists have argued that society's perception of and response to individuals is central to the creation of a deviant career (e.g., Becker, 1963). In the case of a person who commits a crime, this response is most formally codified in our system of law. Yet, despite centuries of experience in developing an elaborate set of procedures and codes, the legal system operates only through the application of individual human judgment to unique cases. Therefore, there exists tremendous variability at all levels of the societal response to the deviant, e.g., sentencing (Hogarth, 1971) and parole (Kingsnorth, 1969).

Second, the parole system has become increasingly important in the criminal justice system with the growing prominence of the indeterminant sentencing paradigm (Miller, 1972). The determination of the actual duration of prison term has become to a great extent the province of parole boards rather than judges.

Third, attention has recently been focused on the need to understand the processes by which the parole decision maker integrates the information he or she has about an individual into a judgment or decision. Previous research approaches to the parole decision have concentrated on describing the relationships of the decision maker's information to the output by correlational techniques (e.g., Scott, 1974) or on improving the decision by making better information available to the decision maker (e.g., prediction tables; Singer & Gottfredson, 1973). However, after reviewing the results of a major project devoted to aiding parole selection, Gottfredson, Wilkins, Hoffman, and Singer (1973) have concluded that, before more progress is probable in improving the parole phase of the correctional system, "fundamental research" is required and that "one important area is that of investigation of the processes of decision-making" (p. 43). In the words of Carter (1967), "The decision-making process is perhaps the most important—and least understood—single dimension of the correctional system" (p. 203).

Fourth, the parole decision clearly involves the active acquisition and use of information about a parole applicant, guided by knowledge the decision maker already has. In other words, the parole decision is an instance of *person perception,* in that the decision maker is called on to examine information about a person, sometimes including a face-to-face interview, and evaluate the person, utilizing any available personal, professional, and cultural sources of knowledge. Issues that have been labeled in the person perception literature as first impressions, stereotypes, similarity-attraction, and so forth, are of obvious importance. The particular concern of this chapter is how the parole decision maker generates a *causal attribution* to explain why the crime has occurred and how this affects the parole decision. The parole decision is also an instance of the exercise of *human judgment,* in which the person has available certain information that must be combined into an overall evaluation pursuant to the goals of the task. It is highly relevant to examine this process utilizing findings from judgment research: what information does the person actually use, for what information does the person search, what information does the person already have, and how is it activated in a given instance, how are these data combined into a single judgment—what are the strategies or heuristics employed by decision makers to turn the parole decision into a manageable task? It is also of central importance to examine how the joint operation of phenomena investigated as person perception or human judgment become understandable as a single process.

Finally, a considerable body of research is developing that describes the parole decision from several viewpoints, in particular the studies summarized in Gottfredson *et al.* (1973), and this serves as a ready data base with which to develop hypotheses.

PAROLE DECISION MAKING

The evaluation of information in parole decision making seems to relate to two primary concerns of the parole authority: punishment and parole risk. For example, Kastenmeier and Eglit (1973) claim that parole board members examine an offender's past history on the basis of two premises: "One is that the board is a moral arbiter, considering a man's past and the offense which he has committed as elements in the decision as to the duration of his present confinement. The second is that the past is indicative of the future" (p. 507). Additional support for this view may be found in studies by Hoffman (1973) and Wilkins, Gottfredson, Robison, and Sadowsky (1973). Hoffman, for instance, has shown two case factors to be most important in predicting youth parole selection: severity of offense (perhaps relating to a concern with accountability, sanctioning, or the serving of a sufficient minimum time) and parole prognosis (relating to a concern with public safety or risk of parole violation). Two other factors studied, institutional discipline and participation in institutional programs, did not contribute as much to prediction.

These results, although admittedly preliminary, suggest an intriguing first approximation of the parole decision process based on a simple two-part model. In the first part, the primary concern of the decision maker is to make the punishment fit the crime. This part requires the decision maker to evaluate the severity of the offense and to determine what will be the sufficient minimum time to be served. Research has shown the agreement on offense severity among parole board members to be high (Hoffman, Beck, & De Gostin, 1973) and for agreement to exist between criminals and guards (Sechrest, 1969). However, there is little evidence whether such a high level of agreement exists between severity of offense and the minimum time to be served.

At the second part of the parole process the primary concern of the decision maker is with parole risk, i.e., the probability that the person being considered for release will again violate the laws of society. The basic model of indeterminate sentencing is that the criminal not be released into society until he is treated or reformed (Miller, 1972), i.e., no longer "dangerous" (Schwitzgebel, 1974; von Hirsch, 1972). In many ways this stage of the parole process may be the most complex. The decision maker must estimate the parole risk and then combine that judgment with other factors into a decision as to when an inmate is to be released. The experience on which the decision maker draws "consists of more or less systematic knowledge about human beings generally and criminals particularly, as well as the separate experience reported or directly observed with each unique individual on whom decisions must be made" (Glaser, 1964, p. 289). We believe that it is in the judgment of risk that parole board members

exhibit the greatest amount of difference, both in how they combine information and in which information they consider important.

A FRAMEWORK FOR THE PAROLE DECISION PROCESS

From our viewpoint, the parole decision process utilizes elements of information
provided in the case, which are sought and interpreted by an active process
within the decision maker. This process calls on the previous knowledge, beliefs,
attitudes, rules of inference, etc. that the decision maker has, which help him to
direct his examination of the information in a way that conforms to the task
structure (making a parole decision).

In Fig. 2.1 we present a preliminary representation of the parole decision task
designed to provide a framework for the reader. The decision maker is provided
with information about the parole applicant (A), and possibly with information
about other people, for example an actuarial prediction (B). Not all of this
information is used or even looked at, but it is available for use. The arrow from
A to D is labeled "a" to indicate that there is a process occurring which selects
and interprets from A; we address this process specifically in one study reported
in this chapter. Similar complexities exist for all the connections in this framework. The information from the task (A and B) and information from the
decision maker's beliefs (C) are utilized by strategies, heuristics, rules, schemas,
or thought models (C) to provide inferences and judgments about the case (D).
From these inferences, judgments of the punishment (E) and risk (F) aspects of
the parole decision are made and lead to the final decision regarding parole (G).
In its present form, this representation can claim to be nothing more than an
organizing tool, not a model in any formal sense. The following discussions
attempt to fill in the picture to some appreciable extent.

Attribution Theory Approaches

It is a general principle of person perception that behavior is not simply judged
by its objective components. Instead, behavior is always an interpretation on the
part of the observer, a set of inferences that partly ignore and partly go beyond
whatever "act" has been performed. In the case of a criminal act, the law
recognizes that the objective crime, as a broken law (*actus reus*), is only part of
the story. There is also a state of mind (*mens rea*) without which the person is
not legally responsible for the act. Even young children utilize information
about a person's intentions when judging the goodness or badness of that person
after some bad act has been performed (Suls & Gutkin, 1973). More generally,
the concern with fitting the punishment to the person, not to the crime, has
generated the indeterminate sentencing paradigm with parole as its gatekeeper.

In the past 15 years, social psychologists have developed a theoretical frame-

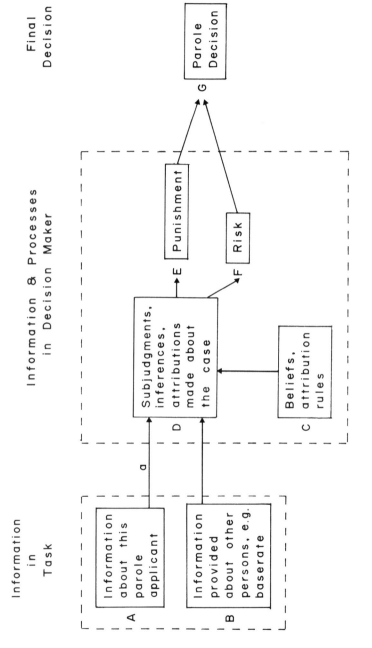

FIG. 2.1 Framework for the parole decision process.

work that may be used to address this issue. This approach, attribution theory, is concerned with how people interpret information about their own behavior and the behavior of others in making judgments about the causes of events, and how these judgments are used and so affect the person's behavior. Attribution theory attempts to specify not the "real" cause of behavior, but how a person infers or attributes cause and what happens once he does. As originally proposed by Heider (1944, 1958), the theory is based on the principle that people attempt to determine the causes of events in order to predict and control their social world. We propose that judgments about people who commit crimes, including the parole decision, are at least in part attribution judgments: to what extent has this person been responsible for the act and to what extent does this reflect a disposition to act in such a manner, i.e., criminality? Attribution theory offers many insights into how the parole decision is made. In this section of the chapter we explore four.

The covariation principle. Kelley (1967, 1971) has proposed that people determine the cause of a behavior by examining the covariation between the effects and possible causes of the behavior and then attributing the effect to the cause with which it covaries. He suggests that people process covariation information in a manner analogous to the way a statistician performs an analysis of variance across three factors: persons, time, and objects/situations. Covariation of an effect within a person over time is called "consistency." The extent to which an effect is localized across objects and situations is called "distinctiveness," and the extent to which an effect is found across people is called "consensus." For example, the set of events—I have always loved my wife, I do not love other women, everyone else loves my wife—is attributed to my wife's great lovability (high consistency, high distinctiveness, high consensus), but if I love all women and no one else loves my wife, it is attributed to my great lovingness. Evidence in support of these principles can be found in Frieze and Weiner (1971), McArthur (1972), and Orvis, Cunningham, and Kelley (1975).

Of concern in the parole decision is the extent to which a person is held responsible for a crime and the extent to which punishment and parole prognosis (see Fig. 2.1) rests on the crime being attributed to the person (e.g., criminality). The covariation principle offers specifications of data about the crime and the criminal that can lead to the assignment of high or low responsibility and risk. The effect of consistency is that the more often a person commits a criminal act, the more likely he is to be judged personally responsible for the crime. The effect of distinctiveness is that the more the person displays criminal behavior only in restricted circumstances, the less he may be held responsible for the crime (e.g., when he is ill, only when in the company of his criminal friends). The effect of consensus is that crimes which fewer people commit are judged the responsibility of the person more than crimes which many people commit.

The prediction for consensus information is of particular interest because controversy has recently arisen over the usefulness of consensus or base-rate information for judgments of causal attribution (Nisbett, Borgida, Crandall, & Reed, Chapter 8) and prediction (Kahneman & Tversky, 1973). In addition, the utilization of base-rate information, such as experience tables, has been a major issue in parole decision research (Hoffman & Goldstein, 1973) and policy making. Glaser (1964) states that "Parole boards face the problem of how to integrate intimate knowledge of characteristics of a particular prisoner with general knowledge about broad categories of offenders. This is one of the most persistently perplexing difficulties of judicial and correctional decision making" (p. 289). Base-rate information is represented as B in the framework presented in Fig. 2.1.

In a pilot study, we asked 32 subjects to rate 20 crime labels (e.g., forcible rape, theft of vehicle for resale, income tax evasion) on several characteristics, including the severity of the crime, how frequent the crime is, how responsible the person who commits the crime is for the crime, and how criminal the person is. Multiple-regression analyses revealed that responsibility was solely a function of severity, whereas criminality was primarily a function of severity with a very small trend for less frequent crimes to be judged the product of a more criminal person (with severity partialled out). More controlled studies will be conducted to explore this issue.

The dimensional approach.   A second major theoretical and empirical body of work on attribution theory is that of Weiner and his associates (Weiner, 1974; Weiner, Frieze, Kukla, Reed, Rest, & Rosenbaum, 1971). They have provided evidence that attribution judgments are divisible into two dimensions,[1] and that the dimensions have separable effects on judgments of punishment and risk. The first dimension, locus of control, considers whether the behavior has originated with the person (ability and effort) or outside the person (task difficulty and luck). The second dimension, stability, considers whether the causes of behavior are stable over time (ability and task difficulty) or variable over time (effort and luck). Research has shown that rewards and punishments or affective responses are mediated by judgments of locus of control. For the same performance, subjects punish most those people who do not try, especially if they have high ability (Weiner & Kukla, 1970). Piliavin, Rodin, and Piliavin (1969) have shown that a person is helped more when his distress is seen as externally caused (illness) than internally caused (drunk, also a failure of effort). Expectancies for future performance, however, are dependent on judgments of stability (Frieze & Weiner, 1971; Valle & Frieze, 1976).

---

[1] Recent work has demonstrated that a third dimension, intentionality, may be important in some of the effects attached to locus of control.

The thurst of Weiner's work in relation to the parole decision is that the two components of the parole decision—punishment and risk—may be mediated by different attributional cues. Punishment may be primarily a judgment based on the locus of control of the criminal behavior, particularly inferred effort. The judgment of risk, in contrast, may be based on the stability of the inferred causes—ability and task difficulty. Hence, an attribution to dispositional factors (e.g., aggressiveness, criminality) would lead to high judgments on both punishment and risk, or the least chance of parole. Attributions to lack of effort to avoid crime (e.g., laziness, mood, did not resist temptation) would lead to high punishment but low risk. Attributions to task difficulty (e.g., his friends, poverty) would lead to low punishment and high risk. In Figure 2.1, these attribution judgments would take place in D, using attributional rules from C and information from A, B, and C.

Hedonic relevance.   Jones and Davis (1965) have proposed that the extent to which an act has consequences for the observer, its hedonic relevance, increases dispositional judgments of the causes of the act. Although the people affected directly by a crime do not judge the criminal in the parole system, we assume crimes the observer himself is concerned about or fears to have higher hedonic relevance in judging a perpetrator of such a crime. To be a useful prediction, this should say something more than the effect of severity, although it is obvious that the primary determinant of the fear of a crime is probably its severity. These feelings about crimes would be part of the beliefs represented in Figure 2.1 as C.

In the pilot study described in the previous section, subjects were also asked to evaluate how much they feared a given crime happening to themselves or their family. The multiple-regression analysis showed judgments of responsibility again to be related only to severity, but judgments of criminality revealed a trend for crimes rated as more feared to be considered more dispositionally caused (with severity partialled out). Again, further research is planned to investigate this issue.

Attitudes of the decision maker.   Wilkins et al. (1973) found that individual parole decision makers considered different items of information important and processed them in different ways. Wilkins and co-workers have suggested that decision makers are of several "types" and that these differences between types are of importance in the parole decision. Kingsnorth (1969) also found wide variation in the use of information by parole agents.

One source of these individual variations in evaluations of parole cases may be the person's "theory" or beliefs about what the principle causes of crime are and what function punishment has as a response to crime. Miller (1973) considers these beliefs to be ideological in nature: the ideological right believes there has been too much leniency toward crime and an erosion of respect for authority; the ideological left believes people are stigmatized as criminal partly on the basis of stereotypes and thereby led into a criminal career. The right blames the person for his acts and advocates punishment, the left blames the social system for crime and seeks to divert the person from institutions or rehabilitate him.

These variations can be conceptualized within an attribution framework relating them to social psychological research. A basic attribution dimension is the degree to which events are seen as internally caused by actors or externally caused by the environment. These beliefs are represented in Fig. 2.1 as C. Individual predispositions to attribute events to traits or dispositions in others, rather than to situations, have been measured by Nisbett, Caputo, Legant, and Maracek (1973). Reed and Reed (1973) found that persons who attribute criminality to dispositions state they prefer less contact with criminals in public or private. A related construct is the extent to which events are seen as controlled by the person, rather than luck or powerful forces, measured by Rotter's (1966) Internal–External Locus of Control Scale. Sosis (1974) found that internals judge defendents more responsible for an automobile accident, indicating a projection of their internality.

Individual beliefs about the causes of events, crimes in particular, therefore lead to consideration of different information about a parole applicant, different inferences about the responsibility of the person for the crime, and different conclusions about the appropriate handling of the case. The study described at the end of this chapter further develops these conceptions.

We have discussed how certain principles from attribution theory may be applied to an investigation of the parole process. In the next section of this chapter we discuss some findings from studies of information processing in decision making and how these results may also be applied to an investigation of the behavior involved in parole decision making.

Information-Processing Approaches

Heuristic processes in judgment. Research in cognitive psychology has made it clear that an individual is a limited information-processing system (cf. Newell & Simon, 1972). In particular, the active processing of information occurs in a memory of limited capacity, duration, and ability to place information in more permanent storage. As a result, people appear to utilize heuristics that serve to keep the information-processing demands of a task within the bounds of their limited cognitive capacity. Heuristic processes "are problem-solving methods that tend to produce efficient solutions to difficult problems by restricting the search through the space of possible solutions, on the basis of some evaluation of the structure of the problem" (Braunstein, 1972, p. 520). Simon and Newell (1971) have proposed that the central process in human problem solving is the use of heuristic methods to carry out highly selective searches of problem spaces. This use of heuristics by individuals, although usually sufficient, can lead them to ignore or misuse items of rationally useful information (Slovic & Lichtenstein,

1971). Parole decision making is obviously sufficiently complex to require the same general type of cognitive processing.

For example, part of the parole decision process involves intuitive prediction, i.e., judgments of parole risk. Kahneman and Tversky (1972, 1973) have demonstrated that humans often resort to heuristic procedures when faced with such tasks as probability estimation and prediction. In particular, a heuristic called "representativeness" has been shown to be important in the process of intuitive prediction. The idea is that people predict the outcome that appears most representative of the evidence. Although this heuristic often leads to correct judgments, it can lead to large and consistent biases that are quite difficult to eliminate. The reason is that there are factors, such as the reliability of evidence and the prior probability of the outcome, which affect the likelihood of the outcome but not its representativeness.

This type of probabilistic information-processing bias is clearly relevant to judgments of parole prognosis, which in many situations involves combining case-specific information with actuarial base-rate information. One particular experiment by Kahneman and Tversky (1973) showed how, as predicted by the representativeness hypothesis, prior probabilities were largely ignored when individuating information was made available. The task was to judge the probability that a brief personality description, allegedly sampled at random from a group of 100 professionals—engineers and lawyers—belonged to an engineer rather than to a lawyer. One group of the subjects was told that the description had been drawn from a set that consisted of 30 engineers and 70 lawyers. Another group was told that the set consisted of 70 engineers and 30 lawyers. It can be shown that the likelihood that any particular description belongs to an engineer rather than a lawyer should be strongly influenced by the prior base-rate information.

In contrast to the normative expectations, the subjects under the two base-rate conditions produced essentially the same probability judgments. Apparently, the psychological procedure employed by the subjects in making their intuitive predictions was dominated by the representativeness heuristic. That is, the important determinant seemed to be the degree to which the descriptions were representative of the two stereotypes, lawyers or engineers, with relatively little regard for prior probabilities or base rate. Kahneman and Tversky (1973) called this "perhaps one of the most significant departures of intuition from the normative theory of prediction" (p. 243). Similar findings regarding the overdependence on case-specific information and neglect of base rates have been observed in a variety of situations (e.g., Lyon & Slovic, 1975; Meehl & Rosen, 1955; Nisbett et al., Chapter 8).

These results are of special importance in view of the report by the National Advisory Commission on Criminal Justice Standards and Goals (1973) regarding the use of actuarial devices, which suggests that the optimal parole decision process should utilize both actuarial and individual case methods. An exploratory study on the use of experience tables in parole decision making was conducted by Hoffman and Goldstein (1973). They found some effect of experience tables. However, as Hoffman and Goldstein note, the limitations of their study are such that "the empirical data should be interpreted extremely cautiously in that they suggest rather than confirm the various relationships" (p. 17).

Clearly, research is needed on the basic question of how parole decision makers utilize base-rate information. Referring back to Fig. 2.1, note that a specific investigation of how parole decision makers combine case-specific information (A) and base-rate information (B) into a final judgment of parole risk (F) provides data relevant to the theoretical issue of whether people operate as naive statisticians (Kelley, 1967, 1971) or use heuristics, and to the practical issue of the value of base-rate information in the parole decision.

Two other forms of probabilistic judgment that have been investigated in laboratory studies are perceptions of correlation and causality. Both would seem important to the study of predictions of parole prognosis. Chapman and Chapman (1969) have described a phenomenon that has been labeled "illusory correlation." They presented judges with two pieces of information about patients in a clinical judgment situation. Later the judges estimated the frequency of cooccurrence of particular combinations of the two variables. They found that a person's prior expectation of a relationship between two variables could lead him to perceive correlation when it did not really exist. The illusory correlation was extremely resistant to contradictory data. It was noted that experts in judgmental situations might be reinforced by the reports of their colleagues, who themselves might be subject to the same illusion. Slovic (1972) has observed that "Such agreement among experts is, unfortunately, often mistaken as evidence for the truth of the observation" (p. 6).

Tversky and Kahneman (1974) have offered an explanation of the illusory correlation phenomenon in terms of a judgment heuristic called "availability." According to the availability heuristic, one judges "the frequency of a class or the probability of an event by the ease with which instances or occurrences can be brought to mind" (p. 1127). Clearly the judgment of how frequently two variables cooccur can be based on the strength of the associative memory bond between them.

Judgments of an offender's chances for favorable parole outcome may also be determined, at least in part, by the use of the availability heuristic by parole decision makers. For example, a parole board member may judge the likelihood of successful parole of an inmate by how easy it is for him to think of persons with similar characteristics who have proved successful on parole.

Availability is a useful procedure for assessing frequency or probability, because instances of large classes of events are usually recalled better and faster than instances of less frequent classes. However, availability can also be affected by such factors as effectiveness of search set, imaginability, and other factors that affect memory without being related to frequency or probability. Consequently, the heuristic can lead to systematic errors, as was the case with the representativeness heuristic.

Task determinants of judgment. Research on cognition has also indicated that the human information-processing system is highly flexible and adaptive (Simon, 1969). In most situations, task characteristics strongly shape the possible ways people can structure their internal representation of the task and hence their information-processing behavior in that task. Within the context of the parole process, two task characteristics have already received attention (Wilkins, 1973). The issue has been raised by Wilkins that parole decision makers may make poor decisions "because there was too much information for human intelligence to cope with" (p. 190). Such a possibility certainly exists given what we know about the limited capacity of the human information-processing system. Results from a number of studies aimed at investigating the effect of amount of information available on judgment behavior (Einhorn, 1971; Hayes, 1964; Hendrick, Mills, & Kiesler, 1968; Jacoby, Speller, & Kohn, 1974; Oskamp, 1965) also seem to support such a possibility. In general, these studies indicate that the effects of increasing the amount of information are to increase the variability of the responses and to decrease the quality of the choices, while also increasing the confidence of the decision maker in his judgments (Slovic & Lichtenstein, 1971).

However, beyond just saying there may be a decrement in performance with increasing information overload, the important psychological question exists concerning how individuals go about dealing with an increasingly complex environment with a limited cognitive capacity. One possibility is suggested by the results of a study by Payne (in press). It was found that as the task became more complex, the decision makers often resorted to simplifying choice heuristics in an effort to reduce cognitive strain. This study used a combination of two process-tracing techniques, explicit information search and verbal protocols, to examine the information-processing strategies individuals used in reaching a decision. It would be interesting to use similar procedures to examine the effects of the amount of information available on the search and use of information by parole decision makers. The decision makers could be asked to explicitly search abstracted case files in which varying amounts of information were available. The expectation would be that the pattern of search, indicative of the heuristic (causal schema) being used to combine information, would differ systematically with the amount of information available.

Another task characteristic that has been of interest to researchers concerned with parole selection (Wilkins, 1973) deals with the interrelationships among sources of information. It is apparent from research on information processing in judgment that interrelationships among patterns of information can influence the manner in which a person utilizes fallable information when making a judgment. For example, Slovic (1966) found that when two important cues agreed in their implications, judgments were dependent on both cues. However, when the two cues had contradictory implications, subjects focused on one of the cues or turned to other cues for resolution of the conflict. Also, subjects were less confident about judgments made for inconsistent patterns of information. Slovic hypothesized that a cue regarded by a subject as having relatively low validity would be used in conjunction with a more valid cue only when it was consistent with that cue. An implication of this suggestion is that subjects may search for cues that are likely to be consistent with the more valid cue. More recently, Mertz and Doherty (1974) have also shown that intercorrelations among cues influence the strategies decision makers use to combine information into a judgment.

In an exploratory study of information use, it was found that parole decision makers had preferences for a method of information presentation which involved redundancy. Wilkins (1973) has recognized the possible importance of information about information in parole decision making and suggests that "correlated rather than uncorrelated items may be preferred" (p. 196).

A possible explanation for the suggested preference for correlated items of information can be given in terms of perceived confidence of judgment, an issue also discussed by Wilkins. We hypothesize that perceived confidence is an important factor in decision making and that it is determined in large part by the interrelationships among the information available to the decision maker. Specifically, it is suggested that perceived confidence or validity of a judgment increases with increased consistency among information, perhaps as a function of the representativeness heuristic (Kahneman & Tversky, 1973). It is further hypothesized that decision makers need to feel confidence or validity in their decisions and tend to search for information that is likely to increase perceived validity. In terms of interrelationships among cues, this implies that highly redundant or correlated sources of information are preferred.

A test of these ideas could be conducted using an information search procedure similar to that discussed previously. That is, an initial set of information about a parole applicant could be provided and an initial evaluation requested. The decision maker would then have an opportunity to search from additional information that would have items varying in their correlation with the original set while controlled for predictive validity. The use of this information could then be monitored and confidence judgments requested. The primary question of interest would be whether parole decision makers search through additional information in a way that implies a preference for sources of information that is redundant to the information already examined.

In summary, it is clear that relatively simple variations in the decision situation, such as the amount of information available and the intercorrelations among the information, can have profound effects on the information-processing strategies used by decision makers. However, there is much still unknown about information search and utilization in decision making in general, and by parole decision makers in particular.

Toward an Integration of Approaches[2]

Attribution theory proposes three classes of ideas: (1) that people spontaneously seek to determine causes for events; (2) that the making of an attribution involves the utilization of judgmental rules, such as the covariation principle; and (3) that attributions are a necessary mediating step in determining how to respond. Despite the centrality of cognitions to this theory, little interaction currently exists with cognitive psychology. The essential unity of thinking processes brings together the study of thinking in attribution situations and the study of thinking in other situations. It is our belief that the information-processing approach in modern cognitive psychology offers theoretical insights and methodological tools that can provide significant contributions to the study of causal attributions.

There has always been a strong effort in Kelley's and Weiner's attribution work to go beyond a description of what attributions are made to how they are made, a process level of analysis. The covariation principle suggests that people collect information along dimensions of time (consistency), object (distinctiveness), and actors (consensus) and evaluate this information in a manner analogous to the way a statistician performs an analysis of variance. Evidence supporting this essentially linear model has been found; yet there are important problems with the model. First, the moderate fit of a linear model may be more a description of the task than of the processes people go through in attributions. Linear models are in general a powerful description of responses at least in part because tasks are constructed so as to best approximate the linear model (Dawes & Corrigan, 1974). Second, evidence of limitations in the information-processing capacities of people suggests that operating as a naive statistician is very unlikely and that other processes are utilized to manage the data which may still produce responses resembling a linear type (e.g., Simon & Newell, 1971; Slovic & Lichtenstein, 1971; Tversky & Kahneman, 1974).

Kelley's own progression away from the covariation principle is evidence that the model has not been fully satisfactory. Orvis et al. (1975) proposed the idea that people have three "information patterns" or configurations of consistency, distinctiveness, and consensus information and that a presented pattern or partial pattern is evaluated by comparisons with the information patterns. This proposal is very similar to the representativeness heuristic of Kahneman and Tversky (1973). It is a much simpler strategy for information use, making more

---

[2] A more extensive discussion is presented in Carroll, Payne, Frieze, and Girard (1975).

modest demands on the attention, memory, and effort of the person, and is therefore more reasonable in the light of the limitations of the system.

Kelley's (1972, 1973; Cunningham & Kelley, 1975) concept of causal schemata is also a step away from the linear model of the covariation principle. Recognizing that people do not always have multiple observations from which to detect covariation (or the desire to do so), Kelley has proposed that information about related events and the present context is used to suggest a causal schema, which is then used to make attributions. Causal schemata specify the combinations of causes expected to generate a given event. Kelley has described three basic types of schema: (a) the multiple-sufficient schema states that any of several causes can produce the event; (b) the multiple-necessary schema states that two or more causes must be simultaneously present to produce the event; and (c) the multiple-compensatory or additive effects schema states that the magnitude of causes add up and one can compensate for another. Kelley (1972) suggests that "each person has a repertoire of causal schemata, each of which is evoked under certain circumstances" (p. 17). Research has shown that there is more use of the multiple-necessary schema with more extreme (Cunningham & Kelley, 1975) or more unusual (Kun & Weiner, 1973) events.

These schemata are directly parallel to decision models investigated by Einhorn (1970) and Payne (in press). The multiple-sufficient schema is similar to a disjunctive decision rule, in which preference for an object depends on that object's exceeding a standard on any attribute. The multiple-necessary schema is similar to a conjunctive rule, in which the object must exceed a standard on all relevant attributes. The multiple-compensatory schema is the common linear additive model. Einhorn (1970) found that different individuals used characteristic but different decision strategies in the same task, whereas Payne (in press) found that individual preferences for decision strategies depended on the nature of the task, specifically the complexity of the task.

The parallels between attribution theory and cognitive psychology led Carroll, Payne, Frieze, & Girard (1975) to argue for an information-processing approach to attribution theory. They proposed that the concept of contingent information processing (cf. Payne, 1973, in press) could be applied to the attribution process—that the pattern of causes and cues examined was contingent on an evaluation of some aspect(s) of the event. A growing number of findings in attribution theory point toward the utility of this interpretation:

1. McArthur (1972) has found that the pattern of attributions differs depending on whether the event is an emotion, accomplishment, opinion, or action. She also found that the use of consensus information depends on whether or not the stimulus is a person.

2. Cunningham and Kelley (1975) found that increasing the extremity of events led to different schemas being employed for different categories of events—e.g., competitive or affiliative. Our extensive knowledge of social events

is therefore brought to bear not simply on the choice of a cause for an event, but even in the determination of how to make that judgment—what information to utilize, what rules to follow, and so forth.

In order to understand processes such as these, which occur very rapidly and often without overt acts, it is necessary to have observational techniques that provide sufficiently dense measurement over time. Attribution theorists are postulating such rapid temporal processes (e.g., Weiner, 1974, pp. 8–31) and may benefit greatly from the accumulated research tools and process-tracing techniques that cognitive psychologists have developed for the study of human information processing. Process-tracing techniques provide a higher density of observations over the temporal course of the process than that yielded by the techniques typically employed in attribution studies, and this expanded set of methodological tools allows a closer observation of the attribution process.

A prime example of a process-tracing technique is the verbal protocol, the running record of everything the subject says while instructed to "think aloud" during the task. Verbal protocols can be used as a source of data against which to test a model, or as a data base from which to derive models of the underlying processes (Newell & Simon, 1972; Payne, in press). Some progress has been made in devising methods for encoding verbal protocols objectively and subjecting them to systematic analysis (Newell & Simon, 1972; Waterman & Newell, 1973). A second example is chronometric techniques, such as response time recording. In attribution theory, it is often postulated that there are several stages in the attribution process. If the intermediate stages do occur, then the attribution process should take less time when intermediate stages have already been completed. A third process-tracing technique is eye movement recording, which can establish to what subjects are attending, in what order, and for how long during the task (Russo & Rosen, 1975). Another related technique is "explicit information search," where subjects must select information sequentially and may choose types of information in any order and stop at any time. This technique has been proved valuable in decision-making research (Payne, in press) and has been used in attribution research by Frieze (Chapter 7).

As an example of the convergent approach to the parole decision process we have been discussing, we have run a study dealing with the effect of differences in the decision maker's attributional outlook on the type of information sought for the parole decision.

ATTRIBUTION BIAS AND INFORMATION SEARCH
IN PAROLE DECISIONS

The conceptualization of the parole decision that we have adopted (see Fig. 2.1) envisions the parole task as consisting of two subgoals: punishment and risk. Each of these subgoals is achieved by the decision maker working through various chains of inference. Attribution theory specifies that an important set of inferences involves the determination of cause or responsibility for the crime committed. In generating this causal attribution, the decision maker applies rules of judgment (e.g., covariation, "good patterns," schemas, and other heuristics) that lead him to examine certain types of information and combine them in various ways.

It is known that parole decision makers vary greatly in what information they use (Kingsnorth, 1969; Wilkins et al., 1973), and we hypothesized that these differences reflect what rules of judgment the decision maker has been utilizing to evaluate the parole applicant. For example, Rotter's (1966) Internal–External Locus of Control (I–E) Scale measures a general tendency of a person to feel in control over his life events, as opposed to being at the mercy of outside forces. If this indicates general tendencies to think about behavior, criminal behavior in this case, in different ways, it implies that different information can be relevant to the different "theories" people possess about crime causation.

Ordinarily, these chains of inference or subjudgments are not observable during the parole decision. One way to make them more observable is to use process-tracing techniques. For this exploratory study, we employed a system of information presentation that allowed us to monitor the information used by the decision makers. The order of use of information was used to indicate the kinds of inference the decision maker was engaged in making. In addition, verbal protocols have been collected and are to be analyzed at a later time in hopes of revealing in more detail the process of the parole decision.

Our study attempts to answer the question of whether people with differ- ent attributional "theories of behavior" utilize different categories of infor- mation in the parole task, presumably indicating different chains of inference or subjudgments.

Method

Forty-one college students, whose scores on the I–E scale had been previously obtained, were informed that they were to act as parole board members who were reviewing a parole applicant. They were to either accept or reject the person for parole. Each subject was run individually on two parole cases, in random order. Each case consisted of 24 categories of information that Wilkins et al. (1973) found to be used often by expert parole decision makers, e.g., age, offense description, type of prior convictions. The case labeled "Smith" was a real parole applicant taken directly from Wilkins et al. The case labeled "Jones" was constructed by us so as to be moderately different on the crime and background information. The 24 categories of information were printed on 3 × 5 inch cards inserted in envelopes arrayed on a board in two columns of 12, in a single random order. The subject could see the title of the category on the card (e.g., "age") but had to remove the card from the envelope and turn it over to get the information for the category (e.g., "person is 28 years old"). All the category labels were explained to the subjects. They were instructed that they could look at any cards they wished, in any order, and could stop at any time and give their overall evaluation of the case (parole/not parole). Subjects were asked to say the category label out loud when looking at a card to aid the experimenter in recording the order of use.

For the second half of the subjects (Nos. 21–41), the procedure was changed in two ways. First, it had been found that a few subjects read down the list of categories, apparently strongly affected by the ordering of the array of categories. Therefore, the order of categories was reordered randomly for each subject and each case. Second, subjects were instructed to "think out loud" and verbal protocols were taperecorded.

Results

Subjects were divided into three groups on the basis of their I–E scores: internals (2–8), middles (9–12), and externals (13–22). Mean ranks of category usage were computed for each group and comparisons were run between internals and externals.

An examination of individual responses revealed considerable differences in number of items examined (varying from four to all 24), which items were examined, and order of use. Across the three groups, strong similarities in category usage were apparent. When we focused our attention on the 14 categories used most frequently (14 was the average number of categories used, with no differences between groups), we found that only one significant and two borderline differences existed between internals and externals. However, an examination of the trends reveals a very interesting pattern: Internals examine information earlier that deals with the crime (crime description, cooperation with police, time served, time left on maximum sentence) and the person (age, prior arrests, previous parole revokations, education level, susceptibility to influence), whereas externals examine information earlier that deals with the environment (release job prospects, recent employment history) and the prison institution (disciplinary problems, changes in attitude noted, prior convictions).

Although such interpretations are ambiguous at best, the pattern does seem to state ideas roughly in accord with the internal–external dimension. This pattern is reinforced and qualified by an examination of the 10 categories used later, only one of which shows borderline significance. Externals looked earlier at living arrangements prior to jail, release living plans, and academic progress in prison. They looked at specific causes earlier: alcohol use, homosexuality, IQ, and drug use. Finally, externals looked at the base-rate prediction earlier. Internals examined financial resources and early home environment earlier than externals among these less used items.

Discussion

Our failure to find strong differences for the groups established a priori by the I–E scale is explicable in several ways. The task of making a parole decision draws on common knowledge shared by all people as a result of various mass media presentations of similar events. Subjects share some ideas of what to do. However, the details of the task were completely novel to our subjects. Individual task performance may therefore be affected by many extraneous factors, such as the order of presentation of information, the relative familiarity of certain category labels, attentional shifts, and so forth. These issues are quite different when dealing with expert decision makers, who have well-established and possibly trained responses to the task environment.

It is also quite possible that the I–E scale is not appropriate to the task. The I–E scale may not embody a set of opinions about the causes of behavior, or these opinions may not be applied to the parole task, or that application may effect the evaluation of information and not the choice of information.

However, the pattern of information use discussed previously is suggestive of meaningful differences between internals and externals. These can be summarized by saying that internals seem relatively more concerned with information about the crime and about the person, possibly dealing with the person's "criminal career." This may reflect a greater concern with punishment than with risk, although this is highly speculative. Externals seem more concerned with information about the environment the person has been in, is in (the prison), and will be in and about specific causes or deviant behaviors. Again speculating, this may reflect a relatively greater concern with risk, and the externals do examine base-rate predictions earlier.

The measures we used, both the I–E scale and the order of category usage, seem inadequate to resolve the many complexities and ambiguities present. The analysis of the protocols may provide new and more sensitive indicators of the processes of the parole decision, and the order of use of information may reemerge as a central variable when this added set of observations is available. We also wish to be sensitive to the many differences that can emerge when we move to an analysis of similar tasks performed by the expert parole decision makers.

CONCLUSIONS

This chapter represents, in our belief, an initial but productive synergy between psychologists trained in separate disciplines. Through a concern with a real-world problem, the issues of application and mutual extension of approaches from social psychology and cognitive psychology become clarified. Cognitive psychology offers a powerful set of theoretical ideas and methodological innovations, loosely termed the information-processing approach. However, this approach has achieved success in part by the restriction of problems to well-defined tasks with well-defined rules. The extension of this approach to poorly defined "social" problems is fraught with difficulty. In a sense, the social psychologist can act as a guide to describe and specify the domain of study. In return, the social psychologist receives a body of theory and enhanced observational tools with which to develop and extend theories of complex social behavior.

The parole decision has offered us an arena in which to learn a great deal about the theories and methods of a related discipline and has caused us to examine our own discipline in a productive way. In addition, we believe that real progress can be made in understanding human behavior in the parole decision, with implications for additional areas of behavior.

ACKNOWLEDGMENTS

Support for this work was provided in part by Public Health Service Grant MH-07722 from the National Institute of Mental Health, and Grant SOC75-18061 from the National Science Foundation.

3
Script Processing in Attitude Formation and Decision Making

Robert P. Abelson

Yale University

This chapter advances a theoretical position on social cognition that departs from views presently predominant among cognitive psychologists studying language, memory, and decision making and among social psychologists theorizing about attitudes and behavior. My disagreement with "classical" positions in these two subdisciplines is that they are overly elementaristic, stilted, and static. By contrast, concern with dynamic, natural cognitive processes has characterized the design of computer simulation models (Abelson, 1968) of human information processing, keyed by the pioneering work of Newell and Simon (1961) at Carnegie. It is therefore fitting for me to participate in the Carnegie Symposium to say, in effect, that the Carnegie School has long been on the right track, even though cognitive and social psychologists out there have been slow to get the message.

SCRIPTS

The theoretical ideas developed here can perhaps help to explain some of the puzzling and provocative findings in other chapters in this volume. The theory rests on the concept of a *cognitive script.* By "script" I mean a *coherent sequence of events expected by the individual, involving him either as a participant or as an observer.* Scripts are learned throughout the individual's lifetime, both by participation in event sequences and by observation of event sequences. (I am using "observation" in a very broad sense here, to include vicarious observation of events about which one reads.) Because individuals have different histories, they may learn some different scripts, although many scripts are culturally so overlearned that they are virtually universal. I hypothesize different kinds of scripts, varying in length of time frame, the number of active characters, and whether or not the separate events in the script are concrete or generic.

It is not central to my purpose in this chapter to develop a precise script taxonomy. (See Schank & Abelson, 1975, for background on the script taxonomy problem.) However, it is important to sketch my concept of the stages of development script material goes through in entering the long-term memory of an individual.[1]

The basic ingredient of scripts I label a *vignette*. This is an encoding of an event of short duration, in general including both an image (often visual) of the perceived event and a conceptual representation of the event. The conceptual representation would not itself be verbal, although it would be such that verbal inputs and outputs could be attached to it, as in Schank's (1975a) Conceptual Dependency theory. The perceptual image might include codes from various sense modalities, and also codes for experienced affect. With the caveats in mind that the image need not be visual nor the conceptual representation verbal, it is nevertheless a convenient shorthand to think of a vignette as "picture plus caption." Vignettes, in short, represent the raw constituents of remembered episodes in the individual's experience.

More interesting than the single vignette, however, is the script—a coherently linked chain of vignettes stored as a unit. If a single vignette is "picture plus caption," a chain is metaphorically a cartoon strip, a sequence of panels telling a story. The simplest version would consist of two panels, one setting up a situation and the second resolving it, for example, a transgression followed by a punishment, or a decision followed by success. Such simple chains constitute the simplest scripts. Before considering them further, let us first set forth a typology for the single vignette.

I hypothesize three processes applicable to the establishment of vignettes. First, vignettes may be stored as single experiences. Second, similarity groupings can then build up categorical vignettes instantiated[2] by many single experiences in a given type of situation. This higher level categorical grouping process is presumably accomplished with the aid of features abstracted from single vignettes. Features help not only to group similar experiences but also to differentiate contrasting experiences. With enough experience in a given domain,

---

[1] There is considerable similarity of parts of our position on memory with that of "episodic memory" theory (cf. Tulving, 1972), and the reader may also recognize essences from various developmental or personality theorists. We are claiming not the invention of an original "script theory," but the organized application of a set of available ideas to areas wherein they have been little used. We therefore do not attempt to unscramble the history of related ideas by referencing the many, many writers who have invoked scriptlike concepts.

[2] In Minsky's (1975) seminal paper on "frames," abstract knowledge structures are postulated that organize generic expectations about objects or situations. When a frame is involved in a particular instance, it is "instantiated"—that is, tokens are created to carry knowledge of a given type into the present instance, although still differentiating one instance from another.

an individual is able to pass to a third level of processing, in which lists of features can be processed instead of the individual or multiple vignettes from which they come. These three levels of processing move progressively from the concrete to the abstract, from the "episodic" to the "semantic." We refer to the three levels, therefore, as *episodic, categorical,* and *hypothetical.*

Chains of vignettes, i.e., scripts, can also be episodic, categorical, or hypothetical (mixed types are presumably possible, but we shall not explore that complication here). To illustrate the three script levels, consider a transgression and punishment script. A child may store an episodic vignette of "the time I sneaked a cookie" together with the subsequent "boy did I get spanked" vignette. This remembered sequence constitutes an episodic script. At a higher level, a generic vignette of doing forbidden things (under which is collected various transgression episodes) may be linked to a generic vignette of getting punished (under which is collected various punishment episodes) to form a categorical script. We view the causal conceptual chain (cf. Schank, 1975b) "Me doing bad things leads to me getting punished" as being stored with this categorical script as an extended "caption." The hypothetical, feature-processing script level is more flexible and complex, possibly including conditional and inferential concepts and abstract rules (Abelson, 1975b) and referring to different possible categorical scripts. "Me doing a bad thing could lead to my getting punished if my parents found out (unless 1 could make it look like my brother did it), but if it weren't too serious or they were in a good mood, or if I could sweet-talk my mother and she could get around my father, then maybe I'd just get a mild scolding." Such a hypothetical script (really, a script ensemble) abstracts critical features of alternative situations, and its employment involves reasoning about those features. Episodic material is not directly involved in a hypothetical script but is indirectly accessible from it through particular categorical scripts.[3]

We assume that scripts at all three levels are available to the individual in familiar content areas. For new material, however, episodic scripts must be constructed before categorical or hypothetical scripts can be established. In turn, the construction of episodic scripts depends on the chaining of episodic vignettes.

HOW THE SCRIPTAL VIEW DEPARTS
FROM TRADITIONAL COGNITIVE PSYCHOLOGY

Within cognitive psychology, there are various views of the nature of understanding. The dominant view, as expressed particularly by Anderson and Bower (1973), Anderson (1976), and Kintsch (1974), is that knowledge is represented

---

[3] In the context of general social behavior, a categorical script is what we have elsewhere (Schank & Abelson, 1975) called a "situational script," and a hypothetical script is what we have called a "planning script."

by propositional networks, and that understanding involves some form of matching of input to known propositions. In the abstract, it is not easy to fault this view. Knowledge obviously requires a network of some kind of conceptual representations (even if visual or motor or affective codes are involved), and understanding requires the use of knowledge. However, in practice there are implicit biases in this dominant view, which I think inhibit a good understanding of understanding.

Three of these biases are that the representation should be noncommital, formal, and surface oriented. In noncommital style, the usual proposed representations avoid primitive concepts. They are eclectically willing to accommodate any proposed proposition for storage in a knowledge base, without major reference to extensive reality. They therefore tend to be implemented with contextless sentential propositions expressing amiable foolishness such as, "In the park, the hippie kissed the debutante," or "The red triangle is above the blue square." In standard experimental designs, we find counterbalanced foolishness where arbitrary subjects and predicates are factorially varied. There are many advantages to using silly sentences in experiments—I have done it myself in studying subject induction (Abelson & Kanouse, 1966)—but exclusive reliance on them guarantees that no attention is paid to pragmatics, that is, to the effects of available episodic or categorical vignettes and scripts on the interpretation of language. A similar point has been made by Spiro (1975).

In one experiment (Abelson, 1974) I was able to show that in rapid sentential processing using the Sternberg (1966) paradigm, the gap in response times between semantic sense and nonsense was not as big as the gap between semantic sense and pragmatic sense. This casts doubt on the contention by Anderson and Bower (1973) that configural or Gestalt properties of sentences are not necessary to their memorization. Their support for this contention is based on silly sentences, which have no configural properties, and so the question is not resolved by their data. (Another more technical critique of their contention is provided by Foss & Harwood, 1975.)

Apart from criticism of specific results, the classical experimental orientation can be questioned because hypothetical vignettes are so often presented without context. The consequent cognitive processing is quite possibly very special and not at all representative of naturalistic processing based on familiar scripts. In part, this tendency is based on the felt need for tight experimental control, but in part it seems to be also based on an "academician's error." Because academicians devote (or aspire to devote) so much cognitive activity to formal operations on abstract materials, it is easy for them to fall into the view that such cognitive activity is generally characteristic. A contrasting view would be that concrete processing of episodic and situational material is often much more compelling. Because people are capable of formal operations does not mean that they prefer them. We shall attempt to justify these opinions in a discussion of script processing in decision making.

THE USE OF SCRIPTS IN DECISION MAKING

Let us consider decision-making contexts such as those discussed by Dawes in this volume (Chapter 1). A faculty admissions committee member must decide on the likely success in graduate school of a set of applicants. What kinds of cognitive processes can or does he go through for these decisions?

As Dawes has so forcefully noted, judges do not make accurate predictions based on combinations of prognostic cues; neither do they even make very good predictive use of individual cues—they behave no better than mediocre linear processors. Yet they often tenaciously resist the suggestion that their judgments ought to be superceded by a more efficient simple statistical model. Why is this? In part, judges may be willing to sacrifice a little predictive efficiency in order to retain a feeling of effectance in determining the fates of the applicants. However, a companion factor concerning the nature of the decision process must also be involved if even this explanation is to make such sense.

If we view the prediction of applicant success in terms of scripts, a minimum chain of two vignettes is required: (1) the applicant as presented in the application folder; (2) the applicant later as a (presumed) student, doing well or poorly. To make a scriptal prediction about a given new case, the judge must match the first vignette of a previously formed script to the new applicant and read off the second (outcome) vignette from the previous script. There are, as outlined earlier in this chapter, three levels at which scripts may originally be formed and therefore three levels of later use: episodic, categorical, and hypothetical.

In the episodic version, a past single case would be recalled, similar to the present applicant. ("Mr. Kolodny reminds me very much of Paul Pippik, who hung around for eight years never writing his dissertation. Let's not get into that again."). Two faculty members with whom I have discussed this process have confessed, smirking, that they are continually seeking as potential new success stories applicants who remind them of themselves when they were that age!

In the categorical variant, a generic type would be invoked by assimilating the applicant to a category ("She's one of those shy women types. They do well in courses, but don't have enough initiative in research," or "He's one of those guys who writes about all this existential stuff, and ends up wanting to go into clinical psych").

At a more abstract level, the applicant can be seen as a bundle of pros and cons, whose success is a hypothetical variable darkly contingent on all the important enumerable features. An obscure computation is necessary to compare one applicant hypothetically with another ("Her letters are better than his, although she's from a less well-known place. Her verbal GRE is much higher than his. On the other hand, he's had more math and his quantitative is higher. However, . . ."). It is at this level that judges evidently function as if they were mediocre linear processors. Introspectively, it is not much fun operating at this level, either—and the consequent decisions are conflictful and unconfident.

These three script levels implicate the judge as observer only. It is possible for the judge to use scripts involving himself as participant. An episodic script of this form would include the judge's initial (perhaps public) stance on a presented case and/or the later (perhaps public) consequences to the judge of the good or bad performance of the applicant. Instead of two vignettes in the script, there are therefore three or four by the inclusion of the judge's response(s) to the stimulus. ("When I saw Hartman's application, I told everybody there was a spark of genius in that kid. He's our most successful graduate, and now we have another applicant much like him." Likewise, "Oh, boy, did I make a fool of myself arguing for Frank Flake. I used up all my idiosyncracy credit on a bad risk, and I'm not going out on a limb for anybody like that again.") Similarly, there could be categorical scripts involving the judge as participant ("I have the best track record in this department for spotting good foreign applicants"). It is less intuitively clear what a hypothetical script with participant judge may be like, but presumably it includes attributes of the judge's diagnostic skills as moderating variables in the computation of the application's prognosis.

Surprisingly, not much is really known about the psychology of natural decision making. The field has been dominated by the model of rational man in economic theory. The decision maker has been seen as a processor of abstract features of the presented options. This is the most mathematically tractable thing to assume, and many of the laboratory decision tasks chosen for study are very well-structured in advance so as to encourage (or force) quantitative reasoning. When one studies messy, real-world decisions, however, either of the one-shot variety explored in this volume by Berl, Lewis, and Morrison (Chapter 13), or of the conflictful, nagging personal problem type (e.g., whether to give up smoking, Janis & Mann, 1976), it is clear that present mathematical decision models are nowhere near adequate to reflect actual cognitive processes or predict actual outcomes. In fact, the author of the most psychologically realistic of all available mathematical models of choice, the "elimination by aspects" model (Tversky, 1972), believes[4] that this model is only one of very many special-purpose components that can be called on by the comprehensive executive program of an individual decision maker.

The trouble partly lies, we believe, in the reluctance to theorize about concrete rather than abstract decision-making mechanisms. Almost all models invoke hypothetical rather than episodic or categorical script processing. There is obviously a great need and opportunity for a renewed empirical look at a whole range of naturalistic decisions. We offer here some speculative expectations on what such empirical study may reveal:

1a. The use of episodic and categorical scripts is very widespread in decision making, the rule rather than the exception.

---

[4] Personal communication, December, 1974.

1b. Available scripts of these types with high-valence outcome vignettes and the judge as participant will play an especially dominant role.

2. The more he is burdened with many similar decisions to make, the more a decision maker is likely to employ hypothetical processes.

3. The attainment of hypothetical processing mode on one decision task does not substantially generalize to another decision task. There is, in other words, repeated reversion to episodic mode on new decision tasks.

4. Hypothetical processing will be rated more socially desirable than episodic processing, especially by sophisticated judges. Thus there is a bias toward reporting hypothetical processing, especially under public rather than private conditions of protocol gathering or interview.

5. Sets of decisions made on the basis of episodic or categorical processing will weakly fit predictions from a feature processing model, because single "good" features will often (although not always) be contained in successful episodes. Weak fits by feature models therefore do not necessarily support hypothetical processing as the operative mode.

The general pattern of results and side effects in decision-making studies seems consistent with these speculations. In particular, the faculty judges and clinical psychologists who doggedly protect their privilege to make inefficient decisions can be viewed as indulging in episodic processing to which they are unwilling to admit publicly. What self-respecting faculty member would confess to being influenced by, say, the facts that the applicant grew up on the Lower East Side and got D's in Physical Education, because these things remind him of himself? Of course, such kinds of irrelevant facts in themselves would not be sufficient to lead a well-socialized judge to fight for a particular candidate—the general pattern of credentials (or a single salient feature) would have to be strong enought to put the candidate into the category of thinkable prospects. This is why, I believe, regressions of judges' ratings on individual relevant features come out nonzero but weak. Judges are attending somewhat to the relevant features but are repeatedly distracted by shifting irrelevant features that cue available episodic and categorical vignettes.

If this is true, then why don't judges who are given only the relevant quantitative information—the usual ground rule condition in the studies Dawes summarizes—make less ragged predictions? We hypothesize that concentrated practice with very large numbers of cases would be necessary to make a notable improvement in performance. In the "lens model" task, where subjects are presented with multiple cues probabilistically related to a criterion, it may take 80 or 100 cases, even with only two cues and the criterion outcome given, for subjects to learn the linear relations well enough to reach their asymptote of good prediction (Hammond & Summers, 1965). In judging student applicants or clinical cases, of course, the judge typically does not have before him the prognostic information from past cases side by side with their outcomes. He is therefore at a disadvantage if he undertakes hypothetical processing. Along the same lines, we note that in N. Anderson's (1968, 1974) studies of information integration, in which judges' impression ratings generally are closely fit by simple linear models, a considerable warmup period is required before the fits are good.

Several of the other chapters in this volume have aspects that may be covered by the above five hypotheses. In particular, the importance of the "risk" variable to parole board officers (Carroll & Payne, Chapter 2) seems very clearly consistent with Hypothesis 1b. The parole officer asks himself how likely the convict is to violate parole. Among the consequences of such a violation is that the parole officer would look like a damned fool and be subject to very embarrassing public recrimination. A participant—categorical script fits the phenomenon well ("This case smells like one of those where you're soft-hearted against your better judgment, the guy goes out and kills somebody, and then the newspapers are all over you").

Of course, we are only speculating here, without proof that this is what goes through the paroler's mind. Our aim is to call attention to a strong type of potential explanation of decision-making phenomena, a type has been almost entirely overlooked. There are a number of peculiar, unexplained findings in the literature on choices among gambles, for example the "Allais paradox" (cf. Coombs, Dawes, & Tversky, 1970, pp. 126—128), which might be explained by invoking some form of "damned fool" script.

Additionally, many of the surprising phenomena discussed by Slovic, Fischhoff, and Lichtenstein (Chapter 11) on judgments of risk make sense in terms of script processes: (1) in estimating probabilities of subsequent events, well-constructed scenarios may be accorded much more credibility than they deserve, distorting the probability judgments; (2) familiarity with a (low-probability) hazard seems to reduce its perceived risk; (3) hazards with delayed consequences are discounted; (4) society is more willing to save a known life in danger than to save a statistical life. It is fairly obvious how an appeal to script processes can give a psychological account for these and related oddities. What is less clear, it must be admitted, is where the boundaries of a script theory lie; that is, how we predict in advance that an episodic script process is going to deform decisions from a hypothetical baseline? Fortunately, the area is eminently researchable.

SCRIPT PROCESSES IN ATTITUDE FORMATION

The present state of attitude theory is frankly a mess. Various rationalizations have been offered for the failure of attitude measures to correlate with overt behavior (Abelson, 1972; Crespi, 1971; Dillehay, 1973; Kiesler, Collins, & Miller, 1969, pp. 22—38; Weigel, Vernon, & Tognacci, 1974; Wicker, 1971), revolving around the difficulty of accounting for situational variance. Extant solutions to the dilemma are not too inspiring, requiring such awkward concepts as "attitude toward the situation" (Rokeach & Kliejunas, 1972), or weighted linear combinations of behavioral intentions and behavioral norms (Ajzen & Fishbein, 1973). I think that the problem lies in supposing the reality of generalized abstract predispositions to respond to objects, especially objects not encountered in ordinary experience. What can be the meaning of attitudes toward Communism or school busing if one never encounters a Communist or that kind of school bus? A humble commonsense test of the nature of attitude is to ask what commerce the individual personally has had or anticipates with the object or any of its manifestations. In other words, that scripts involve the person and the object? In our view, *attitude toward an object consists in the ensemble of scripts concerning that object.* This view, combined with a fuller body of theory concerning how scripts are formed and selected, would give functional significance to the concept of attitude, a significance not clearly possessed by other definitions of attitude.

Not many social psychologists have taken this way of looking at attitudes, although there are some notable exceptions: Kelley (1972), Stotland and Canon (1972), and Tesser (1975) all use the term "schema" to refer to something similar to what we are calling a categorical script, and the "functional theory of attitudes" (Katz, Sarnoff, & McClintock, 1956; cf. also Smith, Bruner, & White, 1956) is on related ground, although it is much more depth motivational than the present more cognitively oriented view.

Why do psychologists so readily suppose that people think abstractly about social issues? As the chapter in this volume by Nisbett, Borgida, Crandall, and Reed (Chapter 8) makes graphically clear, abstract information has feeble effects compared to concrete information. Specifically, the impact of abstract base-rate information about the consensual frequency of an event has virtually no effect on judgments about the motives or future behavior of an actor, in comparison to "distinctiveness" information about other episodes involving the actor. A more recent study by McArthur (1976) has suggested that consensus information is weak in comparison to distinctiveness information, even when the agent of the event is a thing rather than a person. For example, in the sentence "The chemical harms the photograph," the chemical is still seen as primarily responsible for the effect even if almost every other chemical also harms this photograph. Several explanations have been proposed for this particular effect. I suspect that it is mediated by reference to vignettes in which the agent is (almost literally) "seen" as causing the effect. The integrity of such an image is not really affected by statistical information about other agents. There is, as I have suggested elsewhere (Abelson, 1975a), cognitive difficulty in pooling knowledge of different forms.

A further example is presented in Chapter 11, by Slovic, Fischhoff, and Lichtenstein. There it is suggested that the form in which information about risks is presented very much affects the prevailing attitude toward them. Giving the (miniscule) statistical reduction in the average life expectancy of people living within a certain radius of a nuclear reactor produces no alarm, but if the same information is translated into the expected absolute number of radiation-caused deaths (very few), then the outcry is substantial. A notorious unpublished analysis of the supposed deterrent effects of capital punishment[5] comes to the conclusion that "every death sentence for murder saves eight lives." This persuasive technique might be called "sweeping concretization." Script theory holds that in general this technique is persuasive indeed (although the given example is perhaps still a bit too hypothetical to be as effective as a concrete real episode, such as a new murder by a paroled murderer, would be in influencing attitudes on capital punishment).

A remarkable example of an attitude process in which abstract information is weaker than episodic information has recently been provided by Ross, Lepper, and Hubbard (1975). Subjects were given numerical feedback about how well they had performed a judgment task (distinguishing real from fake suicide notes). Later they were clearly told that this feedback was totally arbitrary, an experimental deception taken from a table of random numbers. Nevertheless, subjects knowing they had been falsely told they were good at the task predicted they would do well at a similar future task, whereas subjects falsely told they were bad predicted they would do badly. Ross, Lepper, and Hubbard explain this failure of debriefing in terms of cognitions subjects invoke to explain the feedback when they receive it. If told they are good (bad) at the task, they will invent reasons why, typically involving incidents from their own experience implying high (low) sensitivity to the psychology of the suicide prone, e.g., the presence (absence) of foreboding during the last interactions with particular suicide victims. In our terms, we would consider these cognitions as participant —episodic scripts composed of two vignettes: the foreboding and the tragedy, with the "caption" of self as (non)discerning witness.

In any case, the revelation that the feedback has been false does not cancel out the later impact of these scripts, which are after all true, even if the information which has made them and their captions salient is totally false. The individual may be said to have developed a new attitude about himself in a particular task, based on the increased availability of particular self-relevant scripts in that task situation.

SCRIPT PROCESSES IN BEHAVIOR

We postulate that *cognitively mediated social behavior depends on the joint occurrence of two processes:* (a) *the selection of a particular script to represent the given social situation* and (b) *the taking of a participant role within that*

[5] The statistical techniques were sophomoric, and the piece is unworthy of reference. Yet the conclusion is so graphic that the analysis has found its way into the dialectic of capital punishment advocates and even appears in the Attorney General's brief before the United States Supreme Court in a 1975 test of the constitutionality of North Carolina's capital punishment law (Fowler vs. North Carolina).

script. This postulate is perhaps best explicated (consistent with script tenets) by an example. A few years ago, Ellen Langer and I conducted an experiment on the effects of the phrasing of a request to a stranger for help, on the probability that help would be given. Our analysis was based on the concept of scripts and we in fact used that term in our article (Langer & Abelson, 1972), although at that time I had not tried to articulate a theory of scripts.

There are many scripts that include the behavior of one person helping another, but for purposes of this experiment we concentrated on two major common types: an empathy script, and a social obligation script. In the first, a victim of misfortune states a need, and the listener, feeling sorry for the victim, undertakes to help. In the second, a person having difficulty straightforwardly asks someone for help and the latter person, if he is not pressed by other activities, obliges. In the empathy script, the emphasis is on the plight of the victim and the scene begins with a "victim-oriented" statement, a statement of need. In the social obligation script, the emphasis is on the commitments of the target of the request and the scene begins with a "target-oriented" statement, a statement asking if help is possible.

We assumed that the very first statement of the victim would strongly differentiate these two scripts, making one much more salient at the expense of the other. Accordingly, we arranged for an apparent victim of an injury to approach strangers with the alternative opening lines, "I think I need help. I think I hurt my knee" (victim-oriented), or "Would you do something for me? Would you do me a favor?" (target-oriented). We also varied the favor the victim asked, one version being a legitimate request, worthy of empathy, ("Please call my husband and tell him to pick me up"), and the other a rather selfish, somewhat illegitimate thing for someone with a minor injury to ask ("Please call my employer and tell him I won't be in this morning"). These variations created 2 X 2 design: victim- or target-oriented opening statement crossed with legitimacy or illegitimacy or request. There were 20 subjects per cell.

Our reasoning about the legitimacy variable was as follows. The victim-oriented statement tends to invoke the empathy script. The potential helper must decide whether to become a participant in this script. If the victim then states a legitimate request participation is encouraged, but if the victim states an illegitimate request the script tends to be interrupted and participation discouraged, because the victim does not deserve the sympathy she has attempted to invoke. A critical precondition, or gating feature, for willing participation has been removed. In contrast, with the target-oriented opening statement which presumably calls up the social obligation script, the legitimacy of the request is not a gating feature. Potential social obligation focuses on the willingness of the target person to make a commitment to the necessary time and effort. The victim does not claim that the request is necessarily very worthy. We predict that with a victim-oriented request, therefore, the legitimacy of the favor should make a big difference in probability of helping, but with a target-oriented request, legitimacy should make little difference.

To avoid results contingent on one particular helping situation, the same conceptual structure was also replicated with the victim asking the target to mail a package because of her own haste to catch a train or to go shopping at Macy's. Combining the two replications, the proportions of target subjects helping in each cell of the 2 X 2 design strongly supported the hypotheses. Legitimacy of favor made a large difference with a victim-oriented appeal (75 versus 27% helping), but no essential difference with a target-oriented appeal (42 versus 47% helping).

It is not warranted to claim that these indirect results prove script theory; nevertheless, it is very difficult to account for the results in any simple alternative way.

The most novel problem posed by the present view is the determination of when the individual switches from observer to participant role in the scripts he perceives around him. From childhood, every individual has a lot of experience observing the enactment of scripts in which he does not participate, either because the scenes are distant (e.g., seen on TV), or because he does not yet fit into one of the active roles (e.g., parent, teacher, big kid). Many well-understood scripts may never in a lifetime involve the individual as a participant (winning a state lottery, rescuing someone from drowning, having to beg money to survive, etc.). However, another typical pattern is that there is a critical occasion on which the transition to participant is first made. How might this come about? We call this the "virginity problem."

One common spur to the transition is entry into an assumed role. A very interesting case is the diplomat or other elite role occupant, who having learned his historical scripts overly well seeks to apply them in his role— say, by vigilantly avoiding "another Munich" or "another Viet Nam." This pattern is discussed by Jervis (1976) and May (1973).

There are, however, many scripts with informal rather than formal role participants. Here, possible factors in the assumption of the participant role are strong individual incentives or social pressures. We do not know much about the circumstances under which various factors are sufficient to produce a first instance of a participating behavior in a known script. In effect, our theoretical problem here is very close to the question of what eliciting cues are necessary for social modeling (the imitation of a previously observed sequence of social behaviors). In some types of social modeling, for example, the modeling of aggressive behavior displayed on video, there are confusing contradictory results in the literature. For example, Bandura (1965) found it relatively easy to release specific aggressive behaviors in children by the videotape modeling of those behaviors, whereas Milgram and Shotland (1973) found no effect from the display on an actual TV program of a highly specific aggressive act (smashing and robbing a bubblegum-type charity box identical to charity boxes present on the streets of the city where the program was seen). One of the key factors may well be whether or not the individual has ever before done anything like the modeled behavior.

The first participation in a script, then, is crucial. After that, further episodes of participation become much more likely.[6] As the role of participant in a known script becomes more likely, however, the opposite problem arises: What determines when the individual does not participate? Even a charity box smasher does not smash every available charity box. Some features discriminate subjectively favorable from unfavorable opportunities. These are what we have called "gating features." Their isolation by the individual requires repeated experience with the particular situation and expansion of the script to include outcome vignettes appropriate to self as participant.

This line of theorizing carries us full circle back to our discussion of decision making. We meet again the developmental process of constructing categorical and hypothetical scripts on the basis of abstracted features. This strength of a script theory to address so many phenomena is, alas, also its weakness, for there is an enormous amount of vagueness in what we have laid out in an attempt to be broad and general. This direction, however, seems much more appealing and profitable than the overly rationalistic orientation in social cognition, which has increasingly failed to account for empirical phenomena of decision making and attitude formation.

ACKNOWLEDGMENTS

Work reported in this paper was facilitated by National Science Foundation Grant GS-35768.

---

[6] This proposition may seem like nothing more than the straightforward operant conditioning principle that a behavior (operant) must first occur before it can be reinforced, and that once it is reinforced the probability of its occurrence increases. There is no doubt a theoretical connection between the behaviorist and cognitive viewpoints, but at least one difference between the first participation in a script and the first occurrence of an operant is that the potential participator has a clear concept of what the behavior is to be if he does participate, whereas the operant behavior is often—unless carefully "shaped" beforehand—fortuitous. Furthermore, we assume that mere participation in a script increases future participation probability somewhat, even if the outcome of the situation is not explicitly rewarding.

4
Understanding Human Action: Recognizing the Plans and Motives of Other Persons

Charles F. Schmidt

Rutgers University

INTRODUCTION

Social psychology has typically emphasized the theoretical importance of understanding how persons structure and give meaning to their observations of other persons' actions. The how of this understanding process has consistently eluded our theoretical grasp. The goal of the work to be described here is to develop an information-processing theory of how the observer makes sense of the actions of others.

An information-processing theory is a description of how certain classes of inputs can be transformed to yield certain classes of outputs. Such a theory is verified if it is possible to derive the subject's output from input that is equivalent to the input to the subject. An information-processing theory is further characterized by the following three properties. First, the theory is expressed in a language that can, in principle, be rather directly translated into an executable program. Second, an empirical claim is made that there exists a correspondence between at least some of the temporally ordered states of the computation and some of the temporally ordered states of the human process that is being described by the theory. Third, the derivation of the output from the input is dependent upon the initial knowledge state of the information-processing system. This last characteristic requires that such theories accomplish an explicit decoupling of the knowledge possessed by the system from the processes possessed by the system.

Given this goal, the initial step in theory construction involves choosing the class of inputs and outputs to which the theory is addressed. I have chosen to limit the class of inputs to sets of sentences that describe actions or states of affairs. Additionally, these sentences are partially ordered with respect to time of occurrence. Three general restrictions have been placed on the input sentences. These restrictions are:

1. Only the temporal connectives "and at the same time" and "and then" are allowed to explicitly connect sentences.
2. Only the verb "say" is used to refer to a speech act. Such verbs as "ask," "promise," "order," and so on are excluded.
3. Such verbs as "want," "believe," "intend," and "decide," which refer to psychological states, are excluded.

The exception to the above restrictions occurs when these terms are used to describe what an actor has said. In other words, the actors in an episode may talk to each other in unrestricted English but the narration of the actions must be done using this restricted English grammar.

The class of outputs of the theory has been partially characterized by specifying the kinds of questions that the theory should be capable of answering. Some of these questions are shown in Fig. 4.1. Four classes of questions have been distinguished. The memory questions simply require the subject to describe what has happened, whereas the explanation questions either ask why something has happened or ask questions about an actor's psychological states. The instruction to summarize what has happened is included here because I argue that a summary is best understood as an explanation of what has happened. The postdiction questions require the subject to describe what could have been and the prediction questions inquire about what may happen next.

Within this paradigm the subject is typically allowed to use natural language in answering these types of questions. The requirement that the theory ultimately must account for these linguistic responses affects two aspects of theory formation. First, the language within which the theory is stated refers to processes that operate on symbols rather than processes defined over numeric domains. Second, the process of theory formation can be initially guided by considering examples of the kind of inputs that the theory is intended to accept. Because the response system is natural language rather than an artificial language devised by the experimenter, our intuitions concerning the possible linguistic responses to questions about such examples are quite reliable. It should be further pointed out that the theory is not required to predict the "modal" linguistic response. The modal value is typically 1 because it is virtually never the case that two protocols are identical. Instead, the goal is to derive what can and what cannot be said and still count as an answer to the question asked.

The general nature of this approach having been characterized, the plan for the remainder of this chapter is to first present an overview of the central assumptions that have been made about the social knowledge together with a brief discussion of some recall data that persons use in interpreting the actions of

EXPLANATION QUESTIONS

SUMMARIZE WHAT HAPPENED.
WHY DID ⟨STATE⟩ | ⟨ACT⟩ HAPPEN?
WHY DID ⟨ACTOR⟩ DO ⟨ACT⟩ ?
DID ⟨ACTOR⟩ INTEND TO CAUSE ⟨STATE⟩ ?
DID ⟨ACTOR⟩ BELIEVE THAT ⟨STATE⟩ ?
DID ⟨ACTOR⟩ WANT ⟨STATE⟩ | ⟨ACT⟩ ?

PREDICTION QUESTIONS

WHAT WILL HAPPEN NEXT?
WHAT WILL ⟨ACTOR⟩ DO NEXT?

POSTDICTION QUESTIONS

COULD ⟨ACTOR⟩ HAVE DONE ⟨ACT⟩ ?
COULD ⟨ACTOR⟩ HAVE KNOWN ⟨STATE⟩ ?

MEMORY QUESTIONS

WHAT HAPPENED?
HOW DID ⟨STATE⟩ | ⟨ACT⟩ HAPPEN?
DID ⟨STATE⟩ | ⟨ACT⟩ HAPPEN?
WHAT DID ⟨ACTOR⟩ DO?
WHAT HAPPENED IMMEDIATELY AFTER ⟨STATE⟩ |⟨ACT⟩ ?

FIG. 4.1   Classes of questions that define the output sentences.

others. Second, various examples of input descriptions are examined and used as a basis for determining the nature of the processes that appear to be involved in the observer's understanding of human action. Finally, a sketch of specific aspects of our current attempts at formalizing and implementing the information-processing theory will be presented.

ASSUMPTIONS OF THE COMMON-SENSE THEORY

It is commonly noted that persons who observe the same social events often arrive at a very different conclusions concerning what actually has happened. A study by Hastorf and Cantril (1954) has dramatically documented this phenomenon. Princeton supporters described the events of the Princeton–Dartmouth football game in terms that were quite different from the Dartmouth fans' description of the same game.

This phenomenon is not limited to cases where the observer is emotionally involved in the situation being described. For example, imagine a radio announcer who does not know the plays, rules, or goals of football trying to describe what is happening on the field. Contrast this announcer's description with that provided by a football-wise announcer. Certainly both have access to the same sense information. Nonetheless, the expert describes events that the football-naive sportscaster in some sense has never even seen. For example, the expert does not see simply a person backpeddling with the football, but the quarterback dropping back to pass. It is important to note that this description is not simply a description of the observed physical movements. This observation is obvious as soon as the prediction contained within this description is recognized. That is, the dropping back is being done in order to pass. The quarterback may be tackled before any physical movement involved in throwing a pass could be made. Yet, this would not invalidate the announcer's description because the announcer was not describing physical movements but the play that the quarterback was attempting to execute. However, if the quarterback had simply faked a pass and then actually executed a draw play, then this course of events would invalidate the announcer's description because the meaning of the quarterback's action had been misinterpreted.

The sense in which the expert and football-naive announcers are seeing different things is now clear. The expert is not simply describing occurrances of physical events. The expert is describing the plays or moves of the game. These descriptions refer to what the players are trying to do and not simply to what they have done.

This example has provided a concrete case where the derivation of a person's output seems to depend on both the input and a characterization of the initial knowledge state of that person. In choosing the information-processing framework it has been assumed that the descriptions that observers give of the actions of others are dependent on the knowledge state of the observer. In this sense, the description of human action is *inherently* interpretive because what is seen and reported depends on a property of the observer.

Given this assumption, one of the first tasks is to develop some initial ideas about the nature of the knowledge state that observers use in interpreting human action. Heider's (1958) discussion of the commonsense theory of personal causation was used as the basis for characterizing the general assumptions that the naive observer used in interpreting human action. The basic axiom of this commonsense theory is the *axiom of personal causation,* which may be stated in a first-order logic as

$$(\text{*Act* } A)(P \text{ *cause* } A) \Rightarrow ((\text{Some *Plan* } M)$$
$$(A \text{ *part of* } M)$$
$$(P \text{ *believe* } (P \text{ *is able to* } M))$$
$$(P \text{ *choose* } M))$$

where P stands for person, (*Act* A) is to be interpreted as the universal quantifier read as "for all acts A," and (Some *Plan* M) represents the existential quantifier read as "there is some plan M." This axiom compactly represents the observer's assumption that voluntary actions imply the existence of a plan that the actor has chosen to try to execute and also believes can be carried out.

The terms enclosed within asterisks are intended to be taken as technical terms that refer to the person's internal representation of these notions within the context of the commonsense theory of action. This axiom is meaningless, of course, until the technical terms and relations used in stating the axiom are defined. Satisfactory technical definitions are difficult to state, but each time such technical terms are introduced we must remember that they represent a promise that a further definition is yet to come. I will make a great many such promises, but I will not be able to make good on all of them in this chapter. Nonetheless, the statement of this axiom does now make clear the analogy between the perception of the football game and the more general problem of perceiving human action. The football announcer interprets the actions of the players as part of some play that is simply a particular kind of plan. Furthermore, this notion of plan automatically brings with it intentional terms, such as choosing, believing, and being able. These terms are generally treated as additional operators in modal logics, but the assumption here is that the sense of these terms can be captured by simply representing them as a relation between a person and an internal structure, called a "plan" (cf. Simon, 1966, for a discussion of this viewpoint).

The observer not only assumes that actors have plans but also that persons in general share this assumption. This belief is represented in the *recursiveness axiom* as

(*Person* P)(P *believes* (axiom of personal causation))

This rather innocuous appearing assumption gives social action some special characteristics. Without this assumption there could be no such thing as a strategic act, for a strategic action is one that is done in order to cause an observer to misinterpret the plan that is being executed. For example, the quarterback who is backpeddling with the football recognizes that other persons—in particular, the defensive players—may interpret his action as part of a pass play. It is precisely for this reason that draw plays, bootlegs, and other such strategic plays have been devised. Social action depends in an even more fundamental way on this recursiveness assumption because social actions cannot be successfully carried out unless the other persons who are participants in the action correctly interpret the actor's behavior. For example, one person cannot really give an order to another unless that other recognizes that an order is being given.

Although these two assumptions do not exhaust the general beliefs that persons use in interpreting the actions of others, they do capture some of the fundamental characteristics of this knowledge system. Although the statement of these beliefs as axioms is not intended as a claim that persons hold these beliefs in this axiomatic form, stating them as axioms allows us to point out several things. First, the fact that it is possible to state two very general beliefs that are universally quantified over acts and over persons illustrates one sense in which it is appropriate to refer to a naive or commonsense theory of human action. Another sense in which this nomenclature is appropriate is demonstrated by the fact that these axioms serve to introduce the "abstract" terms of this theory. These include such terms as "plan," "believe," and "choose." Second, it should be clear that the claim is that these statements characterize the assumptions that are implicit in the theory of commonsense human action. They are not intended to specify the assumptions of any scientific theory of human action. Finally, the statement of these axioms implicitly defines in a general way the nature of the information-processing problem. Simply stated, it is to devise a system that accepts acts as inputs and then attributes to the actors plans that are consistent with the data, that is, the observed acts. Additionally, the axioms require that it be possible to assert for each such plan that the actor is able to and chooses to perform the attributed plan.

Having said this much about the nature of the observer's assumptions about human action, it is now possible to arrive at a very general prediction about a person's memory for and the description of human action. Recall that the input to the information-processing theory is restricted to a partially ordered temporal sequence of actions. If persons are organizing these actions into plan units, then the abstract terms of this naive theory can be expected to intrude in their recall of the action sequence. Furthermore, if persons are asked to summarize these input descriptions then the "intrusion" of these theoretical terms should increase because the internal representation of the actions should be organized around the plan units rather than around the sentential units.

In order to initially explore this possibility, Goodson (1975) designed a study in which 20 subjects were presented such a restricted description of a sequence of actions. Fifteen minutes later, and then again 1 week later, these subjects were asked to recall as exactly as possible the list of input sentences. After the last recall session the subjects were also asked to summarize the actions.

In order to score these protocols, the original input description as well as the subjects' recall and summary protocols were represented in a kind of predicate structure (cf. Kintsch, 1974). A somewhat simplified version of the syntactic rules used to perform this translation of the input sentences into this predicate format is given in Fig. 4.2. These syntactic rules also help to make explicit the kind of grammatical restrictions that we have placed on the input sentences. The single asterisk attached to the nonterminal term ⟨Arg⟩ indicates that this term

```
⟨Predicate⟩              ::= ⟨Simple Predicate⟩
                             AND THEN( ⟨Simple Predicate⟩ ⟨Predicate⟩ )
                             AND( ⟨Simple Predicate**⟩ )
⟨Simple Predicate⟩       ::= ⟨Speech Act⟩ | ⟨Act⟩ | ⟨State⟩
⟨Speech Act⟩             ::= SAY( ⟨Arg*⟩ ⟨Utterance⟩ )
⟨Utterance⟩              ::= ⟨Unrestricted Predicate⟩
⟨Act⟩                    ::= ⟨Act Name⟩ ( ⟨Arg*⟩ )
⟨State⟩                  ::= ⟨State Name⟩ ( ⟨Arg*⟩ )
⟨Act Name⟩               ::= MAKE | EAT | HAND TO | ...
⟨State Name⟩             ::= HAS | OWNS | MOTHER OF | BOSS OF | ...
⟨Arg⟩                    ::= ⟨Person⟩ |⟨Object⟩|⟨Place⟩|⟨Time⟩
⟨Person⟩                 ::= JIM | MARY | ...
⟨Object⟩                 ::= ICE CREAM CONE | TABLE| CHAIR | ...
⟨Place⟩                  ::= KITCHEN | BANK | ...
⟨Time⟩                   ::= NOON | MONDAY | ...
```

FIG. 4.2   Predicate syntax for scoring input sentences.

may be selected one or more times. The double asterisk indicates that this term may be selected two or more times. An example of the translation to predicate format would be

Mary gave Jim an ice cream cone and then Jim ate it.
↓
AND THEN(GIVE(MARY JIM ICECREAMCONE)EAT
(JIM ICECREAMCONE))

An analogous but more complicated syntax was defined for the unrestricted English of the subject's recall and summary protocols.

Representing the input and the subjects' data in this fashion allowed us to ask several questions. First, exactly how many of the predicates found in the subjects' protocols were identical to those contained in the original sentences? As can be seen in the first row of Table 4.1, 15 minutes later the average percentage of original predicates that has occurred in the recall is only 9%. This figure dropped to 6% a week later and was 0 for all subjects when they were asked to summarize the original events. These percentages indicate that very little of the recall can be accounted for by assuming that the subject is directly recalling the input sentences. However, these percentages do not give an accurate picture of the quality of the recall. A reading of the subject protocols leads to the impression that the recall of the action sequences was quite good. The "gist" of what has happened is there, but it is expressed at a more interpretive level than that encoded in the original input sentences. Rather complicated scoring procedures are required in order to demonstrate this claim in a fairly rigorous

TABLE 4.1
Average Values of Interpretation Indices

| | Temporal interval | | |
| | Recall | | Summary |
Type of index	15 minutes	1 week	1 week
Original predicates (%)	9	6	0
Psychological predicates (%)	16	15	30
Explanatory connectives (%)	33	32	52

way. Nonetheless, some appreciation of the robustness of this interpretive effect can be gained by computing some rough but simply defined indices.

Recall that psychological predicates—that is, verbs that refer to psychological states, such as "want," "believe," and "intend," as well as verbs that refer to internal actions, such as "decide," and "plan"—have been excluded from the input description. Consequently, any occurrance of these types of terms in the recall or summary were clearly "added" by the subject. In the second row of Table 4.1 the average percentage of such psychological predicates relative to the total number of verbal predicates used by a particular subject is given. This figure of 15% for the recall protocols doubles when the summary protocols are examined in this way.

A final "intrepretation" index was computed by calculating for each subject the number of explanatory connectives relative to the total number of sentential connectives used. Again, recall that the only connectives included in the input sentences were the temporal sense of "and" and "then." Such connectives as "because," "to" in the "in order to" sense, and "since" were identified as explanatory connectives. As can be seen in the third row of Table 4.1, the average percentage of use of these terms is again quite substantial and becomes even more pronounced in the summary protocols.

Because of the coarseness of the analyses, these percentages should be viewed as a lower bound on the degree of interpretation present in the subject protocols. Furthermore, in the memory conditions the subjects were asked to simply recall as exactly as possible the input sentences. Nonetheless, substantial evidence for the existence of an interpretive process was found in each subject's recall protocol. These interpretation indices increased as expected when the subjects were asked to summarize the action sequence.

CHARACTERISTICS OF THE RECOGNITION PROCESS

The form of the observer's knowledge about persons has been shown to be analogous to the form of a scientific theory. In this section the processes involved in interpreting human action are compared to some of the processes involved in using a scientific theory to account for the observed data. Some of the similarities between the theory of human action and a scientific theory are striking. Both the common-sense theory of human action and a scientific theory involve an observer attempting to account for some data. In both cases the account or explanation is abstractive in the sense that certain aspects of the observations are ignored. In both cases the account is interpretive because the explanation goes beyond the data. Both the scientist and the observer of human action may be asked to communicate their explanation to others. Furthermore, they may both be asked to provide the evidence that supports their interpretation. Finally, they can both be wrong, recognize that the explanation is wrong. and revise it accordingly. Parenthetically, it may be noted that some naive observers, such as journalists and FBI agents, also publish their interpretations in their own technical journals.

Each of these surface similarities cannot be examined here in detail. Probably, one of the most important features on this list is the claim that the common-sense theory is interpretive. Scientific theories achieve their interpretive power by using some composition rule to derive the observations. The composition rule may be stated mathematically, logically, grammatically, or in still some other form. The form is unimportant. What is important is that the composition rule is the source of the generative power of a scientific theory. In considering the process of understanding human action, a basic question is whether this understanding is achieved by simply storing and accessing a perhaps very large number of generalizations about human behavior or whether understanding is achieved by a more constructive generative process.

The issue is of central importance to theory construction. If generalizations are stored then some variant of a matching process may be sufficient to account for our ability to understand the actions of others. If the system is constructive, then a true composition or reasoning process must be used in accounting for the observer's explanation of action. I do not know how to definitively answer this question. However, a careful look at the way we use language to describe actions may shed some light on this issue.

Consider the following sentence, which might be used to describe an action:

(1) Joe handed the book to Jim.

In many contexts this particular action can be understood simply as a means by which Joe has accomplished some other action. Stated linguistically, we can all imagine contexts where it becomes possible to say

(2) Joe ⟨verb⟩ by means of handing the book to Jim.

For example,

(3) Joe gave Jim the book by means of handing it to Jim.

The point is that there is some notion of level of description involved here. Sentence (3) states that in this particular context the handing of the book to Jim counted as an act of giving. Further examples of higher levels of description that may be used to interpret Sentence (1) are

(4) Joe returned the book to Jim.

(5) Joe loaned the book to Jim.

(6) Joe apologized to Jim. (The book is a present.)

(7) Joe broke the law. (The book is pornographic and Jim is a minor.)

(8) Joe helped Jim. (Jim needed the book to finish a paper.)

It seems that we can write down many more such sentences. Furthermore, Sentence (1) could also appear in a description as:

(9) Joe handed the book to Jim and asked Jim to deliver the book to Mary.

Now Sentence (9) can be written as

(10) Joe sent the book to Mary by handing the book to Jim and asking Jim to deliver it to Mary.

It appears that we can imagine an indefinitely long list of such "and" connected acts involving "handing to." If this is true, then it is not possible to directly store the relation between "hand to" and higher level generalizations about action because there appear to be indefinitely many such generalizations that can be made. Consequently, it seems that some rules must be used to compose the relation between lower level acts and higher level acts.

The same problem exists in attempting to specify in an a priori way the relation between a higher level description of action and a lower level description of an action that is part of the higher level action description. Higher level acts do not imply the lower level acts. For example, the "giving" of Sentence (3) may have been accomplished by a "handing to" or by sending the book through the mail, or by asking Mary to give it to Jim, and so on. Again, this list of possible means of accomplishing the giving appears to be indefinitely long. Therefore, "giving" does not imply a "handing to," nor the converse. A final possibility would be to argue that the "giving" is identical to the "handing to." However, the identify of two concepts requires that they be implicationally equivalent. Giving implies that the giver wants the recipient to own the object and that the giver no longer owns the object given. Clearly, "handing to" does not carry this same implication.

A somewhat stronger process model would allow that a composition rule be involved in recognizing the plans of others but would argue that the composition simply involved the set union of the implications of the acts that were part of the plan. According to this view, if we had such act descriptions as

(11)   Joe handed the book to Mary.

(12)   And asked Mary to mail it to Jim.

(13)   Joe gave the book to Jim.

then the union of the implications of Sentences (11) and (12) would yield the implications of Sentence (13). This fails as well. In fact, the implication derived from Sentence (13) that Joe wants Jim to own the book is not even in the union of the implications of Sentences (11) and (12). Consequently, no set-theoretic operation on these actions could yield the implications of Sentence (13), and certainly we can imagine situations where Sentence (13) is an appropriate summarization of Sentences (11) and (12).

In order to understand what kind of composition rule can be appropriately defined over this domain, it is simply necessary to examine the axiom of personal causation once more. According to this axiom, actions are terms that imply a plan. Plans are constructed not by any simple set-theoretic operation but by finding a path of actions that can transform the starting situation into a situation where the goal of the plan is achieved. The observer assumes that the actor is such a problem solver. A problem solver's path to a goal can only be recognized by knowing the actor's goal and internal representation of the situation, that is, what the actor wants and what the actor believes to be true about the world. The processes that the observer uses in recognizing plans must therefore include procedures for (1) inferring and representing the actor's representation of the situation; (2) inferring the actors current goals; (3) constructing plans that include the observed acts and the inferred goals of the actor; and (4) evaluating the goodness of fit of the attributed plans to the observations.

Additional information concerning the nature of the plan recognition process can be gained by considering the temporal aspects of this recognition process. First, note that the actions that are observed are linearly ordered in time. However, a plan is not a temporally ordered sequence of actions but a logically ordered sequence of actions. The actions in a plan are partially ordered according to what step or steps in the plan must be accomplished first in order to execute the next step in the plan. Figure 4.3 schematically represents the set of acts A through H that are temporally ordered. These acts are organized into two plans, P and Q, where the acts are now ordered vertically under the "in order to" relation. In the case of Plan P the acts are only partially ordered with respect to time, because A and B both must be done in order to next perform C. The "in order to" relation therefore implies the temporal relation, but the temporal relation does not imply the "in order to" relation.

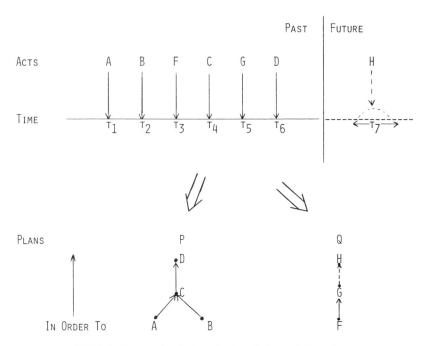

FIG. 4.3   Temporal ordering of acts and plan ordering of acts.

There are several things to note about the relation between acts and plans. First, acts that are part of different plans may be temporally contiguous and acts that are part of the same plan may be quite separated in time. Second, plans group actions into temporally disconnected sets of actions. Consequently, plans have a logically definite beginning and ending point. Finally, because plans have a logical progression, if the end or goal is known then it is possible to predict the kinds of actions that are to occur if the plan is completed. In Plan Q of Fig. 4.3 a dotted "in order to" relation is used to represent such a prediction.

The fact that time is not crucially involved in explaining actions in terms of plans is an important difference between scientific notions of causality and the naive notion of personal causation. Because time is not intimately connected with the commonsense notion of a plan, classically defined notions of acquiring knowledge by induction cannot be used as a basis for explaining how persons recognize the plans of others (cf. Kelley, 1971, for a different viewpoint).

Persons have a limited ability to retain unconnected events in memory. Plans are temporally unconnected events, and plans are opaque unless the goal is known. Furthermore, a particular plan may fail and consequently the goal of the plan is never observed. Additionally, some plans, such as allowing someone to do something, are plans that may involve no action at all but simply a decision not to act. All of these observations support the conclusion that a plan recognition system must be a strongly predictive system the processes of which must be controlled by the state of its space of current plan hypotheses rather than directly driven by input observations. This in turn suggests that the control structure must be not hierarchical and sequential but distributed and determined by an evaluation of the current hypotheses space.

THE BELIEVER IMPLEMENTATION

In the preceding sections our conception of an information-processing theory has been defined, the nature of the knowledge state that is used to interpret human action has been characterized, and properties of the processes involved in the interpretation of action have been discussed. In this section certain general aspects of BELIEVER, the name given the computer implementation of these ideas, will be presented. BELIEVER, as have most such attempts at theory construction using the concepts and techniques of artificial intelligence, has existed or partially existed in several previous implementations (cf. Brown, 1974; Bruce, 1975; Bruce & Schmidt, 1974; Schmidt, 1973, 1975; Schmidt & D'Addamio, 1973).

This current implementation is being developed in close collaboration with N. S. Sridharan and is being expressed using a subset of the meta-description system (MDS) formalism and language developed by Srinivasan (1973, 1975). MDS provides a descriptive formalism together with reasoning facilities within which the BELIEVER theory can be clearly expressed. Such a formally described system facilitates theory construction in two ways. First, it provides a well-defined language within which the structural and process knowledge of the theory can be expressed. Second, it provides a way of explicitly specifying where the psychological claims of the theory stop. When the general reasoning facilities of the MDS system are used to carry out some process, an empirical claim is not automatically being made that persons carry out the computation in precisely that fashion. The claim is simply that some such process is carried out at this point which accomplishes what is accomplished by the system process. For example, MDS provides procedures for checking the local consistency of a relation whenever an attempt is made to instantiate the relation. When this system, called CHECKER, is being used in the psychological theory, no empirical claim is necessarily being made about the form of this computation—only that such a computation is requires at this point in the psychological process.

The MDS formalism cannot be fully presented here, but it will be necessary to introduce certain aspects of this system in discussing the current implementation of BELIEVER. The convention will be followed that technical terms of MDS will be capitalized when introduced and the technical terms of BELIEVER enclosed in asterisks. BELIEVER is activated by the input of an act description (cf. Sridharan, 1975), and some of the basic ideas can be concretely presented by considering the definition of the act *MAKE*. This act definition is the

BELIEVER structure that is activated by the linguistic analyzer when a sentence that refers to someone making an object is encountered. This definition of *MAKE* is shown in Figure 4.4. The cluster of connected boxes represents the static structural information that is directly associated with *MAKE*. This structural information consists of TEMPLATES, represented by the boxes, and RELATIONS, represented by the lines connecting the TEMPLATES. No direction is given to the lines because a relation and its inverse is always defined in MDS. The *PERSON*, *OBJECTS*, and *ARTIFACT* templates also have a great deal of additional structural information associated with them that is not shown here because this information is not directly involved in the definition of *MAKE*. However, it should be noted that this structure shown in Fig. 4.4 is just a piece of a TEMPLATE network. This network differs from a typical semantic net in that TEMPLATES may be of several types; either NODE, SET, TUPLE, or FUNCTION. For example, *OBJECTS* has been defined as a set template.

In addition to the template and relation clusters, MDS allows for the association of SENSE and/or TRANSFORMATIONAL information with a particular template relation. The sense information is represented in an extended first-order logic and expresses the constraints that must be satisfied whenever an attempt is made to create an instance of that particular template relation. The TRANSFORMATIONAL information is specified by using the first-order logic to express the conditions on the transformation and by using the primitive transformations of MDS (e.g., BIND, ASSERT, CREATE) to express the actions that are to be taken if the stated conditions are met.

The use of this information can be appreciated by considering the effect of attempting to ASSERT the relations contained in the sentence "Mary made an ice cream cone." Such an assertion may be initiated by the input analyzer or by the interpretive process, but the effects to be considered here would be the same regardless of the source of the action. When an ASSERT is attempted, then the sense information associated with *MAKE* would be evaluated. In this case, *MARY* would be bound to X and *ICE CREAM CONE* to A in the sense definition given in Fig. 4.4. The expressions would then be checked against the existing hypotheses space, or MODEL SPACE, where the instantiated relations are represented. For example, if it has already been asserted that Mary wants an ice cream cone, then TRUE is returned for this portion of the sense definition. If the negation of this expression had already been asserted, then FALSE would be returned as the value of the subexpression. If neither of these possibilities were realized, then a ? would be returned. The FALSE and ? portions of this sense definition would be retained, but the attempt to instantiate the relation would not automatically fail. Whether or not failure would result would depend on the action taken by the calling function. The evaluation of the sense definition has no direct effects on the model space. The importance of the sense definition is in

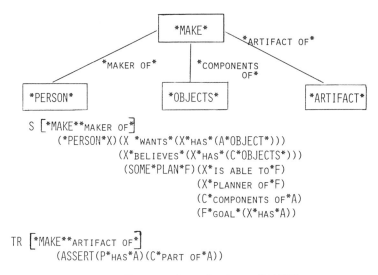

FIG. 4.4   Template cluster for the act *MAKE*.

its use to evaluate the consistency of the proposed assertion with the existing relations present in the MODEL SPACE.

The transformation rule represented in Fig. 4.4 does affect the model space. An anchored transformation rule, such as this, acts as a kind of local demon that is activated whenever the relation is fully instantiated. In this case, if the assertion were instantiated in the MODEL SPACE, then an attempt would be made to assert that Mary had an ice cream cone in her possession and that the components of the make act were now part of that ice cream cone. If the sentence had been that Mary made an ice cream cone out of cardboard and mashed potatoes, then the attempt to assert these as components of the ice cream cone would contradict the sense definition associated with *ICE CREAM CONE*.

This facility to associate constraints and actions at any point within the template network is useful in several ways. First, it allows us to create an active memory network within which a great deal of the psychological and world knowledge can be distributed. Consequently, this knowledge is accessed and utilized in a way that is independent of the nature of the function that originated the command to instantiate a particular template relation. Second, the sense information can be used within BELIEVER to pass information to the BELIEVER control structure concerning the kind of inferences that need to be or can be made in order to support a particular assertion. The transformation rules provide a way to trigger off and make those inferences that are warranted by the instantiation of a template relation. The assertions of these inferences can themselves create side effects through the evaluation of the sense definitions associated with the template relations contained in the inference. Finally, it should be noted that not only the input terms of BELIEVER, such as *MAKE*, can be defined as templates, but also the theoretical terms, such as *PLAN*. In this way, we are able to make the action of hypothesizing a *PLAN* itself have important side effects that can guide the strategy of plan recognition. These facilities together with the specification of the MODEL SPACE as a location within which the currently instantiated structures are represented, can be used to formulate the kind of hypothesis driven strategy of plan recognition that I have argued for in the previous section.

The plan recognition procedure that is currently being implemented can now be sketched. Not all of what is discussed here has been implemented. Nonetheless, the overall strategy does accurately reflect the goals that have been set for the implementation.

The basic logic of the plan recognizer can be simply stated. Plans are recognized by asserting or hypothesizing them into existence. This is simply another way of saying that the process is constructive. This constructive process is achieved by defining a *PLAN* template. The *PLAN* template formally defines the meaning of the term "plan" within the commonsense theory. Because *PLAN* is formally defined, it is possible for a variety of independent knowledge sources to assert a *PLAN* into the MODEL SPACE.

Three such sources of plan hypotheses are (1) the act/plan translater (*OB-SERVER*), which maps acts into plans; (2) the plan builder (*COMPOSER*) that attempts to compose higher level plans from the already generated plans and so performs a mapping from plans into plans; and (3) the process that proposes plans on the basis of the satisfaction of motivational conditions (*MOTIVATOR*) and in this way maps from motives into plans. The job of the BELIEVER *MONITOR* is to evaluate the plans that are proposed by these knowledge sources and to create additional tasks for these knowledge sources by allowing the instantiation of plan hypotheses in the MODEL SPACE. The overall structure of this information-processing system is shown in Fig. 4.5. The arcs in this figure indicate the paths of information flow.

The *OBSERVER* and *COMPOSER* processes have received the most attention in our current work. Consequently, the *MOTIVATOR* will be discussed briefly. The *OBSERVER* is the simplest process and it is considered first. The basic task of the *OBSERVER* is to translate an instantiated act, such as *MAKE*, into a plan structure, again called *MAKE*. If an input act is not translated into a plan, then that act is not interpreted. Because BELIEVER, unlike persons, has nothing better to do, the input acts are always translated into plans.

In Fig. 4.6 a simplified version of the structure of the *PLAN* template is displayed. The meaning of this structure can be illustrated by translating the *MAKE* act template of Figure 4.4 into a *PLAN* template. First, *MAKE*

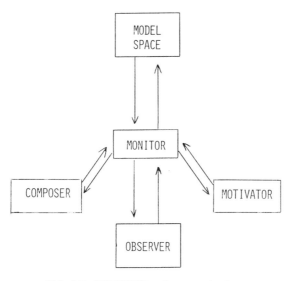

FIG. 4.5 BELIEVER system organization.

would be substituted for *PLAN*, *MARY* for *PERSON*, and so on, if the input sentence were that Mary had made an ice cream cone. Additionally, the expression associated with the sense definition anchored at *planner of* would be fragmented and asserted into the appropriate templates of the *MAKE* plan template. The *STATES* templates are all set templates and can have many single *STATE* templates as elements. The terms in the sense definition that

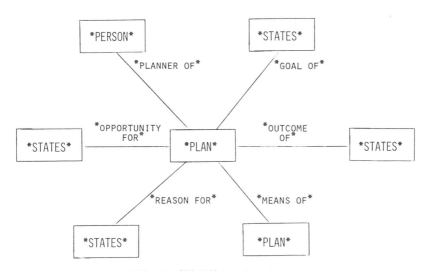

FIG. 4.6 *PLAN* template cluster.

refer to the planner's *wants* [e.g., the portion of the sense definition that now reads as (*MARY* *want* (*MARY* *have* *ICE CREAM CONE*))] would become an element of the template in the *goal of* relation to the *PLAN* template. The *believe* expressions are collected in the template in the *opportunity of* relation to *PLAN* and represent the belief preconditions on plan execution. The (SOME *PLAN* F) expression would be collected as a partially instantiated plan in the *PLAN* template in the *means of* relation to the *MAKE* plan template. Finally, the outcomes asserted by the transformation rule would be associated with the templates in the *outcome of* relation to *MAKE*.

No information is present in the act template concerning the *STATES* that are in the *reason for* relation to the *PLAN*. This is the "why" of the plan, and it is the search for the answer to why the planner has chosen to perform the plan that drives the plan recognition process. The COMPOSER will attempt to answer this "why" question by absorbing the *PLAN* into a higher level *PLAN* under the *means of* relation. This is only a temporary solution, however, because it simply pushes the "why" question up a level. The final "why" answer must be provided by the MOTIVATOR by finding a set of motive conditions that serve as a basis for asserting the observed *PLAN*. This set of motive conditions becomes the elements of the *STATES* template in the *reason for* relation to the *PLAN*.

Before I proceed to a discussion of *COMPOSER*, some of the important side effects that result from the evaluation of the sense and transformational information associated with the *PLAN* template must be discussed. Two such side effects are the assertions of the *ENABLE* and *MOTIVATE* templates shown in Fig. 4.7. The *ENABLE* template collects together those previous *PLAN* templates the outcomes of which have created the opportunity for doing the *PLAN* F that is being asserted. The *MOTIVATE* template cluster collects together those previous *PLAN* templates the outcomes of which have provided a reason for doing the *PLAN* F. In general, these *reason for* states will be empty, but the creation of this structure will allow for the restarting of this procedure if reasons are later adduced.

The *COMPOSER* uses these *ENABLE* and *MOTIVATE* templates as a basis for proposing higher order *PLAN* templates that can account for one or more existing *PLAN* structures. For example, if Mary had scooped the ice cream from the container and put the ice cream in the cone, then we would have *SCOOP* *source of* *ENABLE* *doing of* *PUT IN*. The COMPOSER's task is to take such structures and evaluate whether the "scooping" can have been done in order to do the "putting in." This involves hypothesizing a higher order plan, such as *MAKE* or simply *PLAN* X if no named plan exists, which this substructure is a *means of*. The opportunity, goal, and outcome states for this higher level plan would be composed out of the corresponding sets of the lower level plans with a translation of the psychological predicates to the

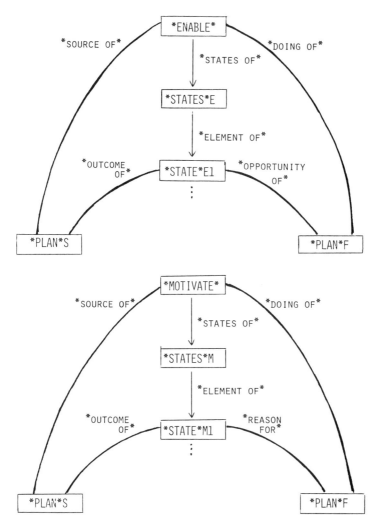

FIG. 4.7   *ENABLE* and *MOTIVATE* template clusters.

time of the first act. The evaluation of this time translated set of predicates serves to assert that the full effects of this higher level *PLAN* template must have been foreseen by the planner. A similar although much more complicated procedure is required when the *PLAN* composition process is applied to *PLAN* templates in the *MOTIVATE* structure.

Note that the composition of *PLAN* templates does not destroy the separate *PLAN* templates used in the composition. Furthermore, the truth values of the higher level *PLAN* are not necessarily equivalent to those of the lower level *PLAN* templates from which it is composed.

Finally, the *MOTIVATOR* uses its knowledge of motivation rules as a basis for asserting *PLAN* templates. These rules are action rules that have psychological and physical states as conditions and the assertion of *PLAN* templates as actions. For example, if Billy is Mary's son and Mary knows that Billy wants to have an ice cream cone to eat, then a motive rule is of the form:

$$(\text{*PERSONS* P Q})(\text{*OBJECTS* O})$$
$$(\text{P *unit* Q})(\text{P *know* (Q *want* (Q *unit* O))}) \Rightarrow$$
$$\text{ASSERT (SOME *PLAN* M) (P *planner of* M)}$$
$$(\text{M *goal* (Q *unit* O)})$$

where *unit* is being used in the sense of Heider (1958). The conditions on this motive rule would then be asserted as the *reason for* this *PLAN*. It is not yet clear whether or not such motive rules can be anchored to the world knowledge of the system or whether they must be organized into an associative network.

The function of the *MONITOR* is to organize the activities of the various subsystems in order to create well-formed *PLAN* structures that account for the observed acts. This is accomplished by bringing together into a single *PLAN* structure the various partial *PLANS* that are proposed by the *OBSERVER*, *COMPOSER*, and *MOTIVATOR* processes. It should be noted that *PLAN* is defined recursively. A particular *PLAN* structure may consist of any number of *PLAN* templates that are organized into a single *PLAN* using the *by means of* and *in order to* relations.

This overall system structure provides a framework that is consistent with the properties discussed in the previous sections. Whether or not it will be sufficient for the task of plan recognition will be answered by our further attempts to implement and test the adequacy of the system. Whether or not the system will be empirically adequate will be answered by the design of experiments to test the various predictions of such a system. However, the point of this chapter has not been to argue for the essential correctness of the particular ideas presented here, but to show how the information-processing framework can be used in theory construction in social psychology.

The BELIEVER project is a collaborative effort and many of the ideas presented here are the result of this collaboration. N. S. Sridharan, A. Sedlak, J. Goodson, and F. Hawrusik have worked extensively on various aspects of the current development of BELIEVER. B. Bruce and G. Brown collaborated on the earlier BELIEVER work. S. Amarel, C. V. Srinivasan, and W. Fabens have continually provided expert support and criticism to this work. E. Soloway generously has read earlier drafts of this paper and this paper has benefitted from his comments. This group has provided much of the stimulation needed to pursue work of this type, and they deserve much of the credit and none of the blame for what is said here.

ACKNOWLEDGMENTS

This research was supported by the NIH Special Research Resource on Computers in Biomedicine at Rutgers University. The paper was prepared while the author was Visiting Associate Professor at the Department of Psychology, University of Massachusetts, Amherst, Mass.

5
Developing a Cognitive Social Psychology

Shelley E. Taylor

Harvard University

The theme of this conference has been described as the marriage of cognitive and social psychology. Although this phrase may characterize the thinking of our symposium participants, some caution is warranted regarding the generalizability of this belief. Whereas social psychology has a strong cognitive tradition and although there has been considerable recent experimentation with cognitive theories and methodologies, there is little evidence of a widespread shift in this direction on the part of all or even most social psychologists. Likewise, although many cognitive psychologists are now exploring social stimuli and situations, this emphasis is by no means universal.

Were one to try to find a marriage reflected in Part I of this volume, our common interests would be clarified only slightly. What we have at present is not a true marriage but a number of sporadic flirtations. Some of the points at which we seem to be drawing together are methodological. A number of common problems have emerged in the two fields simultaneously, so that collaborative solutions seem to be in order. In other cases, the cross-fertilization is indicated by a liberal borrowing of ideas. For the most part, the social psychologists have been the heavy borrowers, testing the implications of cognitively based hypotheses in social settings. However, with the development of attribution theory and its emphasis on the perception of causality, there may come some borrowing in the other direction. Despite these intersections, I suspect many of us still consider ourselves primarily cognitive psychologists or social psychologists who happen to have interests that leak into the adjoining arena. For example, I consider myself primarily a social psychologist, and as such, I address my comments largely to the field of social psychology, where it is now, and how we can expect it to change as a result of these most recent interchanges with cognitive psychology.

WHAT IS COGNITIVE SOCIAL PSYCHOLOGY?

If we ask what the operating assumptions of a cognitive social psychology are, we can identify a general theoretical emphasis and some methodological advances. Theoretically, cognitive social psychologists have shifted toward process models, which focus on how the individual gathers, interprets, and uses information. Whereas an interest in cognitive processes is not new to social psychology, the development of a methodology appropriate to this interest is. In practice, we have begun testing cognitive principles in situations and borrowing measures that attempt to zero in on what is actually going on in the subject's head.

On another level, cognitive social psychology is a shift in theoretical scope. It is an effort to move away from atomistic theories about temporally isolated and fairly specific social events to schematic models that are rich in detail and that attempt to provide a sufficient explanation for individuals' responses over time to a wider range of social events. Here again, the gap between theory and method is substantial, although this theoretical reorientation has resulted in initial efforts to develop computer models of social behavior.

Finally, cognitive social psychology is an emphasis on both the strength and the limitations of cognitive capabilities. Beginning with a naive belief that cognitive processes are infallible, we have now begun to focus on the shortcuts that information processors adopt when seeking explanations for the events that go on around them, which can appear as errors and biases when compared to infallible statistical models. As Dawes (Chapter 1) has pointed out, this has meant a movement away from crediting motivational factors for anything that "goes wrong" in the logical process, in exchange for the position that there are limits on how much information we can consider at any given time and that important aspects of cognition involve an effort to simplify the complexity and diversity of available information. Each of these issues—theoretical and methodological exchanges, a change in the scope of theory, and attention to the limitations as well as the strengths of cognitive capabilities—warrants additional consideration. Let me expand on the issue of theory—method interface.

THE RESEARCH PARADIGM IN SOCIAL PSYCHOLOGY

Whereas social psychology has a long history of interest in cognitive approaches to the study of behavior (an $S-O-R$ approach), we have often behaved like behaviorists. In our most common research paradigm, the experimental episode *cum* analysis of variance, we create a set of stimulus conditions, expose a subject to these conditions, study his outputs as measured by a set of scale responses, and then infer what the mental processes must have been for the subject to have produced those outputs given that particular set of inputs. Making these kinds of process statements from endpoint data is risky. One might say that we have used an $S-R$ methodology to test $S-O-R$ theories.

Several problems are created by this theory—method gap. The first problem is a temporal restrictiveness. My use of the term "outputs" refers in part to the fact that the subject is usually asked to state his reactions to the experiment at its close. In effect, the experimenter is asking, "Now that you have put everything together, what do you conclude?" instead of "How are you putting this information together?" Thus, we have no process measures per se although we discuss experimental results as if we did.

One beginning effort to solve this problem should be to "loosen up" the experimental paradigm in social psychology, and our interchanges with cognitive psychology may help us to do so. Loosening up the traditional experimental paradigm means, in part, a change in temporal emphasis away from studying frozen moments in time to studying process over time. A precedent for this kind of approach can be found in studies of social interaction. Content analysis, the form of social exchanges (e.g., interaction process analysis; Bales, 1950), and nonverbal information indications of affect (e.g., Mehrabian, 1972) are three examples of schemes for studying interaction in progress. One of the major contributions of such efforts has been to stress the importance of gathering a sampling of different classes of outcomes at different points in time, in contrast to waiting until the end of an encounter to see what has happened. For the most part, these efforts have been concerned with interactive situations rather than with information processing by individuals.

Perhaps the clearest indication of a change in social psychology directly attributable to the influence of cognitive psychology has been further changes not only in what temporal portions of interactions are studied but in the nature of the measures that are employed. For example, social psychologists have begun using dependent measures that have somewhat limited usefulness for studying the outcomes of social events but considerable usefulness for studying the dynamics of individual inference. Such measures include reaction time, recall, organization of recall, requests for additional information, eye movements and scanning, and verbal protocols, all of which are efforts to lend construct validity to process models.

A second problem with the traditional experimental paradigm is a "degrees of freedom" problem, i.e., an assumption that a given pattern of group means reflects a single underlying process. It is well known that for a result to be statistically significant, only a subset of subjects need actually show the effect. More importantly, it is usually assumed that all subjects who did show the effect did so for the same reason. Any naive student, if pushed, can come up with about six alternative explanations for any single experimental result. A group of 20 or so subjects can certainly generate even more. The point is that they may well do so. The number of ways a set of means can differ from each other is numerically fixed, given that we usually specify only the direction of differences and not the magnitude of differences we expect among a set of means. The number of ways of getting any pattern of means is potentially much larger than the number of possible patterns. It is therefore entirely possible that five subjects who score high on a set of output measures can do so for five different sets of reasons. Yet we attribute to them the same reasoning process. This picture is complicated further by the use of analysis of variance as the most common statistical procedure. Such summary statistics may tell us what a process looks like when averaged across individuals, but it does not necessarily tell us what any or most individuals are doing with the information provided to them. If we are going to draw inferences about individual behavior, then an examination of what individuals are doing and the use of statistical procedures appropriate to this focus are clearly warranted.

A third problem with the traditional experimental approach is the fact that when we ask questions at the end of an experiment, we make very arbitrary decisions about what the issues in a given situation are and what the subjects wants to and can tell us. For example, at the end of a brief encounter with another person, we may ask our subjects "How much do you like this person?" If the subject says, "I can't answer this," we respond, "Do the best you can." We then conclude that people are likely to like another person under a given set of conditions. Instead, we should take the subjects' objections, "I need more information" or "I can't answer this," more seriously. Unfortunately, because subjects almost always answer any question we ask them, we may be led to assume falsely that we have tapped the most important issues in a situation (when we have not), that the subject's answers to the questions are reliable and valid (when we have few independent assessments of either criterion), and that the subject has told us what he wanted to tell us (when we may not have given him that opportunity). As one place to start addressing this problem, analysis of verbal protocols and examination of open-ended questions and postexperimental interviews can provide some indication of what issues and questions are salient to the subjects.

These, then, are some of the problems and partial solutions facing the social psychological research paradigm if it is to accommodate the renewed and elaborated interest in process models. At this point, let me turn to the papers presented in this panel to see how these and other issues and problems are reflected in the development of a cognitive social psychology. Taken together, the papers indicate the diversity of directions this interface has prompted. Examined separately, each is an illustration of identifying characteristics of social cognition, although each reflects both the advantages and the problems of being in what can only be described as a highly transitional field.

CONTRIBUTIONS OF THE PAPERS

The chapter by Carroll and Payne (Chapter 2) is a clear example of the theoretical and methodological exchanges between the two fields. It illustrates a cognitive approach to a specific social problem, the parole decision process. Using information-processing concepts as a descriptive framework, the authors have derived a large number of testable hypotheses that examine the role of individual differences, various information and task characteristics, and their impact on the selection of problem-solving strategies. There are several features of this chapter that I should like to make explicit, because these characteristics are likely to appear in future such endeavors. The first feature is methodological eclecticism. The use of a large and diverse number of measurement procedures allows them to tap in on the process itself over time, as well as on actual decisions that are made. Relevant to this point, the authors have provided us with some data. Although the evidence they present on locus of control differences in information searches is only one small piece of the picture, it is methodologically more interesting than most locus of control studies in that it examines actual search differences and not merely decision differences. A second significant feature of this paper is its theoretical eclecticism. The chapter draws widely from both cognitive and social psychology to generate specific and, in some cases, contradictory hypotheses. For example, the authors propose to examine Kelley's notion of the naive statistician versus some heuristic problem-solving strategies. Through their examination of information searches, verbal protocols, and actual decisions, the authors can begin to choose among the various schemas and heuristics that may be relevant, should that prove to be the better approach, as preliminary evidence indicates.

Although these modifications in the experimental paradigm constitute one interface of cognitive and social psychology, these are not the only points of confluence which have occurred. As previously mentioned, the blending of cognitive and social psychology has also meant a shift in theoretical scope. Schmidt (Chapter 4) speaks to this issue. His chapter chronicles his development of BELIEVER, a computer model of the observer of social behavior. His approach represents a shift away from an atomistic theoretical orientation in favor of a more broad schematic approach. His goal is a model that is sufficiently rich in detail to predict successfully individual inferential processes that can apply to the general field of person perception. Drawing on Heiderian notions of the naive analysis of causality, Schmidt's model seeks to identify how an observer detects the plans and motives of an actor.

On several points, the Schmidt chapter is very helpful. For example, Schmidt has pointed to the necessity of understanding the norms, expectations, goals, and motives that underly any given act, in this case a simple request. How these features can combine into an interpretive schema for understanding individual acts is a point most experimentalists have ignored. In addition, Schmidt points out some of the holes in our current understanding of person perception. For example, if we look at the traditional method of studying person perception, namely the single-episode experiment, we find one result emerging with considerable consistency. Perceivers of another's behavior tend to reach relatively simple conclusions about the cause of that person's behavior. Behavior is usually attributed to an actor's underlying disposition, an attitude or personality trait.

The misinterpretation of this result lies not so much in the conclusion that people seek single-variable or parsimonious explanations, but in the assumption that the outcome of the reasoning process reflects the process itself. That is, a single-variable solution does not necessarily mean that only information pertinent to that variable has been considered during the reasoning process (see, for example, Jones & Harris, 1967). This, then, is one clear instance of the previously mentioned problem of inferring process from endpoint data. Furthermore, the fact that in experimental studies only person-oriented questions are asked of subjects and a liberal criterion for what constitutes a person attribution is set leaves the experimenter little choice about what conclusions to reach. Open-ended questions, for example, lead one to very different conclusions about the process of person perception (J. Howard & S. E. Taylor, unpublished data, 1974) and so, I suspect, does a modeling approach, in that it requires detailed attention to all phases of the reasoning process. The confluence of these two methods, modeling and experimentation, may at least prevent premature closure on issues of process.

Although Schmidt's chapter is helpful on these issues, on other points we may wish for clarification. The significance of Schmidt's approach is the theoretical concern with rich detail. As such, these very details must be adequately communicated, despite the overwhelming problems of terminology and methodological explication this presents. Some points on which we might ask for more information are the following. First, there seems to be an implicit assumption that all acts are intentional and purposive. One striking capacity of the human observer is his ability to distinguish such things as random events, rhetorical questions, and "thinking out loud" from truly purposive action. In the course of detecting a plan, can the model deal with randomly introduced and properly inputted irrelevancies, and if so, how? If not, does Schmidt regard this as a problem? Second, Schmidt suggests that the detection of "just misses" and procedures for mapping out possible worlds on the basis of a single act have been partially worked out. If this is the case, then we should like to know about the solutions. In sum, if our intermethod exchanges are going to bear fruit, we must have more than a general theoretical overview.

Abelson (Chapter 3) also calls for a large-scale approach to the study of social cognition. First, he rejects the usefulness of two views of psychology: piecemeal, bottom-up approaches to assembling knowledge, which are often adopted in practice if not in theory; and a structuralist approach, which maintains that matching specific experiences to formal structures relatively free of specific world-wise content can provide a basis for understanding social cognition. Abelson's answer to these views is that we should be studying behavioral chunks, not particulars, and that these chunks must take into account a knowledge of how the world works. He has proposed script theory as an alternative way of thinking about behavior, a script being a coherent set of expected events. He proposes that attitudes and behavior depend substantially on what scripts an individual has or can construct regarding social events. My feeling is that this idea forms the basis of an extensive theoretical shift in psychology (although there is by no means unanimous agreement on this point).

In rejecting piecemeal and structuralist approaches to social cognition, script theory also renders unsurprising certain phenomena that are surprising from other theoretical vantage points. For example, several symposium participants have discussed the disturbing fact that concrete information with a high level of immediacy has a greater impact on behavior and some attitudes than does abstract and often objectively better information. Abelson's answer to this is that it is not a problem per se but a very clear illustration of how people impute meaning to social experience. He is asking us to take an information-processing approach several steps further than we already have in considering acts as embedded in a network of prior experience, experience that is concrete, specific, often imageable, and to some extent idiosyncratic.

It becomes clear that script theory is at a metatheoretical level when we ask it to fulfill certain characteristics of theories. There is no test of script theory in the chapter, but rather a set of findings that is consistent with it. The theory is not yet falsifiable, and we are left with little idea of what to do with it.

This last point is quite important, because in the absence of such guidelines, we run the risk of simply adding one new noun, "script," and one new adjective, "scriptal," to our vocabulary, words that subsequently may be interpreted idiosyncratically. One implication of the theory can be directed to artificial intelligence. A mechanical inference system requires a knowledge of how the world works in order to make sense of behavior. An implication for researchers not in artificial intelligence might be a close examination of individual verbal protocols, for summary statistics are unlikely to reveal a scriptal type of reasoning process. Hopefully, once we find out what to do with it, the full impact of script theory can be felt.

Dawes (Chapter 1) speaks to the third concern of cognitive social psychology, namely attention to the limitations of cognitive processes. First, Dawes points out myths about cognition that both social and cognitive psychologists have accepted until quite recently. He exposes the naive assumption that information processing gives us complete and correct answers and that biased, erroneous, or incomplete answers can be traced to motivational factors. Second, he reminds us not only that our cognitive capacities for processing information are extremely limited, but also that one manifestation of this fact is our continued belief that they are not. Through his examples, Dawes has shown that both our theories and our applications of psychology to social problems are badly flawed. We are at our best, he contends, when we stick to figuring out what the relevant variables in a situation are, rather than how they should be combined, and he recommends in situations involving predictive applications (e.g., clinical prognosis, success in graduate school), that we specify the input variables and let the rest of the work fall to linear composite solutions.

Our theories are no less flawed, and within social psychology particularly, an about face on many problems is clearly warranted. The field of stereotyping is one specific example discussed in this volume. Early investigations assumed that stereotyping represents a short circuiting of the normal reasoning process. As a result, the search for what goes wrong persisted for many years and concentrated on individual motives and the social nature of the information. Only recently have investigators returned to the possibility that it is cognitive processes themselves, for example, the use of categorization to simplify incoming information, that may be at fault (see Hamilton, Chapter 6; Taylor & Fiske, in press).

To push Dawes' point a little further, we might consider what the view of man as a limited information processor has to say about our own scientific efforts to understand social cognition. That is, it is easy to see stupidity in retrospect, but our acknowledgements of faulty reasoning about applications to social problems and our recognition of previous arbitrary theoretical distinctions does not render us immune to such errors in the present. Theoretical, methodological, and statistical conventions that are adopted for their popularity rather than their appropriateness or validity may constitute other such blind spots, ones that can be removed only by making the assumptions of our models explicit and developing tools appropriate to examining these assumptions.

THE FUTURE

At this point it may be useful to summarize and reiterate the present status of social cognition. Given the diversity of the chapters in Part I, the field is clearly moving in several directions at once, both theoretically and methodologically. Both kinds of changes suggest a major reorientation in social psychology: much greater attention to the dynamics of individual inference and process. Already, there are indications that the experimental research paradigm is loosening up. In the future, we may find social psychologists returning to the position that one way to find out what subjects are doing is to ask them. An unimpressive history of deceit and trickery has backed social psychologists into a belief that because we do not tell our subjects the truth about what is going on in experiments, they will not tell us what they think they have done. Although in some cases this worry may be valid (see Rosenthal & Rosnow, 1969), there is no reason to assume it is always so. Intensive study of each individual, in addition to the use of summary statistics, need not be directed only toward identifying stable sets of individual differences, nor do subjects' "theories" about their behavior have to be our theories as well. Studies of individuals can identify salient and common styles of reasoning that may in turn lay the groundwork for studying more advanced problems.

In the future we can expect not that we will adopt a common point of view, but that the questions we still ask will become more similar. We can also begin to pose questions to each other with a realistic expectation that some answers can be forthcoming. Social psychologists will want to know more about the dynamics of information integration, categorization, and information storage and retrieval in order to understand problems in person perception, stereotyping, attitudes, and the like. Cognitive psychologists will want to know more about the texture of causal inference to understand social inputs to issues in problem solving and memory. We will both want to know what systems of representation and inference mechanisms the computer modelers are using, so we can know what to look for as we refine our methods of studying process. Newell and Simon's (1972) application of general problem solver strategies to the study of human problem-solving protocols is one example of what we hope to be a growing interchange. In the future, we must also advance our investigations beyond the perception of actor as object to situations that are more truly interactive. How is information processed in these situations and how and how far are contingent courses of action projected into the future? Finally, given our new-found realism about the limitations of our cognitive capabilities, how are we to face the fact that it is these same processes that must perform the work that lies ahead?

Part II

COGNITIVE PROCESSES IN THE PERCEPTION OF SELF AND OTHERS

The chapters in this section offer new theoretical and empirical approaches to person perception, an area of social psychology presenting natural opportunities for the development of a cognitive social psychology.

Hamilton (Chapter 6) shows how the processes of categorization and attention deployment are sufficient to produce group stereotypes without any necessary motivational or factual basis.

Frieze (Chapter 7) examines the importance of causal attributions in academic achievement settings and the selective examination of information used in making these attributions.

Nisbett, Borgida, Crandall, and Reed (Chapter 8) survey several situations in which people fail to use valid but abstract information about base-rate behavior. They demonstrate that concrete information about specific people is heavily utilized in judgments about self and others.

Schulz (Chapter 9) shows that feelings of control over life events is a crucial determinant of physical and psychological wellbeing, specifically among the institutionalized elderly.

Greene (Chapter 10) proposes that social perception can be viewed as the process of solving more or less ill-structured problems, such that their definitions as well as their solutions are partly determined by individual differences.

6
Cognitive Biases in the Perception of Social Groups

David L. Hamilton

Yale University

It is difficult to think of a topic in social psychology that has more obvious and important societal implications and yet has yielded less progress toward increasing our knowledge and understanding than research on stereotypes. The reasons for the lack of progress in this area are not entirely clear. Certainly the persistence of psychologists in adhering to the Katz–Braly adjective checklist method of assessing stereotypes has been a contributing factor. Although this methodology was a useful contribution when it was introduced over four decades ago (Katz & Braly, 1933), it unfortunately became almost the sole paradigm for studying stereotypes in the intervening years (cf. Brigham, 1971, for a critique of this method). One consequence of this reliance on a single paradigm is that a rather narrow range of questions has been investigated in stereotype research. Because the method is essentially designed to *assess* stereotypes, the findings from most studies are limited to providing descriptions of the content of stereotypic conceptions of various ethnic groups. With the exception of the work on ethnic preferences (cf. Brand, Ruiz, & Padilla, 1974), remarkably little research has addressed the questions of how stereotypes develop, the conditions under which they are used, and their consequences for interpersonal behavior. For these and other reasons, the study of stereotyping has become a somewhat stagnant research area, an isolated topic that until recently has remained uninfluenced by developments in other areas of person perception research. Fortunately, there are some recent signs that this state of affairs may be changing.

In recent years there has been a remarkable growth of interest in the cognitive processes involved in the way persons perceive and make judgments about others. Several areas of person perception research reflect this trend, such as the recent research investigating how people use information in forming first impressions, explaining other people's behavior and attributing dispositions to them, making jury decisions, and arriving at clinical diagnoses. In this chapter I summarize a growing body of literature investigating cognitive processes underlying the development of stereotypic conceptions of social groups. These processes involve biases in the way we utilize information, biases that typically play a highly functional role in our adapting to a complex stimulus environment but that can result in distorted and unfounded perceptions of social groups. Before I discuss this research, however, some general comments on the nature of stereotypes are appropriate, because the viewpoint presented here differs in significant ways from the more traditional conceptions of how stereotypes are formed.

CONCEPTIONS OF STEREOTYPES

Traditional conceptions of stereotypes have given little attention to possible cognitive biases that may produce differential perceptions of majority and minority groups. Ever since Lippman (1922) first introduced the term, stereotypes have been viewed as involving rather unique processes that presumably set them apart from other kinds of judgments. From the beginning, social scientists have tended to emphasize the dynamic aspects of stereotyping, arguing that the development and use of stereotypes have motivational roots and are of functional value to the perceiver. In addition, these dynamic forces are presumed to influence the perceiver's cognitive functioning. Stereotyping is therefore regarded as the product of an erroneous and atypical thought process in which the person adopts conclusions he would not normally make.

To demonstrate these points, let me briefly mention three specific assumptions commonly made regarding the basis of stereotyping, according to this traditional viewpoint:

a. First, it is frequently argued that stereotypes develop and are used in order to serve the motivational needs of the perceiver. These needs are often assumed to reside in the person's unconscious realm. For example, perceiving blacks as inferior may provide a person with some sense of power that may otherwise be lacking, or it may enhance (or at least protect) his self-esteem. A related view is that stereotypes are functionally useful for the perceiver in that they provide a means of rationalizing his prejudice and hostility toward an outgroup. The scapegoat theory of prejudice is another outgrowth of this emphasis on the motivational dynamics underlying the discriminatory perception of outgroup members.

b. Second, beginning with Lippman (1922) and continuing through numerous other writers, there has been the belief that stereotypes are arrived at through a "faulty reasoning process" (cf. Brigham, 1971). Somehow, it is argued, the perceiver's normal cognitive functioning is short circuited when he is confronted with some group other than his own, and the judgments made are the result of illogical thinking. Just why or how this deviation from one's usual cognitive processes is triggered has never been made clear.

c. A third commonly held assumption is that, whereas stereotypes may be illogical overgeneralizations and may even perform some useful psychological function for the individual, there is nevertheless some "kernel of truth" under-lying the characterization of the stereotyped group. The strongest form of this position is that a stereotype cannot exist without some actual basis, some real difference (however small) between minority and majority groups.

According to Tajfel (1969, pp. 81–82), stereotypes can be defined as "the attribution of general psychological characteristics to large human groups." Stereotyping thus begins with the differential perception of social groups. If a perceiver differentially evaluates two groups—either two groups of which he is not a part or his own versus some other group—then the particular content of those evaluations provides the basis for stereotypic conceptions. Several lines of recent research indicate that this kind of differential perception of groups can occur simply as a consequence of our normal cognitive functioning. If so, then it may be inappropriate to assume that stereotyping necessarily involves faulty reasoning or unconscious motivations, or even that there is some kernel of truth on which a stereotype is based.

CATEGORIZATION AND INTERGROUP DISCRIMINATION

One line of current research explores the consequences of social categorization on intergroup perception and behavior. As human beings, we exist in a world of many individuals performing many acts. As perceivers, however, we find it difficult to live in such a world and hence we seek out similarities and dif-ferences, reducing the degree of complexity confronting us by sorting people into groups and by sorting acts into behavior patterns. When, as a consequence of this categorization process, the perceiver comes to associate certain patterns of behaviors or traits with certain categories of persons, then stereotyping has occurred. Because persons are the dominant figures in our perceptual fields, it is likely that we construct human groupings and then attempt to identify the attributes or behavior patterns characteristic of those groups, instead of the other way around. The process of categorization and how we apply it to the identification of social groups therefore takes on considerable importance.

Writers have long recognized the importance of categorization as a first step in stereotype formation (see, for example, Allport, 1954; Ehrlich, 1973). If mem-bers of a particular social group are to be singled out and perceived and treated in a discriminatory manner, there must exist some identifiable feature(s) by which they can be identified and classified as belonging to that group. Most previous discussions of this process have emphasized the learned and/or motivational bases of the consequent discriminatory behavior. Recent research to be considered here, however, suggests that the categorization process itself may be a sufficient basis for intergroup discrimination.

One of the most common categorizations or differentiations we make is the classification of people into two groups—those who are like us and those who are not. Of course, the particular dimension on which similarity is judged changes from time to time and depends in part on the situational context, but the basic differentiation between "them" and "us" seems to be almost irresistable. Although this distinction may not be made deliberately, and the person may not attach more importance to it in his own mind, the result is that people are categorized into an ingroup and an outgroup.

A number of recent studies, initiated in the work of Tajfel and his colleagues (cf. Tajfel, 1970), have investigated the cognitive determinants of ingroup–outgroup biases and their consequences, seeking to identify the minimal conditions for the elicitation of intergroup discrimination. It appears from these studies that the necessary conditions are indeed minimal. The procedure in these experiments has typically been as follows. A number of subjects—usually around eight or so—come to the laboratory and two groups are established. The basis for the assignment of subjects to groups is quite arbitrary, usually based on their performance on some irrelevant task. Once they are assigned to groups, the subjects are given a task in which the opportunity to discriminate is present. In some studies, the task has involved allotting amounts of money to the other individuals, who are identified only by a code number and their group membership. In other studies subjects have been asked to make a series of evaluative trait ratings of the other participants. The results of these experiments have been rather striking. When allocating money to others, subjects quite consistently give larger amounts to other members of their own group, even though (a) there is no logical basis for such differentiation and (b) the subjects themselves do not personally gain from it (Billig, 1973; Billig & Tajfel, 1973; Ryen, 1974; Tajfel & Billig, 1974; Tajfel, Billig, Bundy, & Flament, 1971). In addition, subjects typically make more favorable ratings of members of their own group on a variety of personal characteristics (Doise, Csepeli, Dann, Gouge, Larson, & Ostell, 1972; Doise & Sinclair, 1973; Ryen, 1974). The results, then, demonstrate both behavioral and perceptual consequences of group categorization.[1]

---

[1] It should be noted that the minimal conditions for the elicitation of these effects are still somewhat unclear. Two studies (Dion, 1973; Rabbie & Horwitz, 1969) have reported failures to find ingroup–outgroup bias under certain conditions. Rabbie and Horwitz (1969) assigned subjects to groups on a random basis and found that this procedure alone did not produce differential evaluations of ingroup and outgroup. This is not surprising, for purely random assignment would hardly seem sufficient to induce any meaningful concept of "group" in the subjects. The procedure also lacks veridicality, for social categorization does not involve random groupings of others. In Dion's (1973) study, no intergroup discrimina-

The studies by Tajfel and his colleagues are particularly instructive because the methodology employed has permitted an examination of the strategies used by the subjects. When allocating money to two persons, only one of which was a member of the ingroup, subjects did not simply attempt to maximize the ingroup's profits but acted to maximize the difference in profit between the two groups. Hence, purely arbitrary assignment to group membership was a sufficient basis for discriminatory behavior.

Billig and Tajfel's (1973) term "minimal intergroup situation" is certainly descriptive of what happens in these experiments, and one may raise the objection that the situation is so artificial that the findings must be viewed with skepticism. Although the question of generalizability certainly needs to be addressed, the findings are nevertheless instructive as to the consequences of the mere identification of group membership, no matter how nebulous. Moreover, it was not necessary, even in this minimal situation, that the reward allocations be made according to the strategies employed by the subjects. Indeed, a more rational strategy in such an ambiguous situation would have been to maximize the total gain by both groups; after all, in Tajfel's studies the subjects did not even know what individuals were being rewarded and who else was in their own group. Although this "fairness" strategy was used to some extent, the predominant orientation of the subjects was to maximize the difference between their own and the other group. Therefore, our natural tendency to group objects in our environment into classes on the basis of similarities and dissimilarities among them can, under some circumstances, result in discriminatory perceptions and behaviors.

CATEGORIZATION AND THE PERCEPTION
OF SIMILARITY AND DISSIMILARITY

Another consequence of the categorization process has to do with the perception of intragroup and intergroup similarity. Evidence in the literature suggests that when objects have been categorized into groups, the perceiver tends to

---

tion was found in his "low-cohesiveness" condition. In this condition pairs of subjects were told that most groups in the study had been formed on the basis of similarity of predominant personality traits, but that in their case this had not been possible and that the two of them had quite different personality traits. These instructions, then, emphasize the dissimilarity between subjects, which seems to work against the formation of the group notion and to reflect the opposite of what occurs in the social categorization process. So, although the lack of an ingroup—outgroup bias is not surprising in either of these instances, the studies do indicate that the effects cited above do not occur under just any condition in which two groups are formed. Finally, it can be noted that other experimental conditions in both of these studies included procedures that facilitated formation of a "group" concept but that were unrelated to the subjects' task. Under these conditions intergroup bias was observed, as in the studies cited earlier.

overestimate the degree of similarity among members within a group and to overestimate the degree of dissimilarity between groups.

This phenomenon was demonstrated in the perception of physical stimuli in an experiment by Tajfel and Wilkes (1963). Subjects were shown a series of eight lines, which varied in length by a constant ratio. Next to each line there was a label, either A or B. In one condition the four shorter lines were labeled "A" and the four longer lines were labeled "B." In another condition the lines were labeled randomly, and in a third condition no labels were used. The subject's task was to estimate the length of each line. The results showed that in the first condition, but not in the others, subjects systematically erred in their judgments, underestimating the differences between lines with the same label and exaggerating the differences between lines with different labels. When the labels were associated with the lines in a manner leading the subjects to categorize the stimuli into two meaningful groupings, that is, as either "short" lines or "long" lines, significant perceptual distortions occurred.

Two studies provide evidence of similar effects in the perception of social groups. Tajfel, Sheikh, and Gardner (1964) had Canadian college students question two Canadian and two Indian persons about their views on films and books. Afterwards, subjects made a series of descriptive ratings of the persons questioned. The set of rating scales included attributes reflecting both the Canadian and the Indian stereotypes. Results showed that the two members of the same nationality were rated similarly on those attributes associated with the stereotype of that national group. More recently, Taylor and Fiske (in press) have reported an experiment in which subjects listened to a tape of a discussion among six persons, three of whom were white and three of whom were black. The authors reported that, after hearing the group discussion, subjects were able to remember the race of the person who made almost every comment but they could not recall which of the blacks or which of the whites had made the remark. Subjects apparently were successful at differentiating between the two groups but had difficulty differentiating among the various members of each group.

These findings would seem to have important implications. Obviously, categorization of stimulus objects into groups is not only a useful process in simplifying a complex world but also is quite adaptive in many circumstances. However, social objects can be classified in numerous ways, depending on the particular criterion employed. Any given way of classifying others into groups should be of some utility to the perceiver, for example, in helping him make inferences and judgments about others or in anticipating the nature of interactions with them. Conversely, a categorization system that was not useful in these ways would presumably be discarded in favor of some alternative means of cognitively defining important group memberships. The findings described above suggest that the categorization process itself produces perceptual distortions which justify for the perceiver the use of the categories employed. That is, the resulting enhancement of perceived intergroup differences can make those categories seem all the more meaningful and so can provide the perceiver with subjective "evidence" that this particular way of defining social groups has identified important differences to which he ought to attend.

ATTENTIONAL INFLUENCES ON PERCEPTIONS
OF A "SOLO" IN A SMALL GROUP

It is obvious that perceivers cannot possibly attend to all of the stimuli impinging on them. As a consequence, the determinants of what stimuli are attended to has long been a topic of interest to cognitive psychologists. One stable finding in this research area has been that a distinctive stimulus consistently draws the attention of the perceiver. In this section I shall briefly summarize some recent research exploring the implications of this process for social perception.

Members of certain social groups often find themselves in the role of what Taylor and Fiske (in press) have called a "solo" or "token" member of a small group. That is, a black in an otherwise all-white group or a female in an otherwise all-male group are solos within those groups. By virtue of the easily perceived characteristics (skin color, sex) that they bring with them, a person in the role of solo is a distinctive stimulus within the context of the group membership. Taylor and Fiske (in press) have recently reported a study investigating how the perceptions of a group member are influenced by his or her status as a solo.

Based on the finding that distinctive stimuli are attended to more than nondistinctive stimuli, the experimenters hypothesized that more information would be retained about a solo than about other participants in the group. To test this hypothesis, they had subjects listen to a taperecording of a group discussion. While the tape was being played, subjects were shown slides of the participant who presumably was speaking at the time. By using the same tape but varying the slides shown, Taylor and Fiske were able to manipulate the composition of the group while controlling the content of the discussion. In one condition, for example, the slides showed one black and five white males in the group discussion. In the other condition the group was fully integrated, with three participants of each race. Subjects' ratings of the participants in the discussion indicated that the solo was perceived as having been more active and more influential during the discussion than the same stimulus person in the fully integrated group, and subjects remembered more of what the solo had said. In addition, the solo received more extreme ratings on several evaluative dimensions. These effects did not result from the subjects' learned stereotypic conception of blacks, because the same black person in a fully integrated group was not differentially perceived in these ways.

Taylor and Fiske's (in press) findings demonstrate that the distinctive physical characteristics of a minority group member may, when he is in the position of a solo, result in differential attention to his behavior within the group, with consequent misperceptions of him. In contrast to the research described earlier, in which perceptual biases resulted as a consquence of the mere categorization of a person as being a member of an ingroup or an outgroup, the "solo" phenomenon is a consequence of the joint occurrence of two factors, the minority group member's physical distinctiveness and his status as the only minority member of the group. As Taylor and Fiske point out, these findings have implications for a number of naturally occurring situations in which a single member of some socially salient group participates in some larger group context.

DIFFERENTIAL PERCEPTIONS OF GROUPS
BASED ON ILLUSORY CORRELATION

The last area of research on cognitive bases of stereotyping to be discussed grows out of my own research on illusory correlations in interpersonal perception. Several years ago, Chapman (1967) introduced the term "illusory correlation" to refer to the erroneous report by an observer regarding the degree of association between two variables or classes of events. Chapman's interest was in clinical diagnoses, and in an interesting series of experiments the Chapmans (Chapman & Chapman, 1967, 1969) and others (e.g., Golding & Rorer, 1972; Starr & Katkin, 1969) have provided evidence of how cognitive biases can result in erroneous beliefs regarding the relationships between various psychodiagnostic signs and patient symptomatology. My own interest was in person perception, and more specifically in whether the foundation for stereotyping—the differential perception of groups—could be based on the cognitive biases described in Chapman's (1967) research.

The rationale and paradigm used in our research (Hamilton & Gifford, 1976) was based on Chapman's (1967) original demonstration of illusory correlation. In that experiment, Chapman constructed two lists of words, such as the following:

List A: lion, bacon, blossoms, boat
List B: tigers, eggs, notebook

Subjects in the experiment were shown a series of word pairs, each pair combining a word from List A with one from List B. All possible pairings occurred in the sequence an equal number of times. Subjects were then asked to estimate, for each word on List A, the percentage of the occurrences of that word in which it had been paired with each of the List B words. Because all possible pairs had occurred the same number of times, the correct answer in each case was 33.3%. Chapman found, however, that systematic biases were associated with certain kinds of word pairs. In those cases where there was a strong associative relationship between two words (e.g., *lion–tiger, bacon–eggs*) subjects consistently overestimated the frequency of occurrence of the word pair within the series. The other case for which subjects consistently overestimated the frequency of cooccurrence was when the two words paired were distinctive within their respective lists. In each list, one word was considerably longer than the other words. When those two words were paired (*blossoms–notebook* in the above example) subjects recalled the pair as having occurred more frequently than it actually had. Therefore, Chapman argued, an illusory correlation may be based either on the associative meaning that exists between two events or on the pairing of distinctive events. In either case the subject "sees" the two events as "going together" with more regularity than has been actually true.

In our work we have explored the implications of Chapman's findings for social stereotyping. In this context, the associative basis for illusory correlations demonstrated in Chapman's study corresponds to the consequences of learned stereotypic conceptions about social groups. That is, if one has previously learned that blacks are more likely than whites to be lazy and dishonest, then Chapman's results suggest that the person's perceptions of events would be biased in that direction, even in the absence of any difference between blacks and whites in the extent to which laziness or dishonesty are manifested in their behavior. The result for the perceiver, then, is a self-fulfilling prophesy in which "blackness" is seen as being related to laziness and dishonesty, even though no such relationship may exist in the material to which the person has been exposed.

Our research has focused on the other basis for establishing an illusory correlation, the pairing of events that are distinctive. We were interested in this case because of a parallel we saw in contemporary American life. In the everyday experience of the typical white person, interaction with and even exposure to blacks is a relatively infrequent occurrence, so that when one does encounter a black person it is a distinctive event, distinctiveness in this case being defined by infrequency. In addition, undesirable or nonnormative behavior is less frequent than desirable behavior and hence can also be considered distinctive. If this is true, then the implication of Chapman's (1967) finding is that the pairing of "blackness" with "undesirable behavior" can lead the typical white observer to infer a relationship between the two, even if the distribution of desirable and undesirable behaviors has been the same for both blacks and whites. Such an inference would provide the basis for the differential perception of the majority and minority groups, and hence for stereotyping.

In an experiment designed to test this line of reasoning (Hamilton & Gifford, 1976) subjects were shown a series of 39 slides, each of which presented one statement describing a person as having performed some behavior. Each stimulus person was described as belonging to one of two groups. Because we were interested in the effects of paired distinctiveness and not in any associative bases for the subjects' judgments, actual social or ethnic groups were not used; consequently each person was merely identified as belonging to either Group A or Group B. The stimulus sentences were of the following form: "John, a member of Group A, canvassed his neighborhood soliciting for a charity"; "Bob, a member of Group B, lost his temper and hit a neighbor he was arguing with." In the set of stimulus sentences used, there were twice as many statements describing members of Group A than there were for Group B, and desirable behaviors were more frequent than undesirable behaviors. However, the ratio of desirable and undesirable behaviors was identical for both groups. Therefore, there was no relationship between group membership and the desirability of the behaviors described. In addition, the sentence sets were constructed so that the average desirability values of the behaviors characterizing the two groups were approximately equal, based on previously obtained ratings of a larger set of behaviors.

Within the stimulus materials presented to the subjects, membership in Group B and undesirable behavior each were distinctive characteristics. Therefore, sentences describing members of Group B performing undesirable behaviors represented instances of the pairing of distinctive (infrequent) events. Based on Chapman's (1967) finding, we expected an illusory correlation to occur such that subjects would overestimate the degree of association between membership in Group B and the incidence of undesirable behavior. If so, then this might result in differential perception of the two groups, similar to that observed in stereotyping.

Following the presentation of the stimulus sentences, subjects were given a booklet in which they were asked to perform several judgment tasks. In one part, the behavior descriptions from the stimulus sentences were reproduced and subjects were asked to indicate for each one whether it had been performed by a member of Group A or Group B. In analyzing these data, a 2 X 2 table was constructed for each subject with the rows defined by the evaluation of the behavior (desirable or undesirable) and the columns by the group (A or B) attributed by the subject. The subject's responses to the 39 items were then classified in this table, and a phi coefficient was calculated for each subject to determine the perceived relationship between group membership and desirability of behavior. In the set of stimulus sentences, the ratio of desirable to undesirable behaviors was the same for both groups, so a phi coefficient based on the stimulus information was zero. Systematic deviations from zero in the subjects' attributions would therefore reflect a bias in their judgments of the two groups and would constitute evidence for an illusory correlation. To test this hypothesis, the subjects' phi coefficients were converted to Fisher's z scores and averaged, and the mean phi coefficient was found to be significantly greater than zero. Further analyses indicated that this bias resulted primarily from a tendency to overattribute undesirable behaviors to Group B, as would be expected on the basis of Chapman's finding that pairs of distinctive stimuli are overrecalled.

Another measure consisted of the subject's frequency estimates of desirable and undesirable behaviors performed by members of the two groups. The subject was told that there had been 26 statements describing members of Group A and 13 statements referring to members of Group B and was asked to estimate how many of them for each group were undesirable behaviors. Using these estimates, a 2 X 2 table based on behavior desirability and group membership was again constructed for each subject and phi coefficients were determined and averaged. As was true in the attributions of specific behaviors, analysis of these frequency estimates yielded a mean phi coefficient that was significantly greater than zero.

Did the establishment of this illusory correlation influence the subjects' perceptions of the two groups? To examine this question, subjects were asked to rate their impressions of Group A and Group B on a series of 20 descriptive rating scales. Scales were selected from each pole of the social and intellectual dimensions found by Rosenberg, Nelson, and Vivekananthan (1968) in their analysis of the dimensions underlying first impressions. For each of these diminsions, subjects rated members of Group A as being more likely to have desirable and less likely to have undesirable characteristics. These results therefore provided evidence that the subjects formed evaluatively different perceptions of the two groups, even though the average desirability ratings of the individual sentences describing the two groups were equal.

The results of this study, then, demonstrate that distortions in both recall and judgment processes can result from the way in which information about co-occurring events is processed. The consequence was that the two stimulus groups were perceived as being different from each other, even though there were no informational bases for the perceived differences.

This study has recently been replicated by Jones, Stoll, Solernou, Noble, Fiala, and Miller (1975). The procedure in this experiment was highly similar to that used by Hamilton and Gifford (1976), although stimulus persons in this case were described by personality traits rather than behavior descriptions. The findings were consistent with the earlier study in that subjects significantly overestimated the number of undesirable characteristics that had been attributed to the smaller group.

DISCUSSION AND IMPLICATIONS

The studies reviewed above all have the common feature that they provide evidence of the differential perception of majority and minority group members as a function of cognitive processing variables. It has been shown that factors related to the categorization of, attention to, and processing of information about social stimuli can result in social judgment patterns highly similar to those commonly observed in stereotypes of ethnic groups.

Although this growing body of findings emphasizes the importance of cognitive processes as determinants of the differential perception of social groups, it obviously is not my intent to suggest that all stereotypes are based solely on such factors. Much of what persons believe and feel about stereotyped groups is acquired through social learning experiences, and motivational factors may facilitate the acquisition and/or maintenance of the prevailing conceptions of various outgroups. Even when these other processes plan an important role, however, their ultimate effects are necessarily mediated by their influences on the perceiver's cognitive processes. The nature of and the mechanisms involved in these mediating influences have not received sufficient experimental investigation.

In the introduction to this paper three widely held assumptions about stereotypes were noted: that they serve the motivational needs of the perceiver, that they are based on some "kernel of truth," and that they are the product of a "faulty reasoning process." It is instructive to reconsider these assumptions in light of the findings I have summarized. Certainly the results of these studies cannot be understood in terms of motivational forces operating in the perceivers. Most of the tasks employed were highly cognitive in nature, and in most cases deliberate efforts were made to avoid any influences caused by previously developed associations or values the subjects might have had regarding certain social groups. Motivational theories would have particular difficulty accounting for the results of the illusory correlation studies (Hamilton & Gifford, 1976) and of the study by Taylor and Fiske (in press) of the perception of the solo within a group.

Similarly, it is difficult to identify any "kernel of truth" that might underlie the differential perceptions and intergroup discrimination evidenced in these studies. In the "minimal intergroup situation" research by Tajfel and others, the group assignments were made on the basis of criteria quite irrelevant to the intergroup judgments; in the study by Taylor and Fiske the subjects' unique perception of the black solo was associated with his being in that role and could not have been caused by any personal characteristics of the stimulus person, because that same person was not singled out in the observers' perceptions of the fully integrated group; and in the illusory correlation studies the stimulus information about the two groups was carefully equated in terms of desirability, so that no informational basis for the resulting differential evaluations was present. Therefore, stereotyping does not necessarily reflect the overgeneralization of actual differences between groups; aspects of our cognitive functioning may lead us to "see" differences that do not actually exist.

The third assumption about stereotyping is that it reflects a faulty or inferior reasoning process. As noted earlier, this viewpoint holds that the cognitive processes involved in stereotyping are qualitatively different from our characteristic manner of thinking and perceiving. I know of no solid evidence for such a short-circuiting process, and the studies summarized in this chapter indicate that such an assumption is not necessary. Several characteristics of our normal cognitive processing have been cited that have been sufficient to produce differential perceptions of groups and/or intergroup discrimination. Although cognitive strategies, such as categorizing stimulus objects into classes and attending to distinctive stimuli, may be highly adaptive under most circumstances, it has been shown that they may also provide the foundation for stereotyping.

An alternative interpretation of the "faulty reasoning process" notion would be that stereotyping, although not based on qualitatively different cognitive processes, does reflect a rather poor application of those processes to certain classes of social stimuli. This view would simply argue that stereotypic conceptions are unfounded overgeneralizations, that the perceiver has not used the available information in an optimal manner, that he has based his conclusions about a particular social group on poor evidence, etc. In this case the perceiver's processes are inferior or faulty only in comparison to a model of the "rational man." However, the finding that a perceiver does not use information in an optimal manner certainly is not unique to stereotyping; other chapters in this volume provide numerous illustrations of how our cognitive mechanisms fail to approach the specifications of such a model. So, whereas stereotyping may involve a "faulty reasoning process" in this sense, it is not because of anything specific to the perception of ethnic groups. It would seem more appropriate, in terms of both parsimony and potential benefit, to recognize the similarity of these processes to those employed in the judgment of circles and squares of different colors, of lines of varying lengths, and of pairs of words. In doing so, we may not only learn something about the cognitive bases of stereotypic conceptions of social groups, but also discover some of the socially significant consequences of the limitations of man's basic cognitive processes.

ACKNOWLEDGMENTS

Preparation of this paper was facilitated by NIMH Grant MH 26049-01.

7

The Role
of Information Processing
in Making Causal Attributions
for Success and Failure

Irene Hanson Frieze

University of Pittsburgh

Attribution theory is concerned with how people interpret information about their own behavior and the behavior of others in making judgments about the underlying causes of events. It is assumed that people implicitly or explicitly are constantly making causal attributions about every salient event in their lives. These causal judgments or perceptions are believed to be central to people's understanding of their environment and to the formation of predictions about the future.

Although attribution theory is concerned with causal judgments made in a number of situations about many types of events, the focus of this chapter is those attributions made about achievement events—attributions for success and failure. The work within this area grows out of a concern with individual differences in achievement-oriented behavior. Researchers (such as Weiner and Feather) of achievement motivation turned to attributional concepts developed by Heider (1958), Jones and Davis (1965), Rotter (1966), and Kelley (1967) as a potentially fruitful viewpoint for extending the theories and data previously developed for explaining achievement-oriented behavior.

Weiner and his associates (e.g., Weiner, 1974; Weiner, Frieze, Kukla, Reed, Rest, & Rosenbaum, 1971) have done extensive work in investigating the role of causal attributions for success and failure in explaining achievement-oriented behavior. This research has concentrated on three major areas: information processing and its effects on causal attributions; the types of causal attributions made to explain achievement events; and the effects of various causal attributions on affect, expectancies, and subsequent achievement strivings. The first of these three areas is the focus of this chapter but in order that we may understand this work within its larger context, some of the basic findings in the other areas are also discussed.

THE ATTRIBUTION PROCESS FOR ACHIEVEMENT EVENTS

A schematic model of the attributional process, based partly on empirical findings and partly on theorizing, is shown in Fig. 7.1. Although similar models have been suggested for situations in which people themselves are participating in an achievement-oriented activity (Frieze, 1973), this model assumes that a person observes someone else participating in an achievement event, such as taking an exam (the typical situation for much of the achievement attribution research). Within the attribution process, readily available information about the exam and the person taking it is combined with a judgment of the actual test score as either a success or failure (Box 1 in Fig. 7.1) as the first step in determining why this outcome has occurred. Current literature suggests that the causal attribution may be determined in one of two ways. In situations similar to these experienced in the past, the person may quickly assess the readily available information and then match this situation to a previously developed causal schema or decision strategy (Box 2) and form an immediate causal attribution (Box 7). This may take the form of a simple bias toward certain causal attributions for success and others for failure or it may represent a more complex but familiar schema.

In cases where there is no readily available causal schema in memory, the person attempts to develop a new information-processing strategy (Box 3). It is hypothesized that the person systematically considers the available information in arriving at a judgment about why the success or failure occurred. For example, information that may be relevant in attributing the outcome of an exam to one of many possible causes includes knowledge of how well the person has done on past exams of the type given, as well as his or her previous experience on other types of exams. Also, the time spent studying may be important information. This information would be systematically weighted and combined by the person to determine why he or she succeeded or failed the exam. Studies have shown that people have consistent and systematic methods for combining and weighting information in making this type of causal judgment (Frieze & Weiner, 1971; McArthur, 1972). If, in attempting to process the available information, the person finds that the processing strategy developed is not consistent with other previously developed rules or that he or she lacks sufficient information to be reasonably certain of the attribution, the person may seek further information (Box 5), perhaps making a tentative attribution

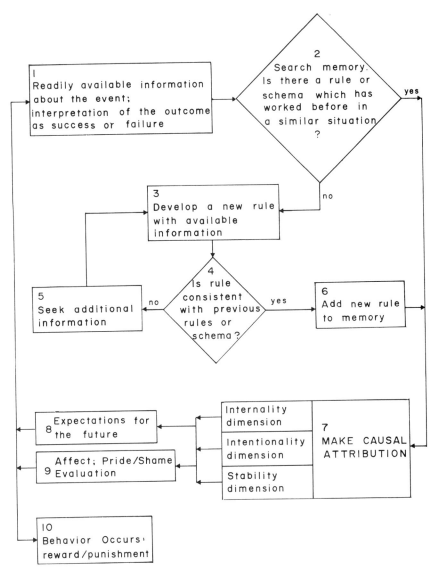

FIG. 7.1   The attribution process for achievement events.

while seeking additional data. For example, in the above instance the person might also want to know who else took the exam and how well they did. Once an acceptable processing rule is developed, this rule is now added to memory (Box 6) so that it can be utilized on future occasions, and the causal attribution is made (Box 7).

Causal Attributions

To return to the example of the person taking an exam, once all available information is processed, a person may then determine that the success on the exam has resulted from one or more of several possible causes: the person's ability in that subject, her trying hard, the exam's being easy, or good luck. Similarly, if he had failed, it might be attributed to lack of ability, lack of effort, the difficulty of the exam, or bad luck. These four causes were specified by Heider (1958) and have been most fully researched by Weiner and associates (e.g., Weiner, 1974; Weiner et al., 1971). More recent work (Elig & Frieze, 1975; Frieze, 1976) has indicated that other causal factors in addition to ability, effort, luck, and task difficulty are frequently employed by people in explaining success and failure. These include stable effort or a consistent pattern of diligence or laziness, other people who may aid or interfere with performance on a task, mood or fatigue or sickness, having a good or bad personality, and physical appearance (see Elig & Frieze, 1975, for a more complete discussion of these causal elements). These attributions may be classified into three dimensions, as shown in Table 7.1. Each of these dimensions (internality, stability, and intentionality) has different relationships to the attributional consequences represented by Boxes 8, 9, and 10.

Consequences of Attributions

As seen in Fig. 7.1, once the attribution of the event is made, certain consequences follow (Boxes 8, 9, and 10). If the performance of a student failing an exam is attributed to lack of effort, he may be expected to succeed in the future if he tries harder. If, in contrast, the failure is attributed to lack of ability, he will be expected to do just as poorly in the future. Weiner et al. (1971) have systematically shown how changes in expectancies for future success on achievement tasks (Box 8) are affected by differential attributions. Weiner, Heckhausen, Meyer, and Cook (1972) and Valle and Frieze (1976) have shown that expectancy changes are related to the stability dimension of the two-dimensional system for classifying attributions. Stable causes produce expectancies that outcomes will continue to be the same, whereas unstable causes at times produce unusual expectancy shifts, such as the gambler's fallacy (e.g., beliefs that success will be followed by failure or that failure will be followed by success). These expectancies are then also used as information for making attributions about future events (Feather, 1967; Feather & Simon, 1971a, b). For example, outcomes at variance with expectations are often ascribed to luck.

Although affect (feelings of pride or shame) may depend directly on the outcome of behavior (e.g., children feel happier after success than after failure, regardless of the information they are given; Parsons & Ruble, 1972), affect also

TABLE 7.1
A Three-Dimensional Model for Classifying Causal Attributions
for the Success and Failure of Others[a]

	Stable	Unstable
	Internal	
Intentional	Stable effort of actor (diligence or laziness)	Unstable effort of actor (trying or not trying hard)
Unintentional	Ability of actor Knowledge or background of actor Personality of actor	Fatigue of actor Mood of actor
	External	
Intentional	Others always help or interfere	Others help or interfere with this event
Unintentional	Task difficulty or ease Personality of others	Task difficulty or ease (task changes) Luck or unique circumstances Others accidentally help or interfere

[a]Modified from Elig and Frieze (1975).

depends on the causal attribution (Box 9). Studies have shown that outcomes attributed to internal factors are experienced with more pride or shame than outcomes seen as caused by external factors (Weiner, 1974). They also result in more positive evaluations by others when successful and less positive evaluations when not successful (Rosenbaum, 1972).

Finally, as a result of the expectations and affect associated with the causal attribution, behavior, such as reward or punishment of the outcome, occurs (Box 10).

EMPIRICAL STUDIES OF INFORMATION PROCESSING FOR ATTRIBUTIONAL JUDGMENTS

A series of studies has been done to investigate how people use information in making attributional judgments. In general, these studies have tended to look for specific information cues associated with specific causal attributions. Studies have utilized both different cue sets and different attributions as dependent ratings. Cues presented in various studies have included the outcome alone, the expected outcome, the outcome in relation to the pattern of previous outcomes and in relation to how other people have reacted or done in similar situations, the type of situation, and the amount of time spent working on a task. Attributions have been made to internal versus external factors or to stable versus unstable factors, as well as to individual causes, such as ability, effort, luck or the unique situation, task difficulty, and other people.

In a typical study, the subject is provided with a number of informational cues in all possible combinations and asked to rate why each event described by a particular cue combination may have occurred. ANOVA models have been used for data analysis, and interaction effects have been equated with configurality in cue usage. Although these studies have used a wide variety of cues, situations, and attribution rating scales, results have been surprisingly consistent.

In general, more internal attributions (see Table 7.1) are made for outcomes unique to the person (Ajzen, 1971; Fontaine, 1974; Frieze & Weiner, 1971; McArthur, 1972). People also see actors as more responsible for success events than for failure events (Chaikin, 1971; Fontaine, 1974; Frieze & Weiner, 1971; Streufert & Streufert, 1969; Weiner & Kukla, 1970). Interpersonally stable attributions, such as task difficulty, are made for outcomes shared by others, whereas causal elements varying across people (personal characteristics, luck, etc.) are utilized when the actor experiences different outcomes than others (Fontaine, 1974; Frieze & Weiner, 1971). As may be further expected, attributions that are more stable over time are made for situations that are consistent with the past, especially if the immediate outcome is expected (Feather & Simon, 1971a, b; Frieze & Weiner, 1971; McArthur, 1972).

When specific causal attributions are considered, ability attributions are most common when the available information implies consistency over time (Chaikin, 1971; Feather & Simon, 1971a, b; Frieze & Weiner, 1971) and, although there is some discrepancy here, when there is high initial success (Beckman, 1970; Feather, 1967; Jones, Rock, Shover, Goethels, & Ward, 1968). Ability attributions are also commonly made for outcomes unique to the person, for outcomes that generalize over similar tasks, and for tasks on which a long time has been spent (Frieze & Weiner, 1971). However, outcomes shared with highly similar other people also lead to ability attributions (Fontaine, 1974).

Effort attributions result from outcomes unique to the person, outcomes inconsistent with past outcomes, and outcomes consistent with their level of importance to the person (Fontaine, 1974; Frieze & Weiner, 1971). Also, success after spending a long time working on the task (Frieze & Weiner, 1971) and low initial success followed by an increasing proportion of successes tend to be attributed more to effort (Beckman, 1970; Jones et al., 1968).

Luck, mood, or unique circumstance attributions are most common with outcomes not shared with others or inconsistent with the past (Fontaine, 1974; Frieze & Weiner, 1971; McArthur, 1972; Orvis, Cunningham, & Kelley, 1975). Antecedents of task attributions are outcomes shared with others and high consistency over time and situation for the person (Frieze & Weiner, 1971;

Fontaine, 1974; Orvis, Cunningham, & Kelley, 1975). Failure after working a long time is also attributed to task difficulty (Frieze & Weiner, 1971).

This research has clearly established that college student subjects can utilize information in meaningful ways to make causal attributions for success and failure. Referring to the model of the attributional process presented in Figure 7.1, these studies further suggest that some of the information-processing rules (Box 2) may be simple relationships between specific informational cues and causal judgments. Although various cues are related to each of the independent causal judgments, there tends to be one cue for each cause that shows a qualitatively stronger relationship: (a) Ability is primarily related to consistency with the past; (b) effort is most related to a covariation of incentive with outcome; (c) inconsistencies over time result in luck or mood attributions; and (d) task outcomes are most common when an outcome experienced by many people.

INFORMATION-PROCESSING ISSUES ADDRESSED BY ACHIEVEMENT ATTRIBUTION RESEARCH

The first studies of the information-processing aspect of the attribution process (Boxes 1–6 of Figure 7.1) were concerned with establishing that subjects did indeed utilize information available to them in meaningful ways to judge the causes of success and failure. The studies reviewed on the last few pages have shown that there are reasonable rules that people consistenly adopt in making causal judgments for success and failure (Box 2). However, these early studies have raised many questions about how subjects combine and weight information—about the process of making causal judgments. There were questions about the procedures employed in these studies and, therefore, about the validity of their results. More recent research has been directed at attempting to resolve some of these issues. Some of the questions being explored in the last few years have concerned the validity of the role-playing techniques utilized so extensively in the attributional studies. A second methodological question was about the appropriateness of the informational cues presented to subjects (Box 1). Another issue was the validity of presenting cues simultaneously rather than in a more natural sequential order (again, a concern with the manipulations occurring in Box 1 of the attribution process). Finally, there was a concern with the nature of individual differences in processing strategies (Boxes 2–6).

Validity of Role-Playing Procedures

Much of the attribution research focused on Boxes 1–7 of the attribution process has used role-playing techniques, in which subjects are presented with a limited set of standardized cues and told to imagine the situation described by these cues and then to make judgments about the causes of these situations. Although similar limitations are not uncommon in information-processing research in general, they are of special importance for a theoretical approach that is attempting to understand human behavior in a variety of real settings. Because the validity of these procedures is essential if any generalizations about the information-processing research based on this methodology are to be made, research about these procedures is a necessary precondition to further exploration of the attribution process for achievement events.

In two different but similar studies, Fontaine (1975) and Frieze and LaVoie (1972) had subjects actually experience a success or failure and state why they felt this event had occurred (real condition). These responses were compared with those of subjects asked to imagine a success or failure (role-playing condition) that was similar to the one experienced by the subjects in the real condition. In both studies, the differences in information utilization between the two conditions were negligible. There were some differences in causal attributions used to explain the outcomes; the subjects in the real conditions tended to be slightly more defensive and were less likely to attribute failures to internal factors.

Other studies in which subjects actually experience success or failure have also yielded similar results to those obtained in role-playing studies (e.g., Bar-Tal & Frieze, 1976). Although these studies have not systematically varied the available information to analyze information-processing differences, the variations in results even for the causal attributions are small enough that role-playing procedures are considered to be valid, at least for the well-defined achievement situations involving success or failure on an exam or similar task. However, the research is still needed to investigate other factors, such as the importance of the situation and the relationship of the observer of a situation to the actor.

Validity of Informational Cues

Within most of the attribution information-processing studies, the information provided to the subjects (Box 1) has generally been selected from a relatively small set of cues: the type of task, how well other people performing the same task have done, how well the person has done in the past, and how much time has been spent working on the task. These cues were chosen because they were felt to be important by the experimenter for intuitive or theoretical reasons. It was assumed that because people did in fact utilize this information that it was the information that they would naturally use to determine why achievement events happened. In order to test these assumptions and to establish the validity of the cues used in previous studies, Frieze (1976) asked subjects to state what information they would want to help them better understand an achievement situation about which they were asked to make attributions. Because the responses were entirely open ended, they did not cue subjects to any particular responses. Based on the information obtained from 80 college students, 13 categories of information were derived from the data. In order of their frequency of requests, there were:

1. Task: specific information about the type of exam or situation
2. Incentive: the importance of the outcome to the person
3. Ability: the ability, skill, or past history of successes of the person
4. Social comparison: the skill or ability of other people involved in the situation or how these other people have performed
5. Effort: the effort exerted by the person
6. Instructor: information about the person teaching the class in which the exam has been given, especially about the teaching skill of this person
7. Mood: the mood or state of mind of the person
8. Exact outcome: detailed information about the exact outcome or score or what items have been missed on the exam
9. Identity of the person: nonspecific information about who the person is
10. Other people: information about other people who intentionally have affected the outcome; the presence of cheating on the exam
11. Cheating: knowledge about whether the person has cheated or let someone else do better intentionally
12. Luck: how lucky the person has been
13. Team effort: information about the outcome being dependent on a group rather than an individual

Over 75% of the information requests were classifiable into these categories (the percentage varied from study to study). Overall, people wanted between two and three types of information to explain each event, even though studies had shown that people might utilize as many as five information cues when they were presented with the information (Frieze & Weiner, 1971).

This study provided data indicating that the types of informational cues which had been made available to subjects in the past were indeed the information they would request freely. However, previous research has neglected to include the important cue of incentive. As a basis of this study, incentive information has been used in subsequent research.

Sequential versus Simultaneous Information Utilization

Another major issue related to attributional information processing also concerns the validity of certain assumptions made in this literature. Nearly all of the attribution studies (as well as most information-processing research) have tended to assume that the procedures used for analyzing large amounts of information available at one time are analogous to a sequential processing strategy. One may assume that people normally obtain cues not all at one time but one by one in nonlaboratory situations. It is fully possible that people make tentative attributions when they know they must wait for additional information (Box 5) and then revise these attributions as more information is made available. However, these tentative attributions may be different from the causal attributions based on full information. If the results of sequential information-processing studies were found to differ in major ways from judgments based on simultaneous cues, the greater apparent validity of the sequential procedure would imply that this should be used in future studies.

There is some evidence to suggest that sequential processing will necessitate some modification in the usual simultaneous models. Although the data are inconsistent, there is some evidence for order effects changing results when information is not available at all one time (Anderson, 1972; Jones & Goethals, 1971; Petronko & Perin, 1970). Jones and Goethals suggest that order effects are produced by differential recall of information presented at different times. However, in addition to cognitive deficiencies, apparent order effects may have specific attributional meanings. Ability attributions result from high initial success followed by continued success (Frieze & Weiner, 1971; Fontaine, 1974) or sometimes from decreasing numbers of successes (Beckman, 1970; Jones et al., 1968). Effort attributions, in contrast, show a more consistent recency effect; low initial success followed by an increasing number of successes leads to greater effort attributions (Beckman, 1970; Jones et al., 1968). These results concern one type of informational cue: the number and pattern of past successes. Other types of patterns and their effects on various causal attributions are not known.

An experiment (Frieze, 1975a) was conducted to investigate more systematically the effects of presenting information sequentially on the causal attributions made. Two questions were of major interest. First, would sequential acquisition of information result in different ultimate causal attributions than if the same information had been given at one time? Although earlier attributional studies implicitly assumed that sequential presentations would not differ from simultaneous presentations, there was other evidence that sequential procedures might result in either primacy (early cues more important) or recency (later cues more important) effects (Jones & Goethals, 1971). Although specific predictions could not be made, it was anticipated that some order effects would occur. However, because the basic cue utilization patterns have been so strong in earlier studies, it was further expected that these basic patterns would not be totally disrupted but only modified by sequential procedures. A second important question concerned the ways in which attributions changed as additional information was made available.

To investigate the sequential processing situation, 30 subjects were given three informational cues: (a) the importance of the exam, I; (b) the person's past exam history, P; and (c) how others had done, N. They were asked to use these cues in determining why a student had passed or failed an exam. Information was given in two different orders in a sequential format. Attributional ratings for ability, effort, luck, task, and mood were made after each new presentation of information. Each subject received a total of 16 different situations.

A series of analyses of variance for the effects of the informational cues after all information had been presented indicated that the order of presentation of information had no major effect on the ultimate cue utilization patterns. There were no main effects from order and only eight of 60 possible interactions involving order were significant.

Table 7.2 shows changes in attributions for success given one, two, and three informational cues. The results of ANOVAs for each part of the three-part series were computed as though all information has been given each time. However, for the first part, only the cue listed on the top row was actually available. In all cases, this one available cue was consistently used to make attributions to ability, effort, and task ease. For the second part of the three-part series, two cues were available. In the third part, all cues were given. Summarizing results of these analyses, when only importance (I) is available, low importance leads to task and ability attributions, whereas high importance leads to high effort attributions. Because importance is such a strong effort cue, these results may indicate a compensatory attributional schema (Kelley, 1972); if the cause is not effort (low importance), therefore, then it may be assumed that it must be ability or task ease. When only past history (P) information is available, good past history leads to ability attributions, whereas effort, luck, and task ease attributions are made for poor past history. As with incentive and effort attributions, past history is the major cue for ability attributions; if the information does not justify an ability attribution, then success is attributed to the other factors. The tendency to use whatever information is available to make judgments, even if the preferred cue is not available, is consistent with other nonattributional studies (Kapla & Brickman, 1971).

After the initial judgment based on one cue is made, subjects are then given one additional cue. When these two cues were available, subjects then chose the cue or cues that would have been used if the two cues had been given simultaneously. For example, either a high number of past successes and/or low norms would be used to infer that ability was a cause of a particular success. If importance was the first cue that had been presented, it would not be sued after these preferred cues were made available (i.e., $p < .05$ for interaction of order and importance information for ability attributions). Nonpreferred cues were used as modifiers if presented after the desired cues but were ommitted from consideration if presented before. These effects can be seen graphically in Figs. 7.2 and 7.3 in the example of ability attributions. In Fig. 7.2, when only importance information is available, there is a slight effect for higher ability attributions for low importance (I− as compared to I+). This effect disappears completely when both I and N are available. As shown by the dotted and solid lines, low norms (N−) contribute to a high ability attribution regardless of the importance information (I+N− and I−N− > I+N+ and I−N+; I+N− ~ I−N− and

TABLE 7.2
Attributional Changes as Additional Information is Acquired

Available information

Condition 1[a]

Causal attribution	I	IN	INP	P	PI	PIN
Ability						
I (Importance)	L*					
N (Norms)		L**	L*			L*
P (Past history)			H**	H**	H**	H**
Effort						
I	H**	H*	H*		H**	H**
N						
P						
Luck						
I		L*			L*	
N						
P			L**	L**	L**	L*
Task						
I	L*				L*	
N		H**	H**			H**
P				L*	L*	
Mood						
I						
N						
P						

Condition 2[a]

	I	IP	IPN	P	PN	PNI
Ability						
I	L*					
N			L**		L*	L*
P		H**	H**	H**	H**	H**
Effort						
I	H**	H**	H**			H**
N					L**	L*
P						
Luck						
I		L*	L*			
N			L*			
P		L*	L**	L*	L*	L*

(continued)

TABLE 7.2 *(cont'd)*

| | Available information Condition 2[a] | | | | | |
Causal attribution	I	IP	IPN	P	PN	PNI
Task						
I	L*	L*				L*
N			H**		H**	H**
P		L*	L*	L*	L*	
Mood						
I						
N						
P						L*

[a]H, High value of cue led to significantly higher causal attribution; L, low value of cue led to significantly higher causal attribution; *, $p < .01$; **, $F > 50$.

I+N+ ~ I–N+). When the third cue, past successes (P), becomes available, high past success (P+) leads to high ability attributions even more than low norms (N–), although norms are still utilized to some degree (I+N–P+ and I–N–P+ > I–N+P+ and I–N–P+ > I+N–P– and I–N+P– > I+N+P– and I–N+P–). This sequence of events can be compared to the effects on ability information when the information is presented in the PIN order (Fig. 7.3). In this case, when only P information is available, there is a very strong effect for high P to lead in higher ability attributions (P+ compared to P–). This effect persists as other information is added with norms having an effect less than that of P.

Another consequence of sequential information presentation can also be seen. When one or more of the cues generally preferred for making a specific attribution becomes available, these cues are used thereafter for making that causal attribution regardless of subsequent new information or the previous information. Instead of the usual order effects, therefore, the result of sequential information appears to be a process of making attributions with whatever information is available, while waiting for the information that is preferred for making the judgment. This also is consistent with the suggestion made by Orvis *et al.* (1975) that subjects have particular configurations of information they employ for different attributions and that they assimilate whatever information they have available to these configurations. However, these results might have also been obtained through a weighted averaging model (Anderson, 1973). Further process-oriented research is needed to totally discount this possibility.

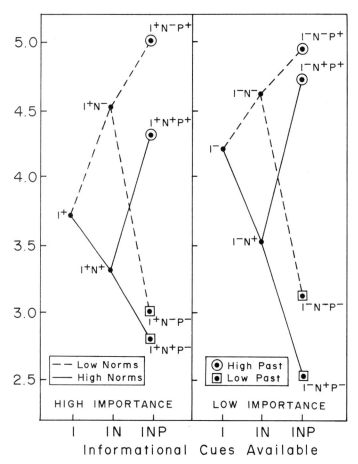

FIG. 7.2 Ability attributions as a function of order and amount of information: Order One (INP)–Condition 1. (– – –) Low norms; (——) high norms; ○, high post; □, low post.

Individual Differences in Information Processing
for Attributional Judgments

Another little investigated issue within attribution theory concerns the mechanism for individual differences in attributional judgments. The general assumption made is that differences in preferences for certain causal attributions are a result of differences in information utilization. Although people may well rely on previous judgments in making many causal attributions (Box 2 in Fig. 7.1), it is assumed that at one time active formation of information-processing rules were necessary in making a causal judgment (Boxes 3, 4, and 5 in Fig. 7.1). Kelley (1972) has suggested that people do have internalized causal schema that

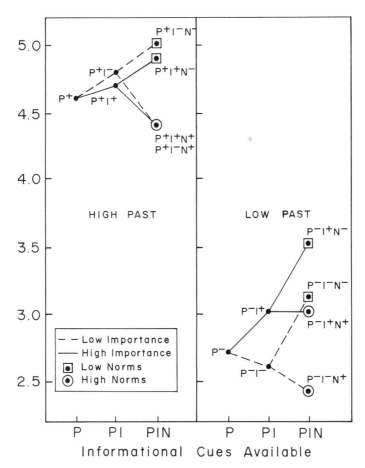

FIG. 7.3 Ability attributions as a function of order and amount of information: Order Two (PIN)–Condition 1. (– – –) Low norms; (———) high norms; o, high post; □, low post.

make a judgment possible with very limited information, but even Kelley has not been able to clearly define those situations in which schema are utilized and those in which new information is needed and/or schemas are developed. Nor does Kelley clearly identify the situations that have to the initial creation of a causal schema. Previous research has suggested that information seeking may vary both as a function of individual differences and according to situational variations. For example, people who exhibit a stable tendency to make internal attributions (internal locus of control) tend to seek more information (Davis & Phares, 1967; Whitley, 1968) and utilize more information (Pines & Julian, 1972) but other studies have failed to replicate these findings (Frieze, 1973). Although studies of nonattributional judgments have identified groups of subjects who tend to use information in similar ways (Hamilton & Gifford, 1970; Hoffman, Slovic, & Rorer, 1968; Wiggins, Hoffman, & Taber, 1969), there has been little analogous work analyzing individual differences in attributional information processing. There have been a number of studies looking at individual differences in preferences for particular types of causal attributions (see Frieze, 1976, or Weiner, 1974, for reviews of this literature).

In one of two studies of this question of information utilization differences Frieze and Weiner (1971) noted that there were wide individual variations in cue utilization patterns for college students making attributional judgments but no systematic study of these differences was done. A second study, reported in detail below, represents one only partially successful attempt to identify meaningful individual differences in cue utilization strategies. Frieze (1975b) wanted to see whether meaningful individual differences in information processing strategies could be identified and whether these differences would be related to the use of different causal attributions.

Frieze (1975b) used 68 UCLA college students who were paid for their participation. Subjects were asked to determine why a series of situations involving success or failure on exams had occurred by making ratings for the causal factors of ability, effort, luck, mood, the exam difficulty, and the instructor. Information about the past history of the student, the importance of the exam to the student, how other people did on the exam, and the teaching skill of the instructor was provided for each of 64 situations (2 X 2 X 2 X 2 informational cues X 2 outcomes X 2 replications). Demographic and personality data were also collected.

Subjects were empirically grouped according to their attributional ratings through a procedure involving a factor analysis of the subject intercorrelation matrices (Hamilton & Gifford, 1970; Wiggins, Hoffman, & Taber, 1969). This yielded three subject factors, representing three groups that accounted for 60% of the variance. Within each of these factors, effort and task attributions were most consistently made, whereas luck and mood judgments were highly variable, again indicating a qualitative difference in these unstable, unintentional attributions from other causal categories. They may, in fact, be avoided by subjects because they offer no predictive value for the future.

Ratings in Table 7.3 demonstrate specifically how subjects within each factor made causal attributions for success and failure. Factor 1 subjects appeared to make high use of all six causes, with their usage of good and bad mood being especially high. The overall higher causal ratings for Factor 1 subjects may also reflect some bias on their part toward high responses. Factor 2 subjects appeared to reject mood and luck as factors, especially as causes for success, whereas they made higher effort attributions than the other groups. Subjects in Factor 3 relied primarily on ability, effort, luck, and task attributions, although they made lower ability ratings than the other groups. Factor 3 subjects were also significantly lower for instructor attributions.

TABLE 7.3
Causal Attributions for Empirically Derived Individual Difference Groups[a]

	Group 1		Group 2		Group 3	
Causal attribution	Success	Failure	Success	Failure	Success	Failure
Ability	3.6	3.0	3.7	3.0	3.3	2.6
Effort	3.5	3.1	3.6	3.3	3.1	3.0
Task ease or difficulty	3.0	3.1	3.2	3.1	2.9	3.0
Luck	3.9	3.4	1.6	1.6	3.2	2.6
Mood	3.8	3.4	2.2	2.1	2.2	2.1
Instruction	2.9	2.8	2.9	2.8	2.3	2.4

[a]Scores are group means on five-point scales, with higher scores indicating that the cause is more of a factor in the outcome.

In addition to overall mean causal attributions, it was of major interest to see how subjects comprising the three factors made use of informational cues in making causal attributions. ANOVAs were done separately for each factor for both success and failure, but there were very few instances of subjects from the different factor groups using cues in different directions. Differences were in the degree to which cues were utilized rather than in the basic pattern of usage. Factor 3 subjects tended to show the most consistent cue utilization patterns. Not only did they demonstrate very strong usage of one cue for nearly every causal attribution, but they also tended to use more cues for making each individual judgment than did subjects comprising the other factors. Factor 1 subjects used the second highest number of cues overall in making causal judgments, whereas Factor 2 subjects had the fewest instances of consistent cue usages within the group. In addition to making high mood attributions for success and failure, Factor 1 subjects were also the only group to make consistent use of information in making the mood judgments. They attributed success when others did poorly to the good mood of the person and failure when the person had done well in the past to bad mood.

Various demographic and personality differences between subjects in the three factors were also analyzed. To summarize this data, subjects belonging to each of the three factors might be described in the following ways if all trends in the data were assumed to represent actual differences.

Factor 1. Scientifically oriented, primarily male subjects who made relatively systematic use of varied informational cues in making attributions primarily to mood, luck, ability, and effort for success and to mood, luck, effort, and task difficulty for failure. Tended to use more external attributions overall than the other groups.

Factor 2. Nonscientifically oriented, older subjects who tended not to use information systematically. Tended to reject mood and luck as causal factors, especially as causes for success.

Factor 3. Scientifically oriented, younger subjects who made highly systematic use of informational cues in making causal attributions to ability, effort, luck, and the task. Idealized Weiner *et al.* (1971) subjects typifying the results of the Frieze and Weiner (1971) studies.

These results suggest that subjects do show strong individual differences in their attributional ratings but they do not differ in the way they interpret various types of information (e.g., high consistency with the past always leads to ability attributions). Subjects did differ, however, in their accuracy or care in using information cues. This meant that although absolute weights attached to the various cues might differ among the groups, the relative weights were similar. Therefore, the hypothesis that information-processing differences could explain different attribution patterns was not supported by this study.

Unanswered Questions and Current Research in Attributional Information Processing

The studies reviewed in this chapter only begin to investigate the information-processing aspect of the attribution process. Current research in this area is attempting to better understand the effects of asking for data about causal attributions using various formats and to more completely explore the types of information utilized by people in making causal attributions. Further exploration of sequential processing and individual differences is also needed to extend and clarify some of the data reviewed in this chapter. A more basic question of when people develop new processing rules or when they rely on past experience in making causal attributions still needs much study. The script notion of Abelson (Chapter 3) may provide valuable insight for such research. Other suggestions for research that may combine some of the methodology and data developed by cognitive psychologists to the study of causal attributions are summarized by Carroll, Payne, Frieze, and Girard (1975).

ACKNOWLEDGMENTS

The author would like to thank Bernard Weiner for his many helpful comments during the execution, data analysis, and writing of the studies presented here and John Carroll and John Payne for their many helpful comments on earlier versions of this manuscript. These studies served as partial fulfillment for the requirements for the doctoral degree at UCLA.

8

Popular Induction: Information Is Not Necessarily Informative

Richard E. Nisbett
Eugene Borgida
University of Michigan

Rick Crandall
*University of Illinois,
Champaign–Urbana*

Harvey Reed
University of Michigan

The cognitive theory that currently exerts the greatest influence on social psychologists is attribution theory, the formalized version of which was introduced by Harold Kelley in 1967. The theory poses a view of man as lay scientist, attempting to infer causes for the effects he observes. The causes he attributes determine his view of his social world, and this view may determine his behavior. An extremely broad range of phenomena, from Asch's conformity research to Schachter's emotion work, may be usefully described as instances of the causal attribution process at work. In fact, it seems quite possible that Kelley's most important contribution may ultimately be seen to have been his creation of a language, or roadmap, with which to describe and interrelate diverse social psychological phenomena.

In addition to his organizational contribution, Kelley posited three formal sources of influence on the causal attribution process. In attempting to attribute causes for events of the form "Actor responds in X fashion to situation A," he suggested that the lay attributor responds to three sources of information:

distinctiveness information (Does the actor respond in X fashion in all situations of the general type, or only in situation A?); consistency information (Does the actor respond in X fashion at all times, under a broad variety of circumstances, or does he respond in X fashion only occasionally?) and consensus information (Do most other actors respond in X fashion, or is the response relatively rare?). Attribution of cause will depend on the answers to each of these questions. The actor is thus seen as the primary cause of his response to the extent that he responds in that way in all situations of the general type and to the extent that his responses are not exhibited by others. The situation is seen as causal to the extent that the actor's response is unique to situation A and to the extent that his response is widely shared.

Kelley's analysis of the attribution process has been acclaimed as well as criticized on the grounds that it is commonsensical in the extreme. Whether one likes or dislikes the theory for this quality, it comes as a surprise to discover that one of its fundamental axioms has found virtually no support in subsequent research. This is the notion that people respond to consensus information in allocating cause. Theory and common sense notwithstanding, there is mounting evidence that people are largely uninfluenced in their causal attributions by knowledge of the behavior of others. Knowledge that the actor's response is widely shared seems not to prompt the inference that the situation rather than the actor is the chief causal agent. Conversely, knowledge that the actor's response is unique seems not to prompt the inference that the actor rather than the situation is the chief causal agent.

In the pages that follow we review the evidence showing that there is little support for the view that people utilize consensus information in making attributions. This evidence concerns both instances where the actor is another person and instances, drawn primarily from our own research, where the actor is the self. We then show the similarity between the failure of consensus information to affect attributions and the demonstration by Kahneman and Tversky (1973) that base-rate information fails to affect predictions. We propose explanations for both failures in terms of the relative impact of abstract (consensus, base-rate) information versus concrete (actor- or target-related) information. Finally, we apply the distinction between abstract and concrete information to questions of communication and persuasion.

CONSENSUS INFORMATION
AND THE PERCEPTION OF OTHERS

There are two studies that examine the effects of consensus information on attributions about the behavior of others. Both studies show a remarkable weakness of consensus information. The first of these is by McArthur (1972). Her study was a direct test of Kelley's propositions about the effects of distinctiveness, consistency, and consensus on causal attributions. Subjects were given one-line descriptions of the form "actor responds to stimulus in X fashion" and were additionally given information on the Kelley dimensions of distinctiveness, consistency, and consensus. For example, subjects might be told that, "While dancing, Ralph trips over Joan's feet," and told additionally that Ralph trips over almost all girls' feet (or over almost no other girl's feet), that Ralph almost always (or almost never) trips over Joan's feet, and that almost everyone else (or almost no one else) trips over Joan's feet. Subjects were then asked whether the tripping incident was Ralph's fault, Joan's fault, or just the fault of circumstances. Subjects were also asked about their predictions for response generalization (How likely would Ralph be to advise Joan to enroll in a social dancing course?) and stimulus generalization (How likely would Ralph be to trip on an icy sidewalk?).

Distinctiveness information accounted for 10% of the variance in causal attribution (summing over all causes) and 63% of the variance in stimulus generalization expectancies. Consistency information accounted for 20% of the variance in causal attributions and 14% of the variance in response generalization expectancies. In contrast, consensus information accounted for less than 3% of the variance in any of the three sorts of inference. These results appear to violate not only the common sense of attribution theory, but any kind of common sense at all. Although subjects appear to believe that it is important to know whether Ralph trips over most girls' feet and whether he usually trips over Joan's feet, it is of no concern to them whether other people trip over Joan's feet!

Common sense—attributional or any other variety—is also violated in the other study concerning the perceptions of others. Miller, Gillen, Schenker, and Radlove (1973) asked college students to read the procedure section of the classic Milgram (1963) study of obedience. Half of their subjects were given the actual data of the Milgram study, showing that virtually all subjects administered a very substantial amount of shock to the confederate and that a majority went all the way to the top of the shock scale. The other subjects were left with their naive expectations that such behavior would be rare. Then all subjects were requested to rate two individuals, both of whom had gone all the way, on 11 trait dimensions heavily laden with an evaluative component, e.g., attractiveness, warmth, likeability, aggressiveness. For only one of the 11 ratings did the consensus information have a significant effect. The knowledge that maximum shock administration was modal behavior was therefore virtually without effect on evaluations of individuals who had given the maximum amount of shock.

CONSENSUS INFORMATION AND SELF-PERCEPTION

Consensus information also appears to have little impact on attributions made about the self. Bem (1967) proposed and Kelley (1967) incorporated into attribution theory the notion that people perform cause—effect analyses of their own behavior in a manner entirely similar to their attributions about the behavior of others. They observe their responses, taking note of the situations in which they occur, and make inferences about their feelings and motive states. For example, the subject in the classic Schachter and Singer (1962) experiment who knows that he has been injected with a drug that produces autonomic arousal, and who is then placed in a situation designed to elicit strong emotions, performs a kind of cause–effect analysis. He feels the symptoms of arousal, which ordinarily he may attribute to the emotional impact of the situation, but instead attributes them to the drug he has taken. The result is that he reports and manifests behaviorally fewer of the symptoms of emotion than subjects who do not know that they have been injected with an arousal agent and fewer emotional symptoms even than control subjects who have not been injected with the arousal agent at all. The subject therefore perceives the cause of his autonomic responses as "external" to himself and feels and behaves accordingly.

Several years ago, we began a program of therapeutic interventions based on this notion that people can be led to externalize the cause of their own reactions. It seemed that whenever an individual has responses that are maladaptive, disruptive, or pathological, there may be something to be gained by persuading the person to attribute his responses to something external to himself. The first study, and the only successful one, was by Storms and Nisbett (1970). The pathological state studied was insomnia. We asked college students who had trouble getting to sleep to take a pill (actually a placebo) 15 minutes before retiring, which they were told would cause increased heart rate, rapid, irregular breathing, a feeling of bodily warmth, and a general state of alertness. These are of course the symptoms of insomnia. Subjects who took these pills reported getting to sleep more quickly on the nights they took them than they had on nights without the pills and more quickly than control subjects who took no pills. Storms and Nisbett reasoned that one or both of two different attribution processes could have accounted for the results. Insomnia is probably caused in large part by arousal at bedtime produced by any number of causes, including anxiety about personal problems, an inconvenient diurnal rhythm, or chronic neurosis. As the individual lies in bed in a state of arousal, his revery includes thoughts with emotional content. The arousal can become associated with, and can amplify, the emotional cognitions. The resulting heightened emotional state intensifies the arousal, and so on, in a vicious cycle. This cycle could be broken, however, by the knowledge that the arousal is exogenous in nature. The person would then infer nothing about how worried he was about his exam, or how angry he was about his roommate, from observation of his arousal state. On the nights with the pills, arousal would be seen as inevitable and thus as dissociated from any thoughts in his head. The cycle of heightened arousal thus broken, sleep could ensue.

Alternatively, or additionally, a somewhat different process with more general applicability might have been at work. Our insomniac subjects reported that they were quite concerned about the fact that they were insomniacs. They took it as evidence of more general pathology and as reflecting badly on their state of psychological adjustment. For a subject with such worries, the knowledge of inevitable, extrinsically produced arousal should be reassuring. At least tonight, the subject might reason, the insomnia could not be taken as evidence of general psychopathology. To the extent that such a concern was itself partially responsible for the insomnia, sleep should have occurred more quickly on the nights with the pills.

Attempts to Manipulate Depression

Armed with this successful intervention with insomniacs, we began a series of attempts to modify states of depression. The technique in all studies was a consensus manipulation, designed to externalize the cause of the depressive affect by convincing the subject that it was widely shared. To the extent that the state is shared by similar others, its existence reflects less negatively on the self. It should seem less rooted in the subject's own unique, possibly pathological reactions to his particular circumstances and environment. With worry and concern about one's ability to deal with one's life situation reduced, the depression might be partially abated.

Study I: The Sunday Blues

Many college students experience a general letdown feeling on Sundays. Although the day may begin well enough with brunch, coffee, and the Sunday papers, a sense of ennui often begins in the afternoon. There is much to be done for the week ahead, too much to seriously consider a Sunday outing, although perhaps not enough to begin work just this minute. By late afternoon, no excursion and no work have taken place, the Sunday papers, including perhaps even financial and travel sections, have been rather too thoroughly absorbed, and a long evening of tedious study looms ahead. By evening, if all has gone as badly as it often does, work is proceeding painfully, or not at all, and a gray mood of malaise and self-doubt has settled in.

It occurred to us that if the phenomenon were general, and if people knew this, the Sunday blues could be lessened in intensity. If the individual student knows that the dormitories around him are full of people in the same stale state, then his own negative emotions should be somewhat mitigated. Instead of deciding he is not cut out for the academic life or brooding on the possibility that he may never have a fulfilling relationship with a woman, he may simply acknowledge that people tend to be low on Sunday and let it go at that.

In order to test this notion, we requested a large number of male undergraduates at Yale University to fill out a number of mood scales at 4:00 p.m. and 10:00 p.m. on Sunday. The mood scales were several Wessman and Ricks (1966) scales loading highly on their euphoria–disphoria factor. In addition, subjects were requested to fill out a questionnaire at 10:00 p.m., reporting on their academic and social activities for the day and on the number of instances in which they gave vent to some disphoric affect, for example, by shouting or weeping. Finally, subjects took a packet of cartoons out of a folder and rated them for funniness.

After this initial Sunday premeasure, subjects were sorted into three groups, each with 18 subjects. One, a control group, was simply told that the investigators were studying mood patterns on Sunday and participants were asked to fill out on the following Sunday the same package of materials they had filled out the previous Sunday. For a second group, the Sunday blues syndrome was described in detail and subjects were given (false) statistics to indicate its widespread occurrence in the college population. Subjects were told that 92% of Yale students reported having experienced the phenomenon at least occasionally, whereas 65% experienced it on most Sundays. A third group was given the same consensus information as the second group and, in addition, was given a theory to account for the phenomenon. Subjects were told that it is caused by an "arousal crash" on Sundays: The normal weekday arousal is typically followed by even higher arousal on Saturday; then on Sunday, there is an arousal trough. This lack of arousal is often interpreted as, or converted into, depression.

The anticipation was that subjects in the latter two experimental groups would reinterpret their sour experiences on Sunday, personalizing them less and becoming, as it were, less depressed about their depression. If so, they should have shown a decrease in disphoric affect on the mood scales from the premanipulation Sunday to the postmanipulation Sunday; a decrease in disphoric behavior, such as blowing up or weeping; an increase in both academic and social activity; and a higher average rating of the funniness of the cartoons in the package for the second Sunday. They did none of these things. Not by a single indicator did the mood of experimental subjects improve as compared to control subjects.

Study II: Chronic Depression

Insufficiently daunted, we attempted a similar intervention with male undergraduates who described themselves as chronically depressed. Twenty subjects were recruited by means of an advertisement in the University of Michigan's student newspaper that called for "depressed male upperclassmen to participate in a study by the Institute for Social Research on depression."

On arrival at the laboratory, subjects were randomly assigned to one of two groups. Control subjects were told that a new mood scale had been developed and that it was important to obtain daily mood reports, using the scales, from people who described themselves as being depressed. This would help to assess the validity of the scale and its ability to detect mood changes.

Experimental subjects were given the same story and in addition were told that the experimenters were in the final stages of testing a theory of depression in young male adults. The theory, based on fact at least in its particulars, went as follows. Subjects were told that it had been known for some time that mood maintenance in adults depended in part on the presence of gonadal hormones—in the male, on testosterone. There had been until recently a paradox, however, in that children almost never become depressed. Because children have extremely low levels of all gonadal hormones, this seemed a contradiction of the general rule that hormones are promotive of good moods. The paradox had recently been solved by the discovery that the limbic lobe, the emotional center of the brain, switches over in adolescence to a dependence on gonadal hormone for mood maintenance. In most males, the switchover is timed fairly well to correspond to the rise in testosterone level, which reaches a peak at about age 25. In many young men, however, the switchover is completed before the "fuel," so to speak, is available in sufficient quantities to maintain mood.

The strong implication to the subject was that he was such a young man. It was anticipated that the manipulation would cause an improvement in mood for three confounded reasons:

1. A time limit was implied for the depression.
2. The negative affect was "externalized" in the sense that it could now be attributed to an unfortunate biological incident rather than to the web of the subject's own life and any pathological inability to come to grips with it.
3. The negative affect, and the reasons for it, were shared by many others in a way suggesting nonuniqueness of the subject's problems and his response to them.

All subjects were requested to fill out the Wessman and Ricks mood forms at the end of each day for a 2-week period. The questionnaire also included a report on how the subject had slept the night before, because sleep disturbances are frequent symptoms of depression. Finally, subjects' grade point averages were obtained at the end of the semester in which the study took place.

There were no differences in the mood reports of experimental and control subjects at any point in the 2-week period, nor were there any differences in report of the quality of sleep. There were, in fact, no hints of any trend in the direction of the hypothesis on these variables. There was a tendency for experimental subjects to get somewhat higher grade point averages, as predicted, but this fell short of statistical significance ($.05 < p < .10$).

Study III: The First-Year Faculty Member Syndrome

A final attempt to manipulate depressive states employed as subjects first-year faculty members in the physical and social sciences at a large number of universities. Many young academics find their first year as a faculty member to be a stressful and depressing episode in their lives. Torn from a network of the friends and familiar activities of several years, cast abruptly from one side of the educational desk to the other, confronted with the difficulties of conducting research in a new environment, faced with the change from the graduate student social life to the sedate dinner party routines of academe, strapped in all probability by unexpected large financial burdens of house, new car, or wardrobe, it is a rare first-year faculty member who does not experience considerable stress, anxiety, and self-doubt.

In an attempt to dilute this unhappy syndrome, we provided consensus information to half of a sample of hundreds of new faculty members in the physical and social sciences at 100 major American universities. The sample was first made contact with in early October of 1973. Half of the respondents were simply told that we were studying the adjustment of first-year faculty members and were asked to fill out a background questionnaire preparatory to a more extensive survey at the end of the year. The other half of the respondents—the consensus information group—was told specifically that we were interested in the very widespread phenomenon of stress and depression in first-year faculty members. It was emphasized that negative reactions to the first year were the norm. The syndrome was described in general terms, reasons for it were proposed, and four lengthy vignettes of first-year faculty members and their travails were presented.

Then, at the end of the year, respondents were requested to fill out a detailed questionnaire asking about their moods during the year and their satisfaction with their teaching, research, and social life. In addition, questions were asked concerning various behaviors pertinent to the effectiveness of their functioning—number of papers written, number of research projects started, whether a grant application had been submitted, how many cigarettes they smoked, and how many alcoholic drinks they consumed. Sixty-two percent of the subjects returned both the initial and the final surveys, and return rates for the two groups were equal (N was 187 for the consensus information group and 218 for the control group). Each respondent was also requested to give a form reporting on his adjustment to someone who knew him well, such as a spouse, colleague, or friend.

It was expected that faculty with consensus information would perform better. The knowledge of widespread stress and poor functioning for people in their position should have made them less upset about their own negative reactions and this should have been reflected in lowered stress and heightened effectiveness. In fact, however, the manipulation produced no net improvement in functioning. There were fewer mean differences between experimental and control subjects than would have been expected by chance. However, there was a distinct possibility that the manipulation had real but countervailing effects on different individuals in the experimental group. For more than a quarter of the 32 dependent variables, the variance was greater for people who got consensus information. This was true for ratings of satisfaction about accomplishments for the year, estimated probability of academic contract renewal, percent time spent over the year in the happiest and in the three unhappiest mood categories, reported number of nights with sleep disturbances over the week preceding the completion of the final survey, and change from beginning to end of the year in both cigarette consumption and alcohol consumption. For one of the six peer-reported variables, namely rated satisfaction with the job, the variance was greater for consensus information subjects. For only one subject-rated variable and for none of the peer-rated variables was there a greater variance for control than for consensus information subjects.

It is always hard to know how to interpret variance differences. Post hoc explanations for such findings tend to have a speculative ring to them. Nonetheless, some attempt to interpret the findings is incumbent on us. The explanation that is both the most congenial and the most plausible to us goes as follows. Perhaps the hypothesis actually "took" for some of the individuals. That is, some people read the materials at the beginning of the year and accepted the fact that stress and unhappiness were to be expected in their new role. Their difficulties were then viewed in light of this consensus information and the perceived cause of them was externalized. They then functioned more effectively because they were less upset and depressed by their difficulties. Other individuals in the consensus information group, however, may have been adversely affected by the manipulation. Being told at the beginning of the year that they were going to be miserable might have been depressing in itself for some individuals and, in a fatalistic mood, they might have worked less vigorously to overcome any problems that did occur. Alternatively, the subjects in the consensus information group who reported worse functioning might not have been adversely affected by the manipulation but might simply have been more willing to admit to the difficulties and unhappiness they experienced. The manipulation may well have carried an implicit encouragement to report any and all negative feelings on the final survey.

The results are therefore not without promise from the practical standpoint of the ultimate feasibility of attribution therapy by mail. However, their implications for the theoretical point at issue—the extent to which people make the proper attributional use of consensus information—are negative. Consensus information produced no net improvement in functioning or reported satisfaction.

Casting the harsh glare of hindsight over these three experiments, it is not hard to see why they might all have failed. The state of depression is notoriously difficult to alter and the manipulations were mere one-shot, verbal interventions. Still, we can easily recall the excitement with which these studies were planned and the optimistic assumption we had about their outcomes. We are therefore not very receptive to the observation that it is obvious that these studies were doomed to failure. And we insist that no one has a right to make such an observation who has ever attempted to comfort someone else by saying "Anyone in your situation would feel the way you do," or "Most people would have reacted like you did."

Attempts to Manipulate Perceptions
of One's Own Beliefs and Reactions

Consensus information apparently does not readily serve to externalize the perceived causes of depression. There is evidence to indicate that such information also fails to prompt the expected inferences concerning less intransigent states.

In his 1967 paper, Kelley argued that in the low-justification conditions of dissonance experiments, subjects move their beliefs in line with their behavior in part because they lack the consensus information available to the experimenter. If subjects knew that almost all their fellow subjects had also agreed to perform the requested behavior, they would realize that the situation, rather than either the weak explicit justification or their own inclinations, had elicited the behavior and so would infer nothing about their own beliefs. In order to test this proposition, Cooper, Jones, and Tuller (1972) requested Princeton students to write a counterattitudinal essay advocating that no student be allowed to be a member of the Communist party. Subjects were paid either $.50 or $2.50 to write the essay. Cross-cutting this manipulation was a consensus information manipulation. Some subjects were told that almost all previous subjects had complied with the request to write the essay; others were told that almost no previous subjects had complied; and still others were told nothing about the behavior of previous subjects. The knowledge that almost all previous subjects had complied should have reduced the insufficient justification effect. Subjects should have realized that because the pressure of the situation was so strong, their compliance was in no way caused by a predisposition to agree with the stance taken in the essay. Conversely, subjects who believed they were relatively unique in complying should have shown a heightened insufficient justification effect. They should have been doubly compelled to find an explanation for their compliance in terms of their own personal predilections. In fact, however, consensus information had almost no effect. The same insufficient justification effect was found in all consensus groups, with each group simply showing the traditional effect such that $.50 subjects reported more agreement with the position in the essay than $2.50 subjects. Subjects therefore appeared to infer nothing about the power of the situational pressures from knowledge of the rate of compliance.

Study IV: Interpretation of Sensory Reactions and Motivational States

An additional study by the authors failed to find substantial effects of a consensus manipulation on self-perceptions. Male undergraduates at Yale were requested to sample crackers and rate them on several taste dimensions. Between crackers, they were asked to sip a "neutralizing solution" to prevent the taste of the preceding cracker from influencing the succeeding one. This "solution" was a room temperature mix of water, lemon juice, and sugar. Subjects rated how much they liked the solution (and three other concoctions) before they tasted the crackers and again, on a scale with a different format, at the end of the experiment.

Just as each subject finished the cracker-rating task, the experimenter became terribly busy. The "next subject" arrived, the phone began ringing, and, in his distraction, the experimenter asked the subject to "take his bottle of neutralizing solution into the next room where the other bottles for the day are." In the next room, the subject encountered a consensus manipulation. The other bottles for the day were either much more full or much more empty than his own. The subject thus learned that he had drunk either much more or much less neutralizing solution than other subjects.

On returning to the now calm experimental room, the subject was asked to rerate the solutions and fill out a final questionnaire. Among filler items, the subject was asked to indicate on a 30-point scale, labeled "very little" and "a great deal," how much of the neutralizing solution he had drunk. In addition, he was asked three questions that would seem to be exhaustive of the possible reasons for drinking a small or a large amount of neutralizing solution: (1) how pleasant he found the taste of the solution, (2) how thirsty he was just before he started tasting the crackers, and (3) how thirsty the crackers had made him.

The consensus manipulation was quite strong, with virtually no overlap in subjects' reports of the amount of solution they drank (22.6 vs. 7.09). Despite the effectiveness of the manipulation, there was little evidence that it produced the required causal attributions. Pre–post ratings of the taste quality of the neutralizing solution did not differ between the two groups; nor did the relative rank of the taste quality of the four solutions, nor did reported original thirst nor the degree to which the crackers made them thirsty. It should be noted that Ns were low (10 and 8) and that there was a trend in the direction of a consensus effect for the question about how thirsty subjects had been before tasting the crackers. Although it can scarcely be claimed that the null hypothesis has been proved, therefore, it is the case that even an unambiguously strong consensus manipulation was insufficient to trigger causal inferences of comparable magnitude.

ATTRIBUTION AND THE PSYCHOLOGY OF PREDICTION

Kahneman and Tversky have demonstrated an inferential failure that seems highly pertinent to the inferential failure observed in studies of the effects of consensus information. These investigators, in a paper titled "The Psychology of Prediction" (1973), have shown that people ignore population base rates when making predictions about the category membership of a target member of the population. For example, they asked their subjects to read brief descriptions of the following type:

Jack is a 45-year-old man. He is married and has four children. He is generally conservative, careful, and ambitious. He shows no interest in political and social issues and spends most of his free time on his many hobbies which include home carpentry, sailing and mathematical puzzles [Kahneman & Tversky, 1973, p. 241].

Their subjects are informed that Jack is a member of a population containing either 70 lawyers and 30 engineers or 30 lawyers and 70 engineers, and then asked to judge the likelihood that Jack is an engineer. Base-rate manipulations have literally no effect on the judged probability that Jack is an engineer. This is true even when the description of Jack is much less suggestive of his being an engineer than in the above paragraph, and even when the description is of highly dubious validity and acknowledged as being of such a dubious character by subjects.

If subjects are not influenced by base-rate information in their predictions about the category membership of a target case, then their attributions seem scarcely likely to be much influenced by consensus information. Consensus information is precisely base-rate information. It is base-rate information about behavioral responses rather than about category membership. An attribution, moreover, is a more complicated and indirect inference than a prediction. Kahneman and Tversky ask their subjects to produce a rather direct and uncomplicated chain of inference: "If the majority of the members of the population belong to a particular category, then odds are the target case does also." Their subjects fail to make such an inference. In the attribution research we have been discussing, a still more elaborate chain of inference is requested: "If the majority of the members of the population behave in a particular way, then the situation must exert strong pressures toward that behavior, and there-fore it is unparsimonious to invoke personal idiosyncracies to account for the behavior of the target case if his behavior is modal."

It remains to be tested, of course, whether subjects are unwilling to apply behavioral base rates to predictions about target cases. If they are, then the question we have been pursuing must be shifted from "Why do people fail to alter their attributions in response to consensus information?" to the more fundamental "Why do people treat base-rate information as if it were uninformative?"

Study V: Behavioral Base Rates, Prediction, and Attribution

In order to examine the question of people's willingness to alter their predictions in the face of behavioral base-rate information, two psychology experiments were described to subjects (Nisbett & Borgida, 1975). University of Michigan students read detailed descriptions of (a) an experiment by Nisbett and Schachter (1966) in which subjects were asked to take as much electric shock as they could bear, and (b) an experiment on helping behavior by Darley and Latané (1968) in which, as several students discussed problems of college adjustment over earphones from separate cubicles, one of the "subjects" began to have what sounded like a seizure. The two experiments were chosen because in our teaching experience, college students' guesses about behavioral base rate were wide of the mark. Whereas students tend to assume that few subjects take much electric shock, the modal behavior is actually to tolerate the highest intensity the apparatus can deliver, enough amperage to cause the subject's entire arm to jerk involuntarily. And whereas students tend to assume most people would quickly leave their cubicles to help the seizure victim, the typical subject never does anything to help the victim in the six-person condition of the Darley and Latané experiment.

Because subjects were ignorant of the true behavioral base rates, it was possible to give some of the subjects the actual base rate from the two experiments and thereby create differential base-rate information conditions. Subjects with knowledge of the base rate (consensus information condition) were shown brief videotaped interviews with students described as subjects in the original experiments (or, in one variation of the consensus information condition, shown brief written descriptions of the backgrounds and personalities of the students). Consensus information subjects then were asked to predict how the target cases they viewed or read about would have behaved. It is therefore possible to compare the predictions of consensus information subjects with both the actual base-rate information they possessed and with the guesses about base rate made by subjects lacking consensus information.

Figure 8.1 shows the results for the shock experiment. The top bar graph shows the actual base-rate data given to consensus information subjects. The second row shows the estimates about base rate made by subjects lacking knowledge of the base rate. It may be seen that estimates by these no consensus information subjects are quite different from the actual data. They assume taking a moderate amount of shock to have been modal behavior. The third row presents consensus information subjects' guesses about the behavior of the target cases they have viewed or read about. Although these subjects were fully cognizant of the base rate, it may be seen that the distribution does not resemble even remotely the actual base rate. Instead, the distribution is highly similar to the guesses about base rate made by subjects lacking knowledge of the base rate. Results were entirely similar for the helping experiment.

The experiment allowed an opportunity to test another hypothesis, this one suggested by Tversky and Kahneman (1971) in an article entitled "Belief in the Law of Small Numbers." These authors argued that even scientists are rather insensitive to sample size and are willing to draw recklessly strong inferences about populations from knowledge about even a very small number of cases. In order to test this notion in the present context, some subjects were left ignorant of the base rates in both experiments and were shown brief videotaped

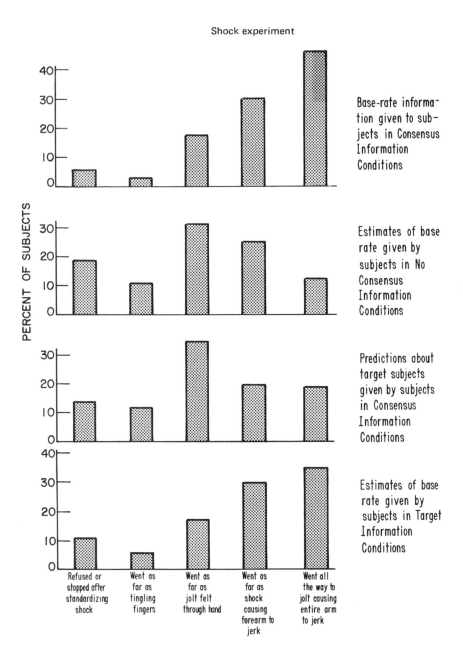

FIG. 8.1 Base rate, estimates of base rate, and predictions about target subjects in the shock experiment.

interviews with two subjects from each experiment. Subjects in this target information condition were told that both subjects in both experiments had behaved in the most extreme possible way, i.e., that the two subjects in the shock experiment had both taken the maximum possible shock, and the two subjects in the helping experiment had never helped the victim. Subjects in the target information condition were then asked to indicate what they thought the distribution of the entire subject population of the experiments would have been. For both experiments, subjects were willing to infer that the population mode was identical to the behavior of the two subjects whom they had observed. It may be seen in the bottom row of Fig. 8.1 that estimates for base rate in the shock experiment were remarkably similar to the true base rate. Estimates were not so similar for the helping experiment but were nevertheless rather close to the J curve form of the actual base rate. Subjects were as willing to infer that the population mode was similar to the behavior of the two cases they viewed when sample selection procedure was unspecified as when it was repeatedly and vividly brought to their attention that the two cases had been selected at random from a hat containing the names of all original subjects.

In summary, subjects did not employ base-rate information when called on to make predictions about the behavior of target cases. It is important to note that, in addition to the prediction questions, several attribution questions were asked, e.g., whether situational forces or personal inclinations were responsible for the behavior of a target person. There was no substantial effect of consensus information for any of these attribution questions. The latter failure seems virtually inevitable given the former failure. Therefore, the question as to why people should ignore consensus information in making attributions should be reduced to the more fundamental question as to why base-rate information should be disregarded for even such a simple inference as prediction. Any answer to this more fundamental question about people's failure to be informed by base-rate information ideally should account simultaneously for the other major finding in the present study. This is the finding that subjects are, in effect, "overly" informed by target case information, being willing to assume that extreme behavior is modal when told that as few as two subjects have behaved in the most extreme possible way.

ABSTRACT VERSUS CONCRETE INFORMATION

Kahneman and Tversky (1973) themselves have not speculated at length on the reasons for people's failure to be influenced by base-rate information. Their basic explanation appears to center on the idea that people are simply not very good at dealing with probabilistic data. Even in the sphere of gambling, where people know that the laws of chance are operative and have at least some rudimentary schemata for dealing with likelihoods, people can show remarkable blindness and biases. Outside of such situations people may utterly fail to see the relevance of such "merely" probabilistic information as base rate. Or, lacking any notion of how to properly combine base-rate information with target case information, they may opt for simply ignoring base-rate information altogether.

There is surely considerable truth to this notion that people lack good schemata for working with probabilistic information. In fact, it has the virtue of accounting for the single exception in the attribution literature to the rule that people ignore consensus information. This is the clear evidence of utilization of success and failure base rates when making attributions about the ability of a particular individual (Weiner, Frieze, Kukla, Reed, Rest, & Rosenbaum, 1972). If most people fail at a particular task, then the target is perceived as having high ability; if they succeed, the target is seen as having lower ability. Of course, we have all had a lifetime of experience in estimating ability in relation to the performance of others. Ability, in fact, is by definition a base-rate derived inference.

It seems to us, however, that another principle may be at work as well. Almost by its very nature, base-rate or consensus information is remote, pallid, and abstract. In contrast, target case information is vivid, salient, and concrete. In the depression studies, we were attempting to pit the memory of rather dry, statistical information against vivid, pressing reactions to stimuli in an all too real world. In the cracker-tasting study, consensus information abstracted from evidence concerning the level of liquid in bottles was pitted against sense impressions. In the study describing the shock and helping experiments, tabular frequency data were pitted against a videotape or a written description of a real human being with parents, career plans, hobbies, and personal quirks. The logical pertinence of the base-rate information notwithstanding, such information may simply lack the clout to trigger further cognitive work.

This hypothesis, as it happens, is not original. In 1927, Bertrand Russell proposed that "popular induction depends upon the emotional interest of the instances, not upon their number" (p. 269). In the experiments by Kahneman and Tversky, and in those by ourselves and others on the effects of consensus information, sheer number of instances has been pitted against instances of some emotional interest. Consistent with Russell's hypothesis, emotional interest has in every case carried the day.

We may speculate that concrete, emotionally interesting information has greater power to generate inferences because of the likelihood of such information's calling up "scripts" (Chapter 3) or schemas involving similar information. The inference then proceeds along the well-worn lines of the previously existing script. Abstract information is probably less rich in potential connections to the associative network by which scripts can be reached. Consistent with this speculation, Nisbett and Borgida (1975) found that consensus information concerning the behavior of others in the shock experiment and the helping experiment not only failed to affect subjects' predictions about how they would have behaved had they been in the experiments but was never mentioned by a single subject in the postexperimental interview concerning why they had made their predictions. Instead, subjects seized on particular concrete details of the experimental situation and related them to similar situations in their own histories. "I'm sure I would have helped the guy because I had a friend who had an epileptic sister."

Russell's hypothesis has some important implications for action in everyday life. A homely example will serve as an illustration. Let us suppose that you wish to buy a new car and have decided that on grounds of economy and longevity you want to purchase one of those solid, stalwart, middle class Swedish cars—either a Volvo or a Saab. As a prudent and sensible buyer, you go to *Consumer Reports*, which informs you that the consensus of their experts is that the Volvo is mechanically superior, and the consensus of the readership is that the Volvo has the better repair record. Armed with this information, you decide to go and strike a bargain with the Volvo dealer before the week is out. In the interim, however, you go to a cocktail party where you announce this intention to an acquaintance. He reacts with disbelief and alarm: "A Volvo! You've got to be kidding. My brother-in-law had a Volvo. First, that fancy fuel injection computer thing went out. 250 bucks. Next he started having trouble with the rear end. Had to replace it. Then the transmission and the clutch. Finally sold it in three years for junk." The logical status of this information is that the N of several hundred Volvo-owning *Consumer Reports* readers has been increased by one, and the mean frequency of repair record shifted up by an iota on three or four dimensions. However, anyone who maintains that he would reduce the encounter to such a net informational effect is either disingenuous or lacking in the most elemental self-knowledge.

Study VI: Influenceability by Abstract versus Concrete Information

It seemed worthwhile to operationalize the *Consumer Reports* thought—experiment (Borgida & Nisbett, in press). Because our most readily available subject population consisted of psychology students at The University of Michigan, we chose psychology courses at The University of Michigan as our consumer goods. Ten upper level lecture courses in psychology, differing in their reported quality, were singled out. Groups of underclasspersons planning to become psychology majors were greeted in a classroom by a faculty member experimenter. The experimenter told the students that he was on a faculty committee concerned with long-range planning for the department. One of the problems with planning concerned determining how many students would be taking which courses in the future. Subjects were told that in order to get some indications of projected enrollment, they were being asked to fill out a tentative course schedule for their undergraduate careers in psychology.

Control subjects then were asked to look over a catalog (actually a mockup consisting of 27 courses and excluding labs, statistics, and cross-listed courses) and put a check next to the 5–10 courses they expected to take and to circle their check marks for any courses they felt certain they would take.

The two experimental groups were told that in order to help them in making their decisions, they would be given extra information on the high-enrollment lecture courses. For both groups, this extra information consisted in part of a detailed description, more comprehensive than the catalog blurb, of the content and format of each of the 10 courses. Then for one experimental group (face-to-face condition), subjects were introduced to a panel of upper level psychology students. These students then proceeded to make brief comments about each of the courses on the list of 10 that they had taken. Between one and four students, usually two or three, commented on each course. Each comment began with an evaluation of the course employing one of the following five terms: "excellent," "very good," "good," "fair," "poor." The student then made a few remarks about the course. An example, in its entirety, is below:

> While there's a lot of material to cover, it's all very clearly laid out for you. You know where you are at all times, which is very helpful in trying to get through the course. It's a very wide and important field of psychology to become introduced to. But the reason I rated it very good instead of excellent is that the material isn't particularly thought-provoking.

In the other experimental condition (base-rate condition), subjects were told that they would read mean evaluations of the course based on the scales filled out by all students in the course at the end of the preceding term. Beneath the description of each course was a five-point scale, labeled from excellent to poor. A mark was placed on each scale to indicate the mean evaluation, and the number of students on which the mean was based was indicated. These Ns ranged from 26 to 142. The mean evaluation of each particular course was rigged so as to be identical with the average of the evaluations given by the confederates in the face-to-face condition.

The design therefore makes it possible to compare the effectiveness of recommendations based on first-hand hearsay, i.e., the brief comments of two or three students who have taken the course, with the effectiveness of much more stable, broadly based information. Table 8.1 presents the mean number of recommended (mean evaluations 2.50 or better), nonrecommended (mean evaluations 3.75 or poorer), and unmentioned courses chosen by the three groups. Beside each category is the weighted choice tendency, an index that gives a weighting of 0 to a course if it has not been chosen, 1 if it has been chosen, and 2 if it has been circled as a definite choice.

It may be seen that the face-to-face method had a much larger impact on course choice. Subjects in that group were much more inclined to take recom-

TABLE 8.1
Mean Number of Courses Chosen and Weighted Choice Tendency

Condition	Recommended courses		Nonrecommended courses		Unmentioned courses	
	Number chosen	Weighted choice tendency	Number chosen	Weighted choice tendency	Number chosen	Weighted choice tendency
Face to face (N = 22)	4.73^a	$8.31^{a,b}$	$.50^a$	$.77^{a,b}$	$3.09^{a,b}$	$4.32^{a,b}$
Base rate (N = 18)	4.11	6.33^b	.94	1.56^b	4.17^b	5.89^b
Control (N = 18)	3.33^a	5.22^a	1.39^a	2.17^a	$5.39^{a,b}$	7.17^a
F (2, 55)	6.14*	10.34**	6.59*	6.65*	13.24**	8.19**

^{a}Column means sharing this superscript differ from each other at the .01 level by the Newman–Keuls test.
^{b}Column means sharing this superscript differ from each other at the .05 level by the Newman–Keuls test.
*$p < .005$; **$p < .001$.

mended courses and much less inclined to take nonrecommended or unmentioned courses than control subjects. In contrast, the base-rate method affected only the taking of unmentioned courses.

It might be argued that the face-to-face group had more information than the base-rate group. One version of this argument is precisely the point we wish to make. Our students behaved as if they had extracted more information from the *in vivo* comments of a couple of people than from the dry, statistical summaries of entire populations. A different version of this argument, however, is that the comments made by students in the face-to-face condition contained genuinely valuable information not available in the base-rate condition, concerning, for example, course organization, grading procedures, or teacher accessibility.

In order to deal with the latter objection, we replicated the study with one important variation. The base-rate group was given a verbatim written transcript of the comments made by face-to-face confederates. Moreover, those comments were explicitly described as *representative* views of the students taking the course, culled from the entire stack of evaluations at the end of the term. Subjects in this condition, with access to stable mean evaluations based on large and complete populations, with the verbatim comments of confederates, and with the "knowledge" that these were representative comments, were less affected in their choices than subjects who simply heard the confederates verbalize their comments in the face-to-face condition.

COMMUNICATING WITH CREATURES OF CONCRETENESS

It is not hard to see the implications of Bertrand Russell's dictum about popular induction, and the above illustration of it, to general questions of communication and persuasion. If people are unmoved by the sorts of dry, statistical data that are dear to the hearts of scientists and policy planners, then social and technological progress must be impeded unless effective, concrete, emotionally interesting ways of communicating conclusions are developed. We have collected several "case studies" of persuasion that we believe are well understood in terms of the distinction between abstract and concrete information. We present them below in the hope that they may serve as a source of real-world inspiration and guidance for research on questions concerning the nature of information and its persuasive impact.

1. An early version of the Green Revolution was made possible in the early 1930s by advances in agricultural technique. The government duly proceeded to inform the nation's farmers of these techniques by means of county agricultural agents spouting statistics and government pamphlets and sat back to await the glowing reports of increased crop production. No such reports followed and it soon became clear that farmers were not converting to the new techniques. Some clever government official then set up a program whereby government agricultural agents moved in on selected farms and cultivated the crops along with the farmers, using the new techniques. Neighboring farmers watched the crop results and immediately converted to the techniques.

2. The waiting lists at cancer detection clinics, as of this writing, are months long and have been since the fall of 1974. This was not because of the issuance of new statistics by the Surgeon General, AMA, or any other organization. The long waiting lists date from the time of the mastectomies performed on Mrs. Ford and Mrs. Rockefeller.

3. Timothy Crouse, in his book on the press coverage of the 1972 Presidential campaign titled *The Boys on the Bus* (1974), reported that on election eve a large group of the reporters following the McGovern campaign sagely agreed that McGovern could not lose by more than 10 points. These people were wire service reporters, network television reporters, and major newspaper and news-magazine reporters. They knew that all the major polls had McGovern trailing by 20 points, and they knew that in 24 years not a single major poll had been wrong by more than 3%. However, they had seen with their own eyes wildly enthusiastic crowds of tens of thousands of people acclaim McGovern.

4. *The New York Times* (Kaufman, 1973) recently carried an interview with a New York subway graffitist who had been badly burned in an electrical fire started by a spark that ignited his cans of spray paint. The boy, whose *nom de plume* was "Ali," admitted that 2 weeks before his accident he had read of a boy named Bernard Brown who was crushed to death while painting graffiti on

trains. "Maybe if we knew the name he used, say 'Joe 146' it would have made an impression," he said, "but I remember laughing about it thinking he must be some kind of dude who didn't know what he was doing."

5. It is doubtful whether domestic opposition to a foreign war was ever greater than the opposition of the American public to the Indochinese intervention. It is possible that this is because the war was particularly heinous and unjust or that morality is on the upswing. Another strong possibility, however, is that this was the first war for which the carnage was portrayed in color in the homes of citizens. At any rate, this hypothesis gains credence from a pronouncement by Senator Mansfield just before the fall of Viet Nam, opposing further American aid to Southeast Asian combatants: "I am sick and tired of seeing pictures of Cambodian and Vietnamese men, women and children being slaughtered by American guns and American ammunition" (*Detroit Free Press,* March 6, 1975).

We believe that the present research and examples drawn from everyday life show that some kinds of information that the scientist regards as highly pertinent and logically compelling are habitually ignored by people. Other kinds of information, logically much weaker, trigger strong inferences and action tendencies. We can think of no more useful activity for psychologists who study information processing than to discover what their subjects regard as information worthy of processing.

ACKNOWLEDGMENTS

The research described here was supported by Grant GS 40085 from the National Science Foundation. We are indebted to Gordon Bear and David Glass for assistance in conducting the research and to Michael Kruger and Linda Temoshok for criticism of an earlier version of this paper.

9
Some Life and Death Consequences of Perceived Control

Richard Schulz

Carnegie–Mellon University

Psychological variables are now almost universally recognized as important determinants of physiological decline in humans. In part, this is because of the publicity recently given by the popular press to research in this area. It is not uncommon to find articles in the medicine section of *Newsweek* or *Time* magazine discussing how fear, depression, or even excitement can terminate or extend life.

Reporting on research carried out by Bogdonoff, *Newsweek* (1965), for example, described how fear may result in death. Bogdonoff told volunteer participants in his study that they had severe heart conditions, causing his subjects to have severe physiological reactions, including increased blood pressure, a slowed heart rate, and a sharp increase in the strength of heart contractions. Bogdonoff speculated that severe emotional shock brought about death by either causing a clot in the coronary artery or disturbing heart rhythms. Similarly, in an article entitled "How recession can kill," *Newsweek* (1970) again pointed to psychological variables as mediating life–death outcomes. The magazine summarized M. H. Brenner's statistical evidence showing an increase in the incidence of ulcers and asthma, as well as deaths caused by heart attack, following economic recessions.

Although a variety of psychological variables has been identified as playing an important part in both the etiology and course of physical disease, probably one of the most important is hope. This paper focuses on the concept of hope as a mediator of life–death outcomes. The discussion that follows is divided into three parts. First, I examine some of the existing observational and correlational evidence highlighting the importance of hope in maintaining life and, conversely, hopelessness in fostering deterioration. Second, I derive a more specific conceptualization of hope and hopelessness and argue that they are mediated by individuals' cognitions about the predictability and controllability of their environments. Finally, an experiment and data testing this conceptualization are presented.

EVIDENCE FOR HOPE MAINTAINING LIFE

Working with archival data, David Phillips (1969) reported results showing how a strong desire or reason for living might lengthen life. He examined birth and death dates of 1,251 famous Americans and found that death occurred least often the month before birthdays and most often the months after birthdays. Similarly, in cities largely populated by Jews, the death rate declined significantly the month before Yom Kippur, the high holy day of atonement. Even elections have induced people to stay alive long enough to find out the outcome. The death rate declined before every United States election from 1904 to 1964.

In observations of American prisoners of war, Nardini (cited in LeShan, 1961) noted that "where the will to live was for any reason weak, death seemed to come readily even with lesser physical ailments. On the other hand, where the will was firm even in the presence of serious physical illness, life often continued" (p. 321). The relationship between hopelessness and shortened temporal distance to death was also observed by Weisman and Hackett (1961), LeShan (1961), Beard (1969), Kimball (1969), and Kubler-Ross (1969). Weismann and Hackett (1961), for example, discussed five surgical patients whose physical condition did not indicate imminent death. However, on admission to the hospital, the patients overtly expressed hopelessness about their chances of survival and, contrary to medical prognosis, died shortly after admission. Similarly, Kubler-Ross found that when terminally ill patients no longer anticipated recovery they were likely to die soon afterwards.

Several researchers have suggested that the will to live is especially important to the physical wellbeing of kidney patients and their adjustment to hemodialysis (Eisendrath, 1969; McKegney & Lange, 1971). As did Kubler-Ross, Eisendrath (1969) concluded from interviews of chronic renal patients that feelings of depression and hopelessness precede death. In a study of 25 dialysis patients, McKegney and Lange (1971) observed that for those who died "hope wanes as the expectation of a transplant, good health, and freedom from dialysis are constantly disappointed" (p. 271). Before their death the nonsurvivors lost all hope, explicitly rejecting the life prescribed by their disease.

Less subjective and more convincing evidence of the relationship between hope and distance to death comes from correlational studies of the seriously ill. Paloucek and Graham (cited in LeShan, 1961) attributed the negative response to treatment of some of their patients with cancer of the cervix to hopelessness.

They divided their patients into two groups, matched for state of the disease and type of treatment. Members of the first group were said to have had a "miserable childhood, a bitterly unhappy married life, and a bleak, hopeless future" (p. 328), whereas members of the second group were said to have had happier childhood and marital experiences and were more hopeful about the future. Fifty-seven percent of the first group responded poorly to treatment, whereas only 15% of the second group responded poorly. When asked, all the women in the first group viewed their future as "hopeless or totally unacceptable," whereas only 15% of those in the second group felt this way.

Similar findings were reported by Verwoerdt and Elmore (1967). Of 30 terminally ill patients, the 11 who were most hopeless died within 2 months of the assessment date, whereas another 11 lived from 1 to 7 months longer. Physical status, which was assessed at the same time the hope questionnaires were administered, was not related to time of death. Kastenbaum and Kastenbaum (1971) found that patients rated by the medical staff as high on will to die tended to die sooner than predicted from medical status alone, but level of will to live was not related to survival. The Kastenbaums attributed the lack of strong findings to the tendency of medical staff to make unrealistic judgments in the direction of favorable prognoses.

Methodological Problems

Problems in both research techniques and design leave the important question of causality unanswered. It is not clear from the research described above whether hope affects the course of illness or vice versa. It could be, for example, that patients somehow become aware of their physiological decline and hopelessness is simply a response to this awareness. Or, it may be that medical personnel somehow become aware of the patient's prognosis and convey this information to him. In addition, problems with assessment techniques magnify interpretive difficulties. The most frequent methods of data collection rely on individual observations and interviews and these techniques are subject to individual biases that threaten validity and reliability. A controlled experimental study manipulating level of hope could provide solutions to these problems. How this should be done raises the questions of what we mean when we are talking about hope and hopelessness, and what are the specific psychological mediators of hope.

THE MEANING OF HOPE AND HOPELESSNESS

Although many researchers use these words, few have attempted to clearly specify what they mean. Several have focused on the individual's cognitions about the perceived probability of certain events as determinants of level of hope. Kastenbaum and Kastenbaum (1971) describe hope as a psychic or phenomenological state pointed toward the future with a predominantly positive affective glow. Hope exists only if there is an element of uncertainty or suspense present. That is, one hopes only if the subjective probability of an event is greater than 0 and less than 100%. Furthermore, hope and expectations are not synonymous. An individual may have certain levels of expectations for particular contingencies but a probabilistic forecast that has no affect attached to it is merely an expectancy and not hope. Stotland (1969) and Melges and Bolby (1969) in general propose that the higher the perceived probability of attaining a goal and the greater the importance of that goal, the higher the level of hope and the greater the positive affect experienced by the organism.

The existing definition of hope and related concepts focuses primarily on the perceived probability of specific events. Columns 1 and 2 of Table 9.1 indicate, for example, that hope is high when the perceived probability of a good event is high or the probability of a bad event is low. That is, one can hope for something good to happen or for something bad not to happen. However, as depicted in Columns 3 and 4 of Table 9.1, hope can also be viewed as a general phenomonological state dependent on the individual's perceived effectiveness in controlling future outcomes. That is, an individual is hopeful when he perceives himself to be generally in control of his future outcomes and perceives others to have relatively little control over his outcomes. In short, he views himself as master of his fate. This definition of hope differs from Rotter's (1966) concept of internal control in that hope is viewed as a transient state that comes and goes as a function of experiences with one's environment rather than a personal disposition.

If hopelessness is the opposite of hope, then it should follow that the organism is hopeless when the probability of positive events is low or the probability of negative events is high. However, Kastenbaum and Kastenbaum (1972) label this dread. An individual dreads the anticipated absence of a positive outcome and the presence of a negative outcome. A generalized state of dread may result when an individual feels control over his future outcomes lies within other individuals rather than himself. The affective state associated with dread is anxiety (see Table 9.1).

The hopeless person, in contrast, does not believe that outcomes are contingent on his behavior nor does he believe that anyone else can provide meaningful outcomes for him. The perceived probabilities of either positive or negative events for the hopeless individuals are low and associated affective state is extreme depression and psychological and physical withdrawal (Seligman, 1975). As LeShan (1961) puts it, the hopeless person lacks the belief that outside objects can bring any satisfaction, has no faith in development or the possibility of change, and does not believe that any action he or anyone else may take can ease his aloneness.

Closely related to the concept of hopelessness is helplessness. As Table 9.1 indicates, the helpless individual feels incapable of controlling his own outcomes but perceives the possibility of others providing outcomes for him.

TABLE 9.1
Differentiation of Hope and Related Terms

	Perceived probability of positive or negative event		Perceived effectiveness of self and others in determining outcomes for self		
	Positive event	Negative event	Self's control of future outcomes	Others control of future outcomes	Affective state
Hope	High	Low	High	Low	Positive glow
Dread	Low	High	Low	High	Anxiety
Helplessness	Low	Low	Low	High	Depression
Hopelessness	Low	Low	Low	Low	Extreme depression

These definitions of hope and the related concepts of dread, hopelessness, and helplessness focus on two issues: (a) the perceived probability of good and bad events, and (b) beliefs about control over the environment exercised by the individual relative to others in his environment. This latter issue becomes increasingly important because of the convergent evidence in other areas of experimental psychology on the importance of control and predictability as mediators of an organism's physical and psychological functioning. This literature is briefly examined in the next section.

CONTROL AND PREDICTABILITY

Seligman (1975) has convincingly argued that feelings of helplessness or hopelessness are the result of prolonged experiences of noncontingency between behavior and outcomes. Relying on extensive animal and human experimental research, Seligman states that the motivational, cognitive, and emotional disturbances seen in helpless individuals are brought about when the individual perceives himself incapable of exerting any personal control over his environment.

Personal control is generally defined as the ability to manipulate some aspect of the environment. In his recent review of the control literature, Averill (1973) distinguishes three types of control—behavioral, cognitive, and decisional—and points out that each type is beneficial in alleviating the negative effects of a stressor. It is not clear, however, whether these beneficial effects are attributable to control or to increased predictability. For example, stimulus regulation, a type of behavioral control where the subject determines either when an aversive stimulus is delivered or who delivers it, is found to be stress reducing only when accompanied by the reduction of uncertainty regarding the threatening event (Averill, 1973). Similarly, the reduction in experienced stress resulting from signaled, as opposed to unsignaled, shock is readily attributable to the greater predictability of the former.

Control is therefore confounded by predictability, in that having control over a stimulus also means that it is predictable. It becomes important to ask, therefore, whether the ability to control adds something over and above the ability to predict.

The only experiment specifically designed to answer this question was carried out by Geer and Maisel (1972). Subjects in the control group could terminate aversive photographs of dead bodies. Subjects in the predict group knew when and how long the photographs would be presented but had no control over when they would be terminated. Subjects in the no control–no predict group could neither control nor predict the occurrence of the photographs.

The results revealed that subjects with control over the termination of the aversive stimulus exhibited lower GSR reactivity to the stimulus than those subjects with prediction alone. Although these results strongly suggest that control is more than just predictability, some alternative explanations for these results have been suggested (see Geer & Maisel, 1973; Seligman, 1974).

The Geer and Maisel study is undoubtedly not the last word on the predictability–control issue but it does make two points salient. First, researchers doing control studies should, if possible, include conditions necessary to evaluate differences between predictability and controllability. Second, such differences should be maximal to the extent that powerful control manipulations are used.

The existing literature on control focuses almost exclusively on the effects of having control over aversive events. Only a few investigators have used positive stimuli, such as food or money, in the context of a control experiment. In an experiment carried out by Engberg, Hanse, Walker, and Thomas (cited in Seligman, 1975), three groups of hungry pigeons received food under different contingencies. One group learned to jump on a pedal for grain, whereas the second group received the same grain but the food was independent of their behavior. A third group received no grain. All pigeons were then placed in an autoshaping task in which a subject had to learn to peck a lighted key to get grain. The group that had previously attained food through pedal pressing autoshaped fastest, the no grain control group was second, and the "welfare state" group was last. Following this procedure, all three groups were shifted to a schedule in which they had to learn to refrain from pecking to get grain. The pattern of results was the same as before. The pedal-pressing pigeons learned fastest, the no experience group was second, and the "learned laziness" group was last. Similar effects have been observed with rats.

Other animal studies have demonstrated that organisms prefer working for positive reinforcers over securing them for free. Carder and Berkowitz (1970), Jensen (1963), and Neuringer (1969) have all reported that rats prefer response-contingent food over response-independent food, suggesting that response-contingent stimulation is probably more positive than the same stimulation when it is response independent.

Using human subjects, Lanzetta and Driscoll (1966) examined the preference for information about a potential outcome as a function of whether it was negative (shock) or positive (monetary reward). In a repeated measures design, subjects had the option of receiving information about three types of possible outcomes: (a) shock–no shock; (b) monetary reward–no reward; and (c) shock–reward. Lanzetta and Driscoll found that subjects preferred to have information as opposed to no information about an anticipated event, regardless of potential outcomes. This suggests that information that may be useful in achieving cognitive control is just as desirable when the outcome is positive as when it is negative.

In her dissertation, Wortman (1975) examined the effects of perceived control on the evaluation of a positive outcome (prizes valued at either $3.00 or $.20). Some of the subjects were induced to feel that they had control in causing the outcome they experienced, whereas others were induced to feel that the experimenter was responsible for their outcome. Subjects in this study did not evaluate outcomes differently as a function of whether or not they felt they controlled them.

In summary, the studies reviewed above suggest that controllable positive events are preferred over uncontrollable ones and that experience with uncontrollable positive events may cause motivational deficits in that response initiation and the learning of response–reward contingencies become retarded. Because these conclusions are based primarily on animal research, a cautionary note is in order. Little is in fact known about how humans react to controlled versus random positive events.

RESEARCH ON CONTROL
AS A DEVELOPMENTAL VARIABLE

More than a decade ago, Robert White (1959) concluded that many of an infant's diverse behaviors were motivated by a biological drive that prompted the organism to find out how to deal effectively with its environment. More recently, the importance of synchrony between behavior and outcome for the normal development of organisms has been demonstrated in both humans (Seligman, 1975; Skeels, 1966; Spitz, 1962; Watson, 1970) and animals (Bainbridge, 1973; Joffe, Rawson, & Mulick, cited in Seligman, 1975; Harlow, 1968). Learning deficits as well as defects in the ability to carry on normal social interactions with other organisms are typical results of prolonged dissynchrony experiences.

Although less is known about human development beyond childhood and adolescence, one characteristic of adult development is that most individuals continue to expand their realm of competencies. For example, increased social and financial status enables many individuals continually to enlarge control over the environment as they grow older.

Typically, however, retirement and old age precipitate an abrupt decline in control. Retirement means the loss of one of the most meaningful sources of instrumental control in life, the work role. Closely related is the loss of income, often resulting in further shrinkage of an individual's control as it becomes necessary to curtail activities requiring money. In addition, many individuals at this age experience some deterioration in physical condition, representing a further shrinkage of their sphere of control. Finally, aged individuals suffer the loss of the child-rearing role, which has undoubtedly been an important source of competence and environmental control in their younger and middle years.

In addition to the role losses associated with retirement, many aged individuals experience further declines in their ability to manipulate and control the environment as a result of institutionalization. Gottesman (1971) describes institutionalization of the aged as the "least desirable and most extreme form of treatment . . . because it removes the person into an encapsulated portion of the world, and in doing so it generally removes all autonomy" (p. 54).

Most institutionalized aged are located in nursing homes, where restrictions are so severe that patients are permitted little normal behavior within them or with the outside world (Gottesman, 1971). This lack of autonomy is even more distressing when it is realized that healthy aged individuals are often encouraged to enact a sick role because nursing homes are paid more if their patients are sick. As Schulz and Aderman (1973) have noted, a patient's adverse reactions to institutionalization are probably mediated by feelings of helplessness, born out of the patient's perception that the institutional demands for passivity represent a real loss in his ability to control the environment. The consequences of such a loss of control usually include withdrawal, depression (Schulz & Aderman, 1974; Streib, 1971), and sometimes early death (Schulz & Aderman, 1973). Experimental studies with animals (for a review, see Seligman, Maier, & Solomon, 1971) and humans (Roth & Kubal, 1975) amply demonstrate the negative effects of loss of control. Seligman (1975) attributes motivational, cognitive, and emotional deficits to any prolonged experience with lack of contingency between individuals' behavior and their outcomes. Roth and Kubal demonstrated that subjects working on an important task who received large amounts of exposure to a noncontingency situation behaved helplessly in a subsequent task situation.

The study presented here was designed to assess the effects of increased control over and predictability of a positive outcome on the psychological and physiological wellbeing of the aged. The intent of this research was twofold. First, because this was a manipulative as opposed to a correlational study, it was expected that cause and effect statements could be made about the importance of predictability and control to successful aging. Second, viewed from the perspective of the theoretical literature on control, this study was designed to answer some important questions on the effect of having control over positive outcomes.

In order to give some of the aged subjects the opportunity to exert control over a positive event in their environment, it was decided to make a student visitor available to them for a 2-month period. Because institutionalized aged persons are often very lonely (Streib, 1971), being visited by a friendly college student was conceptualized as a significant positive event. Control subjects could exert control over the frequency and duration of visits they received, giving them the opportunity to both regulate and modify the positive event.

To assess the effects of predictability, a second group of subjects was informed at what time and how long they would be visited but was not given any control over these details.

A third group of subjects was visited on a random schedule. They were not given any control over the duration or frequency of visits. This group served as one of two "control" conditions.

Finally, a fourth group of subjects served as a baseline comparison group. These individuals were not visited except to collect data.

In order to hold amount of visitation across all three groups constant, individuals in the predict and random visitor groups were yoked to the control visitor group. The duration of the visitation period was 2 months, with the average number of visits per person being slightly more than one a week. A total of five students (four females and one male) served as visitors. Each was assigned subjects in sets of three, one in each of the visitation conditions.

Data on the psychological and physical status as well as activity level of each subject were collected before the visitation program began and again after 2 months of visits. Data from the no visitation control group were collected at the same time.

Initial Interview—Premeasures

If the subject was still able to read and write, the experimenter left a folder containing three questionnaires with the subject. Before leaving, the experimenter explained each questionnaire in detail. To those individuals too blind to read or too shaky to write, the experimenter administered the questionnaires verbally. A fourth questionnaire, the "Wohlford Hope Scale" (Wohlford, 1966) and some health status questions, were administered verbally to all subjects at the initial meeting.

The four questionnaires administered at the interview were entitled "Activities," "My Usual Day," "Future Diary," and the "Wohlford Hope Scale." The "Activities" questionnaire contained eight open-ended items designed to assess activities inside (e.g., watching TV, reading newspapers, visiting neighbors in the building) and outside (e.g., attending meetings, visiting friends) the home. An activity index was calculated by adding together the frequency per week of those pursuits requiring active participation. These included number of visits to neighbors in the building, number of visits outside the building, number of times the building was left for activities other than visiting, number of club meetings attended, number of visits to church, and number of phone calls made.

In response to the "Usual Day" questionnaire, subjects recorded all the activities they engaged in from the time they got up in the morning to the time they went to bed at night. Activities mentioned by the respondent were divided into two major divisions—active and passive. Active pursuits were composed of (1) domestic activities, such as household chores, or special duties at the home, such as being a receptionist at the front door; (2) active hobbies requiring some physical activity; (3) active social activities requiring some physical activity; and (4) active social activities requiring some effort, such as preparing for visitors or leaving the home. All other activities were classified as passive pursuits. A score was computed for each subject representing the percentage of waking time spent in active pursuits during a day.

The "Future Diary" questionnaire was used to assess the percentage of time devoted to special commitments during the waking hours of the next 7 days. This included such activities as going to church or to the beauty parlor, having a luncheon date, or attending a scheduled bridge game. Committed hours included traveling time estimated by the respondent in getting to and from an appointment. A future commitments score was calculated for each subject as the percentage of waking hours in the week committed to such activities.

In administering the "Wohlford Hope Scale," the experimenter simply asked the subjects to "name ten things that you have talked about or thought about in the last week or two." The experimenter then read back each of the things mentioned and asked the subject to "decide whether at the time you thought about it, the idea or topic referred to something mostly in the past, present, or future. Finally, I want you to give me the actual data or approximate data when the thing occurred or probably will occur. If it occurs over a period of time, give your best estimate of the range of dates." The following tabulation scale was used to weight each item either negatively if it occurred in the past or positively if it occurred in the future:

0 = under 2 hours
1 = 2 hours to 1 week
2 = 1 week to under 1 month
3 = 1 month to under 4 months
4 = 4 months to 1 year
5 = 1 year to 4 years
6 = 4 years or over

A mean score ranging from −6 to +6 was obtained for each subject, where the higher the number (the more future oriented), the greater the level of hope.

Postinterview

To assess the effects of the manipulations, the three visitation groups and the no visit comparison group were interviewed by two experimenters approximately 2 months after the initial interview. Experimenter 1, the same individual who carried out the initial interview, administered the same battery of questionnaires used in the first interview. With the exception of the "Wohlford Hope Scale," all responses were scored the same way for this set of questionnaires as they were for the first set. In scoring the "Wohlford Hope Scale," all references to the visitor were excluded in order to make comparisons between the visitation groups and the no visit comparison group valid. Difference scores representing pre- to postmanipulation changes were calculated for all measures. Experimenter 1 was blind as to which condition each subject was in.

Experimenter 1 also administered two additional nine-point Likert-type scales to the activities director at the home. The activities director was asked to rate each subject on two scales entitled "Health Status" (the two extremes were labeled "in perfect health" and "extremely ill") and "Zest for Life" (the two extremes were "extremely enthusiastic about life" and "completely hopeless"). The activities director had worked at the home for many years as a nurse before taking on this new position and was as a result personally acquainted with all the participants in the study. However, she knew nothing about the study and was therefore blind as to which condition each subject was in.

Experimenter 2 introduced himself to the subject as a friend of Experimenter 1 who was "helping him collect some information." Experimenter 2 verbally administered three questionnaires entitled "Background Data," "Visitation Questions," and "Tri-Scales."

The "Background Data" questionnaire included questions on the demographic background of subjects and questions on the percent of time subjects perceived themselves lonely and bored. The "Visitation Questions" survey included several manipulation checks pertaining to the visitor and items assessing the subjects liking of the visitor and the visits.

The final questionnaire, "Tri-Scales," consisted of 10 nine-point Likert-type scales tapping such dimensions as happiness, health status, and usefulness. In order to give subjects a reference point, the midpoint of the scale was always labeled "Average American." Given this midpoint, subjects were first asked to rate themselves on each of the 10 dimensions as they perceived themselves at present by placing an X on the scale. A second rating was obtained to indicate a subject's "best year" on each dimension. This was done by placing a B on the scale. Finally, a subject made a third rating by placing an O on the scale indicating where they perceived other old people to fall on each dimension. A composite score similar to one used by Schonfield (1973) for each of the 10 dimensions was derived as follows. Assessing an individual's status on each dimension should first be based on where he perceives himself at present (the X score). The disparity between "best year" and present state (B − X) was subtracted from present state because this represented self-assessed deterioration. When there has been no deterioration (B − X = O) the X score is not decreased, indicating that the individual is aging successfully (Schonfield, 1973). Self-assessed present superiority over other old people should add to feelings of wellbeing, whereas feelings of inferiority should reduce such feelings. The difference between present state and other old people (X − O) was therefore added to the present state score. This difference could either be positive or negative. The formula finally arrived at was X − (B − X) + (X − O) = 3X − B − O. In order to ensure a minimum score of 1, the constant 16 was added. The possible range of scores was 1 (when X = 1, B = 9, O = 9) to 40 (when X = 9, B = 1, O = 1).

Experimenter 2 administered all questionnaires verbally and, although he knew whether or not a subject was visited, he was unaware of the contingencies under which these visits occurred.

RESULTS

Manipulation Checks

Subjects assigned to the visitation groups were visited an average of 1.3 times a week with the mean length of each visit being 50.8, 49.0, and 50.0 minutes for the random, predict, and control groups, respectively. Therefore, there were no differences in the frequency or duration of visits among the three visitation groups.

To check on the effectiveness of the control manipulation, all subjects in the visitation groups were asked "Who decided when the visitor should come?" Nine of 10 control subjects responded that they determined when he came. Two of eight predict subjects felt they determined the delivery of the reinforcer, whereas only one of 10 random subjects felt this way. Fisher's exact test showed the differences between the control and other two visitation groups to be significant (control vs. predict, $p < .005$; control vs. random, $p < .005$). For the question, who determined how long the visitor stayed, eight of 10 control subjects felt that they determined the length of visits, whereas only two of 10 predict and three of 10 random subjects felt this way. Comparisons between the control group and the other two groups were again significant ($p < .025$ Fisher's exact test).

The effectiveness of the predictability manipulation was assessed by the question "Did the visitor let you know when he was coming?" As expected, control and predict subjects felt they had been informed, whereas random subjects reported not being informed. Nine of 10 control and nine of 10 predict subjects reported being informed. None of the random subjects felt this way.

Fisher's exact test again revealed highly significant results when comparing control with random ($p < .005$) and predict with random ($p < .005$). The control subjects also perceived the visitor as significantly more dependable when compared to predict and random subjects.

It can safely be concluded from these results that the manipulations have had their intended effects. As expected, control subjects felt they controlled both the frequency and duration of visits. Predict subjects reported knowing when visitors would come, and random subjects perceived neither forewarning nor control over the delivery of the reinforcer.

Major Analysis

Because of the large number of dependent variables, it was decided a priori to limit the primary analysis to those variables most directly relevant to the hypotheses. Fifteen dependent variables were selected such that the effects of the manipulations on health status, psychological status, and activity level could be assessed.

The general plan of the analysis was as follows. Initially, three orthogonal comparisons were carried out for all variables. They were (a) no treatment vs. random, to determine the effects of a positive reinforcer per se; (b) predict vs. control, to test the effects of control over and above predictability; and finally (c) no treatment + random vs. predict + control, to determine the effects of experimental treatment relative to the two "control" conditions. A multivariate analysis of variance for each comparison yielded a significant multivariate F only for the comparison of no treatment + random with predict + control (multivariate $F_{15,22} = 2.50, p < .025$). Univariate Fs for all comparisons are reported.

Health Status Indicators

Five different indicators of health status were used to assess the effects of the experimental manipulations. The comparison of no treatment + random against predict + control yielded several significant results. The predict + control groups were rated as significantly healthier by the activities director at the home than a combination of the no treatment and random groups ($F_{1,36} = 4.457, p < .042$). Analysis of change scores on quantity of medication taken per day revealed a significant effect for the same contrast ($F_{1,36} = 5.953, p < .02$). Table 9.2 shows that mean increases in quantity of medication were smaller for the predict + control groups than the no treatment + random groups. A marginally significant difference for the same contrast was found when the change scores for number of different types of medication taken per day were analyzed ($F_{1,36} = 3.041, p < .09$). The means in Table 9.2 show that, although all groups increase their intake of the number of different types of medication, the increase is smaller for the predict and control groups.

TABLE 9.2
Mean Health Status
Indicators by Condition

	Condition			
Variable	No treatment	Random	Predict	Control
Health status as assessed by activities director at home[a]	5.100	4.700	6.100	6.900
Triscale composite on health	19.800	20.300	21.200	20.800
Change in number of types medication used per day[a]	+.700	+.800	+.400	+.400
Change in quantity of medication taken per day	+2.400	+2.400	+.900	+.800
Change in number of trips to the infirmary per week	+.700	+.850	+.300	+.850

[a]The comparison of no treatment + random with predict + control yielded $p < .05$ or better.

Psychological Status Indicators

Six dependent measures were analyzed to determine the effects of the manipulations on psychological status. Again, only the comparison of predict + control with no treatment + random yielded statistically significant results for these variables. Relative to the no treatment and random groups, the predict + control groups perceived themselves as signiticantly happier ($F_{1,36} = 7.134, p < .011$) and were judged to have significantly more "zest for life" ($F_{1,36} = 8.072, p < .007$). Table 9.3 reveals that both no treatment and random groups evidenced a decline in level of hope, whereas the predict and control groups showed an increase ($F_{1,36} = 5.467, p < .025$). Marginally significant differences for the same comparison were found for the variables percent of time lonely ($F_{1,36} = 3.682, p < .063$), percent of time bored ($F_{1,36} = 3.046, p < .089$), and usefulness ($F_{1,36} = 4.008, p < .053$). The means in Table 9.3 reveal that, for all dependent variables, the predict and control groups were superior in psychological status when compared to the no treatment and random groups.

Activity Level Indicators

All four indicators of activity level revealed significant differences when predict + control were compared against no treatment + random. Predict + control group subjects evidenced more positive change in the time devoted to

TABLE 9.3
Mean Psychological
Indicators by Condition

	Condition			
Variable	No treatment	Random	Predict	Control
"Zest for life" as rated by activities director at home[a]	4.300	5.000	6.100	7.000
Change in level of hope[a]	−.308	−.073	+.197	+.421
Percent of time lonely	8.000	11.000	3.000	1.000
Percent of time bored	7.000	15.500	4.000	4.000
Triscale composite on happiness[a]	19.500	20.900	22.700	23.300
Triscale composite on usefulness	17.400	17.500	18.900	21.600

[a]The comparison of no treatment + random with predict + control yielded $p < .05$ or better.

active pursuits in a "Usual Day" ($F_{1,36}$ = 4.744, $p < .036$), in the time devoted to "Future Commitments" ($F_{1,36}$ = 11.71, $p < .002$), and on the "Activity Index" ($F_{1,36}$ = 10.736, $p < .002$) than the no treatment + random groups (Table 9.4). In addition, predict + control subjects perceived themselves as significantly more active ($F_{1,36}$ = 6.133, $p < .018$) than no treatment and random subjects.

TABLE 9.4
Mean Activity
Level Indicators by Condition

	Condition			
Variable	No treatment	Random	Predict	Control
Change in "Usual Day"[a,b]	−1.492	+1.307	+1.467	+2.178
Change in "Future Commitments"[a]	−.398	+.052	+.266	+.498
Change in activity index[a]	−.600	.000	+1.300	+1.000
Tri-scale composite on activity[a]	19.400	19.500	22.100	22.300

[a]The comparison of no treatment + random with predict + control yielded $p < .05$ or better.
[b]The comparison of no treatment with random yielded $p < .05$ or better.

The comparison between random and no treatment groups revealed one significant ($F_{1,36}$ = 5.08, $p < .03$ for change in "Usual Day") and one marginally significant ($F_{1,36}$ = 3.849, $p < .058$ for change in "Future Commitments") univariate F. On both measures, the random group was superior to the no treatment group. However, because the multivariate F for this comparison was not statistically significant, these univariate Fs must be viewed with some caution. It is possible that they are merely chance effects.

Conclusion

Because several of the dependent measures have been change scores, it is possible to say something about the directional effects of the manipulations. That is, did the manipulations inhibit a progressive decline or did they actually effect improvement? The mean changes for indicators of physical status in Table 9.2 show that all groups increased their intake of drugs and number of trips to the infirmary, but that this increase was smallest for the predict and control groups. In the case of health status indicators, therefore, the manipulations effectively inhibited a progressive physical decline. Mean changes in indicators of psychological status and activity level suggest, however, that the manipulations actually reversed the pattern of progressive decline. Tables 9.3 and 9.4 show that, on the average, predict and control groups evidenced a positive increase, whereas the no treatment and random groups showed a slight decrease.

DISCUSSION

The most significant finding of this study is that predict and control groups were superior to the no treatment and random groups on indicators of physical and psychological status, as well as level of activity. The absence of significant differences between the predict and control groups and between the random and no treatment groups suggests that the relatively positive outcome of the predict and control groups is attributable to predictability. However, instead of arguing that the effects of controllability result from predictability, it is also possible to argue the reverse: the effects of predictability may be due to controllability.

Although control subjects reported having greater control over the frequency and duration of visits than the predict subjects, individuals in the latter condition may have felt that they had potential control. That is, they may have felt that they could, if they desired, tell a visitor not to stay as long as the visitor intended. It is possible, then, that predict subjects felt that they had a choice in deciding whether or not to receive a visitor and for how long. Unfortunately, no data on perceived choice were collected from the residents of the retirement home. Therefore, this alternative explanation cannot be adequately evaluated.

Although the majority of the evidence indicates no difference in effectiveness between predictability and controllability as these variables have been operationalized in the present study, some of the data can be interpreted to suggest such a difference. First, the direction of differences between predict and control groups was the same on 11 of 15 dependent measures. The control group was consistently superior to the predict group. Second, in their evaluation of the visitor, the control group reported significantly less disparity between their liking of the visitor and the "most favorite person in the world" than did the predict group. These findings appear to suggest that there are effects from controllability over and above predictability. Although this conclusion must remain very tenuous, it is nevertheless important to know what may account for such apparent differences. Another look at the way in which controllability and predictability have been operationalized in the present study suggests some possible answers. Even if it were assumed that predict subjects felt that they had some control over the visitor, their power was still much more limited than the power available to control subjects. The former group could potentially turn a visitor away, but they could do nothing to make him come or make him stay longer than the prescribed time once he was there. The control group, in contrast, had the power to do both.

It should be noted, however, that even the control group probably felt somewhat limited in its ability to exercise control. Unlike laboratory subjects given control over some inanimate, impersonal event, the control subjects in this study had to deal with a complex, highly personal organism. Undoubtedly, their exercise of control over another human being was limited by their consideration for how their demands might be perceived, as well as by situational demands against inappropriate behavior. For instance, the fact that meetings lasted an average of approximately 50 minutes suggests that control subjects decided what the appropriate length of a visit should be on the basis of the initial visit, which also lasted about 50 minutes. Approximately 45 minutes into the first meeting, the visitor remarked that he did not want to take any more of the subject's time than the subject could afford. The meeting usually terminated shortly after this remark was made. It is possible that the subject took this statement as a cue indicating that the visitor wanted to terminate the meeting. The subject could easily have reached the conclusion that about 50 minutes was the appropriate amount of time for such meetings. In summary, the predictability manipulation may have been contaminated by controllability and the controllability manipulation may not have been as strong as intended. A future test of the hypothesis that controllability is better than predictability should strive for a clearer separation of these two variables operationally.

It was also expected that subjects in the random group would benefit from being visited even though the visits were not predictable. Because being visited was conceptualized as a positive event, it was thought that a visit would be analogous to being pleasantly surprised. Apparently, this was not the case. Random subjects were not significantly or consistently superior to the no treatment subjects in any category of variables. Several explanations may account for this absence of differences.

First, it is possible that, because of its unpredictability, the quality of the interaction between visitor and random subjects was very inferior, perhaps even aversive, when compared to the quality of interaction occurring in the predict and control conditions. The subjects' ratings of their enjoyment of the visitation experience contradicts this explanation, however. Random subjects reported enjoying the visits just as much as predict and control subjects. The differences between the subjects' enjoyment of the visits and their enjoyment of "their favorite activity" were also not significant across the three conditions. Subjects in the random group therefore apparently enjoyed the visits just as much as subjects in the predict and control groups. It is possible, then, that a positive event has generalized benefits only to the extent that the individual has the opportunity to look forward to it (it is predictable) or have it whenever he wants it (it is controllable). Extensive correlational and observational research with hospital patients supports the notion that having something positive to look forward to is beneficial to a speedy recovery (Schulz, 1973).

The relevance of these findings to the process of aging is evident. This study demonstrates that the decline in physical and psychological status and level of activity associated with increased age can be inhibited or reversed by making a predictable or controllable significant positive event available to aged individuals. The study further supports the conceptualization that the many negative consequences of aging may be mediated by increased unpredictability and uncontrollability and that, to the extent that the aged individuals are able to maintain a predictable and controllable environment, they should experience relatively less physical and psychological deterioration with increasing age.

The idea that the aged should have the opportunity to retain as much autonomy in their lives as possible is not new to gerontologists. Eric Pfeiffer (1973), at a recent conference on alternatives to institutional care for older Americans, remarked that total care for the aged is just as bad as no care at all. Elaine Brody (1973) is at present carrying out some research on alternatives to institutionalization that emphasizes the importance of enabling the aged individual to retain some autonomy in his or her environment. These gerontologists appear to have reached their conclusions on the basis of intuition, personal experience, and a large body of correlational research. The present investigation supports their points of view and suggests some specific psychological variables that appear to be causally related to successful aging.

Although there is not direct evidence that subjects' level of hope was elevated as a result of the predictability and control manipulations, several dependent measures suggest that this was indeed the case. Subjects in the predict and control groups were judged to have greater zest for life, became more future oriented, and perceived themselves as happier. These data suggest then that the minimal condition for increasing hope is the introduction of a predictable positive event into the individuals life space. This statement is made cautiously, however, subject to the numerous qualifications mentioned earlier when the problems in operationalizing predictability and control were discussed.

Future research in this area should be focused on clearly differentiating controllability from predictability at the operational level. Experience gained from the present investigation suggests that this may be easier to accomplish if the thing to be predicted or controlled is something inanimate, such as a food menu or aspects of the physical environment, instead of another human being. Giving one human being control over another is very problematic.

It is probably also useful to think about and investigate how relevant a particular control manipulation is to an individual's perceived competence. A control manipulation that increases environmental control as well as enhancing a subject's feelings of competence should result in greater beneficial effects than one just increasing environmental control. Although no data assessing the effect of the manipulation on perceived competence have been collected, it is probable that the obtained effects have largely not been mediated by increased feelings of competence. Nevertheless, this line of research should be pursued.

Finally, it would perhaps be useful to carry out a conceptual replication of this study in the laboratory. Although field studies permit a wider and sometimes more meaningful range of independent and dependent variables, laboratory studies permit finer tuning when attempting to operationalize a conceptual variable.

10
Social Perception as Problem Solving

David Greene

Carnegie–Mellon University

Most of our data about human information processing come from laboratory experiments. It is not difficult to think of most experiments as problem-solving tasks, involving, particularly, a set of instructions and a set of possible solutions. Yet it was quite difficult for me, at one time, to think of many interesting social–psychological phenomena for which an explanation in terms of problem-solving processes was satisfying. Surely, I thought, no two people view their social world exactly alike. Clearly, then, no two subjects in a social psychology experiment are trying to "solve" the same "problem." From these premises, it followed that only problems that would be interpreted by most subjects in the same way were worth studying in the laboratory.

ILL-STRUCTURED PROBLEMS AND DESIGN PROCESSES

What began to turn me around was the concept of an ill-structured problem. As Simon and Hayes (1976) put it, "a problem is ill structured to the extent that it puts demands on the knowledge and repertory of problem-solving skills of the solver" (p. 278). Of course, individuals differ in what knowledge and problem-solving skills they bring to problems. Different problems therefore appear more or less structured to different persons, depending on whether the knowledge necessary to supplement the task instructions is easily accessible or not.

The concept of an ill-structured problem may provide a useful frame of reference for discovering how individual differences manifest themselves in problem-solving behavior. Because very few real-world problems have unique optimal solutions, differences among individuals are likely to contribute to different satisfactory solutions to ill-structured problems. We should therefore be able to derive fruitful hypotheses from an analysis of the processes by which problem solvers contribute to the definition of ill-structured problems.

Such an analysis has been done by Herb Simon (1975) for the processes by which an architect designs a house. To put it simply, there is more than one way to build a house according to its owner's specifications. Most of the information necessary to define the task is in fact stored in the architect's long-term memory, where it has been placed through professional training and experience. The task "design a house" evokes from memory some overall program for the design process itself. At any moment, the architect may be working on some well-structured subproblem or component, but the coordination of the various subtasks is built into the organization of the process as a whole.

The program's essential features are outlined in the following quotation:

> The design program consists of one or more generators and a number of tests. When the program is furnished a set of constraints, i.e., a set of criteria for determining when a satisfactory solution to a design problem has been obtained, it proceeds to generate elements for consideration as components in the design [Simon, 1975, p. 298].

Generators ordinarily are designed to satisfy some design constraints automatically, but they also have what Simon has called "autonomous" characteristics. Similarly, not all of the tests applied by the design program will come from problem constraints.

Specifically, there are at least three different classes of characteristics of the design process that contribute to a product recognizable as the architect's own. First, there are those components of a design generator that specify the order in which various elements are to be considered. In any satisficing (as opposed to optimizing; see Simon, 1957) process, the order in which possibilities are examined should influence which solution is discovered. Second, most design programs include a number of stored "prefabricated" assemblies that constitute solutions to subproblems that arise repeatedly in different contexts. Some subset of these is likely to be retrieved from memory in the course of any design project. Third, there are the designer's unique values and preferences—what he should like to see in the finished product. Again, only a small subset of these constraints will be involved in any single application.

These three elements of the design process may be considered hypotheses about how individual differences help determine different satisfactory solutions for ill-structured problems. These hypotheses form the basis for the following speculative attempt to look at social perception as a special case of problem solving. In the rest of my discussion, I propose to sketch a rough outline of this approach and then to comment on previous chapters from the present point of view.

SOCIAL PERCEPTION AND PROBLEM SOLVING

Instead of an architect designing a house, I want to examine an individual constructing an explanation of pertinent events in his social world. As a working definition, I shall define the goal of the social problem solver as having reasonable confidence that the current explanation of the object of his attention is sufficient to permit him to behave adaptively. At any moment, the problem solver can apply a test to determine whether the current explanation meets the several criteria of sufficiency. If it does not, he can either search for new information or construct a different explanation from the same information. The criteria of sufficiency will necessarily vary from moment to moment, depending on several factors.

For example, does "adaptive behavior" require a very elaborate explanation, or does a sketchy one suffice? A person about to make a decision with important long-range consequences may set criteria involving extensive expert advice, social consensus, and an exhaustive consideration of alternatives. A person planning to walk to the mailbox on the corner, in contrast, may merely want to see if it is raining before deciding whether or not to reach for an umbrella. In the same vein, "reasonable confidence" may involve anything from a wild hunch (when little is at stake) to virtual certainty. Also, of course, an individual's personal capacities and priorities will affect his notion of sufficient explanation. For example, we can imagine a university professor and a manual laborer with very different criteria for "understanding" a scientific proposition. Indeed, in day-to-day life, a current explanation may shift suddenly from sufficient to insufficient and vice versa as a result of a change in plans, new information, or simply a change in focus of attention.

To be more specific about the last point, a basic question concerns the conditions that initiate this kind of problem-solving behavior. As Frieze has discussed in Chapter 7, we know virtually nothing about when people rely on previous judgments as opposed to when they actively seek new information. I propose that there are at least three specific classes of events that require a person to revise or construct a new problem space of possible explanations.

First, and most obviously, a person may be asked to explain some social event, either in a conversation or in an experiment. Alternatively, he may generate the same kind of task instructions for himself while planning some future course of action. Second, a person must construct a problem space of possible explanations when an event occurs that is inconsistent with his expectations. In this category I would include, for example, one's own behavior when one perceives it to be either insufficiently or oversufficiently justified (e.g., Lepper, Greene, & Nisbett, 1973). Third, a person must question his current explanation when what he attends to seems ambiguous, particularly unusual, or particularly important. I am explicitly making the assumption that the same basic processes underlie the construction of explanations in response to each of the preceding classes of instigators.

What, then, does a person do when he lacks reasonable confidence that his current explanation satisfices? In part, the answer depends on the precise nature of the task environment. To the extent that the task environment is relatively simple and unambiguous, a more satisfactory explanation is likely to be discovered with minimal problem-solving activity. Put somewhat differently, the more well structured the problem is, the less differences among problem solvers should contribute to which solution is discovered. A person facing an unusual, ambiguous situation, however, will have to begin by generating an overall plan for explanation. Presumably, different individuals will start with different elements of the situation. Another source of variation among individuals should be the conditions under which they begin seeking more information to resolve the ambiguity, as opposed to generating alternative explanations for the same information. Individuals should also differ in the effectiveness of their criteria for terminating unproductive searches. These and other differences among individuals are the "autonomous" characteristics that should play an important role in determining which of many satisfactory solutions to an ill-structured problem is discovered.[1]

How does the problem solver know that he has found a sufficient explanation? The basic answer is that he is continually applying a means–ends analysis, and when no constraint remains unsatisfied, he is finished. However, the answer in this form obscures an important characteristic of the program, namely, the role of feedback and heuristics in increasing the efficiency of the process. The person is not making a simultaneous choice among a set of possible explanations. Instead, he makes a series of choices among sets of promising components that are gradually built into a consistent, coherent pattern. Putting it somewhat differently, the synthesis of an explanation is cumulative.

The number of potentially relevant components may as well be infinite; however, the range of possible components can be narrowed considerably by making use of feedback and/or heuristics. For example, in conversation, we can always ask each other questions. In principle, at least, each question answered should reduce any search by at least a factor of two (cf. the "twenty questions" game). In problem solving, worked-out examples often serve as useful surrogates for real feedback. By analogy, representative individuals may serve as useful surrogates for information about an entire population; alternatively, a stereotype

---

[1] Mischel (1973) has proposed a set of individual difference variables that lend themselves to this approach. One of his categories is labeled "construction competencies," and refers to individuals' abilities to generate particular cognitions and behaviors. Another of his categories is labeled "subjective stimulus values," referring to acquired preferences and aversions. I see these variables as possibly corresponding to descriptions of generators and tests in a program to construct explanations of social events.

may summarize a lot of information in one chunk (cf. Nisbett *et al.*, Chapter 8, and Hamilton, Chapter 6, in this volume). These and other procedures may quickly reduce the number of promising components to manageable proportions.

Without a doubt, the single most useful heuristic is to test for consistency. If I have considered two components in turn, at the very least my explanation for one cannot be inconsistent with my explanation for the other. The consistency heuristic exemplifies a general point, that the dynamics of synthesizing an explanation reveal the utility of a variety of shortcuts, which may have dysfunctional applications in other contexts. In the present case, for example, as a person cumulatively builds an explanation out of components that are consistent with one another, he may very likely overlook a better alternative explanation that contains components inconsistent with the current theory.

THIS MORNING'S PAPERS

Let me turn now to relate these ideas to this morning's papers. In the first place, imagine how a social problem solver such as I described would react to helplessness training. Random events will tax the system to its limits. Put differently, the system must recognize regularities in its environment in order to function. Although I have not used the precise term "control" to describe the goal of our social problem solver, I would not object to the assertion that its *raison d'être* is to feel in control of events. Schulz's (Chapter 9) findings about the physical and psychological well-being of his aged population, for example, are completely consistent with the present analysis.

I want to comment more generally about the findings reported by Nisbett and his colleagues (Chapter 8). There is evidence accumulating that focus of attention and salience are critical determinants of the attribution process (e.g., Ross, 1975; Storms, 1973; Taylor & Fiske, 1975). This evidence is often juxtaposed with other evidence that subjects make poor use of objectively more useful information (cf. Tversky & Kahneman, 1974). Clearly, these findings are not well explained by current theories, unless ascribing them to subjects' use of heuristics is considered a good explanation. In my opinion, our current list of heuristics is just the tip of an iceberg. In reference to our social problem solver, concrete or salient data are likely to be processed first. They become the kernel around which the synthesis grows. As long as a consistent explanation can be built around them, no other explanation is considered. Once the explanation is complete, persons can always shift around less "central" components to adjust for small inconsistencies—in a word, rationalize.

A related point concerns redundancy. It has often been noted that redundant information is logically uninformative, yet people prefer to have it and typically ignore sample size and other objectively important indices of the informativeness of data. From the present point of view, these facts are themselves very informative, because redundancy obviously serves important functions for a social problem solver. For example, it is absolutely essential for any heuristic based on internal consistency, as Simon and Hayes (1976) have noted. In addition, Haviland and Clark (1974) have recently published some data supporting what they call the "given–new" distinction. They argue that sentences typically contain redundancy precisely because new information has to be integrated with existing structures. Redundant information helps the listener to understand new information, to know where to put it. Again we have evidence that the human information processor is more concerned with coherence than with objective informativeness. These findings, of course, dovetail nicely with the notion of the social problem solver, gradually synthesizing a coherent, sufficient explanation.

Hamilton (Chapter 6) provides further support for this line of thinking. The findings he describes remind me somewhat of the initial stages of processing that occur in the visual system. I am thinking specifically of the sharpening of contours, the exaggeration of differences between adjacent stimuli to make separate objects stand out. His description of the minimal conditions to produce stereotyping suggests that we process some social stimuli in an analogous fashion. I see these processes as another example of how we must simplify our social world in order to keep up with it.

The last topic I want to discuss is the general implications of thinking about social perception from a problem-solving point of view. It is a truism that to understand information processing we must understand the task environment. I see the work that Frieze summarized in Chapter 7 as an eloquent testimony to that truism. The research in attributions for success and failure has progressed admirably for at least three reasons. First, it has built on years of study of the social structure of what is known as "achievement motivation." Put simply, a lot was known about the task environment of persons striving to achieve a standard of success. Second, this research is notable for having broken down the process into sequential steps. This strategy has enabled Weiner and his associates to isolate difference stages of the processes mediating achievement-oriented behavior. Third, there has been a very constructive tradeoff between nomothetic and idiographic approaches in their work. Specifically, by looking separately at subjects previously designated as high or low in achievement motivation, these investigators have been able to identify different patterns of attributional thinking for different groups of people.

I see a parallel between this approach and where I think a problem-solving approach to social perception should lead. We cannot study individual differences by putting people in highly structured situations. At this point, we may have progressed far enough in information-processing psychology to be able to apply its ideas and techniques to ill-structured problems. Carroll and Payne (Chapter 2) have offered a good example of how to study the order in which different individuals consider different sources of information. In the same spirit, we should be able to study individuals' social problem-solving strategies by alternating between assessment of their assumptions and other "autonomous constraints," on the one hand, and careful analysis of their information-seeking behavior and verbal protocols while solving ill-structured problems, on the other.

As a postscript, I want to suggest that our cognitive capacities have obviously evolved in a less complex environment than we presently inhabit. The utility of the hodgepodge of heuristics that we employ may be far greater for some purposes than for others. Where we can make the value judgment that we must improve our ability to make complex decisions more rationally, we should devise schemes to accomplish this purpose that do not rely on any substantial change in our capacities.

I have one example to offer. In Carroll and Payne's work, it looks as though one of their major problems will be to get decision makers to make rational use of base-rate information. The evidence is pretty convincing that people do not do so if other information is more salient. There is also evidence that an initial starting point has undue influence on decision makers' judgment—the so-called "anchoring" heuristic. Here is a case in which two biases can be pitted against each other. If parole decision makers were required to start with base-rate information and then allowed to adjust from this anchor according to the individual case, they might end up taking base-rate information into account, so to speak, in spite of themselves.

Part III

COGNITIVE PROCESSES
AND SOCIAL DECISIONS

The chapters in this section examine important social decisions as a setting in which the cognitive social psychologist can explore human behavior and offer insights capable of improving public policy or personal choices.

Slovic, Fischhoff, and Lichtenstein (Chapter 11) look at situations, such as flood danger and nuclear power plants, in which judgments of risk cannot accurately be based on previous experience and new decision methods are required for both policy maker and layman.

Staelin and Payne (Chapter 12) investigate how consumers use information in making product choices and offer a new model based on processes of human thinking.

Berl, Lewis, and Morrison (Chapter 13) explore alternative models of high-school students' decision about which college to attend.

Shanteau and Nagy (Chapter 14) describe the decision process in dating choice and examine several issues from the perspective of human judgment.

Klahr (Chapter 15) observes that social psychology has begun to tackle bigger and more important problems. He sees the information-processing approach as potentially the newest part of a sophisticated methodology appropriate to the problems.

11

Cognitive Processes
and Societal Risk Taking

Paul Slovic
Baruch Fischhoff
Sarah Lichtenstein

Oregon Research Institute

Our world is so constructed that the physical and material benefits we most desire are sprinkled with the seeds of disaster. For example, the search for fertile fields often leads us to floodplains, and our attempt to make less fertile fields productive forces us to rely, at some risk, on fertilizers, pesticides, and fungicides. The wonder drugs that maintain our health carry side effects proportional to their potency, and the benefits of energy are enjoyed at the risk of damage from a host of pollutants. People today have some control over the level of risk they face, but reduction of risk often entails reduction of benefit as well.

The regulation of risk poses serious dilemmas for society. Policy makers are being asked, with increasing frequency, to "weigh the benefits against the risks" when making decisions about social and technological programs. These individuals often have highly sophisticated methods at their disposal for gathering information about problems or constructing technological solutions. When it comes to making decisions, however, they typically fall back on the technique that has been relied on since antiquity—intuition. The quality of their intuitions sets an upper limit on the quality of the entire decision-making process and, perhaps, the quality of our lives.

The purpose of this chapter is to explore the role that the psychological study of decision processes can play in improving societal risk taking. Over the past 25 years, empirical and theoretical research on decision making under risk has produced a body of knowledge that should be of value to those who seek to understand and improve societal decisions. After we review relevant aspects of this research, we will focus on some of the many issues needing further study.

The chapter is organized around three general questions:

1. What are some of the basic policy issues involving societal risk?
2. What do psychologists already know about how people behave in decision-making tasks that is relevant to these issues?
3. What more do we need to know and how may we acquire that knowledge?

BASIC POLICY ISSUES

The issues involved in policy making for societal risks can best be presented within the contexts of specific problem areas. Two such areas, natural hazards and nuclear power, are discussed in this section.

Natural Hazards

Natural hazards constitute an enormous problem. Their mean cost in the United States is approaching $10 billion annually (Wiggins, 1974). A major earthquake in an urban area could cause $20 billion in property damage (Gillette & Walsh, 1971), not to mention the accompanying human misery, anguish, and death.

The question facing public policy makers is: What sorts of measures should be employed to maximize the benefits of our natural environment, while at the same time minimizing the social and economic disruption caused by disasters? In the case of floods, policy options that have been tried or considered include compulsory insurance, flood control systems, strict regulation of land usage, and massive public relief to victims.

Not surprisingly, modern industrial countries have opted for technological solutions, such as dams. It is now recognized, however, that these well-intended programs have often exacerbated the problem. Although the United States government has spent more than $10 billion since 1936 on flood control structures, the mean annual total of flood losses has risen steadily (White, 1964). The damage inflicted on Pennsylvania in 1972 by flooding associated with Hurricane Agnes exceeded $3 billion despite the area's being protected by 66 dams. Apparently, the partial protection offered by dams gives residents a false sense of security and promotes overdevelopment of the flood plain. As a result of this overdevelopment, when a rare flood does exceed the capacity of the dam, the damage is catastrophic. Perpetuating the problem, the victims of such disasters typically return and rebuild on the same site (Burton, Kates, & White, 1968). The lesson to be learned is that technological solutions are likely to be inadequate without knowledge of how they affect the decision making of individuals at risk.

Current debate over public policy is focused on whether or not disaster insurance should be compulsory. Kunreuther (1973) has noted that, whereas few individuals protect themselves voluntarily against the consequences of natural disasters, many turn to the federal government for aid after suffering losses. As a result, the taxpayer is burdened with financing the recovery for those who could have provided for themselves by purchasing insurance. Kunreuther and others argued that both the property owners at risk and the government would be better off financially under a federal flood-insurance program. Such a program would shift the burden of disasters from the general taxpayer to individuals living in hazard-prone areas and would thus promote wiser decisions regarding use of flood plains. For example, insurance rates could be set proportional to the magnitude of risk in order to inform residents of those risks and deter development of high-risk areas.

Without a better understanding of how people perceive and react to risks, however, there is no way of knowing what sort of flood-insurance program would be most effective. To take another example, it seems reasonable that lowering the cost of insurance would encourage people to buy it. Yet, there is evidence that people do not voluntarily insure themselves even if the rates are highly subsidized. The reasons for this are unknown. Knowledge of how psychological, economic, and environmental factors influence insurance purchasing may suggest ways to increase voluntary purchases—or indicate the need for a compulsory insurance program.

Nuclear Power

The problem of determining our level of dependence on nuclear energy is so well known as to require little introduction. Policy decisions must weigh the risks and benefits of a technology for which relevant experience is so limited that technicians must extrapolate far beyond available data. Policy makers must also guess how the public is going to react to their analyses and decisions.

One major issue in the nuclear power controversy involves determining the locus of decision-making authority and the nature and amount of public input. At one extreme are those who argue that decisions about nuclear development should be left to technical experts and to policy makers trained in sophisticated decision analytic techniques. Resistance to this view is exemplified by Denenberg (1974), who insisted that "Nuclear safety is too important to be left to the experts. It is an issue that should be resolved from the point of view of the public interest, which requires a broader perspective than that of tunnel-visioned technicians."

At present, the weighing of benefits versus risks has degenerated into a heated controversy over the magnitude of the risks from loss of coolant accidents, sabotage, theft of weapon's grade materials, and long-term storage of wastes. Some experts argue that nuclear power is extraordinarily safe; others vigorously dissent and have mobilized numerous public interest groups in opposition to the nuclear menace. If the opponents of nuclear power are right about the risks, every reactor built is a catastrophe. If they are wrong, following their advice and halting the construction of reactors may be equally costly to society. What contributions can cognitive psychologists make toward resolving this controversy? Several possibilities exist. First, they can help develop judgmental techniques to assist engineers in assessing probabilities of failure for systems that lack relevant frequentistic data. Second, they can attempt to clarify, from a psychological standpoint, the advantages and disadvantages of various methods of performing risk–benefit evaluations and determining acceptable levels of risk. Third, they can assist the layman trying to understand what the professionals' analyses mean. Even the most astute technical analysis is of little value if its assumptions and results cannot be communicated accurately to the individuals who bear ultimate decision-making responsibility. Fourth, psychological study of man's ability to think rationally about probabilities and risks is essential in determining the appropriate roles of expert and layman in the decision-making process. Fifth, such study can help the public understand how much faith to put into experts' subjective judgments. Given the biases to which these judgments are susceptible, the public may sometimes decide that the experts' best guesses are not good enough.

PSYCHOLOGICAL KNOWLEDGE RELEVANT TO SOCIETAL RISK TAKING

Early Work

The classic view of peoples' higher mental processes assumes that we are intellectually gifted creatures. A statement typical of this esteem was expressed by economist Frank Knight (1921): "We are so built that what seems reasonable to us is likely to be confirmed by experience or we could not live in the world at all" (p. 227).

With the dawn of the computer era and its concern for information processing by man and machine, a new picture of man has emerged. Miller (1956), in his famous study of classification and coding, showed that there are severe limitations on people's ability to process sensory signals. About the same time, close observation of performance in concept formation tasks led Bruner, Goodnow, and Austin (1956) to conclude that their subjects were experiencing a condition of "cognitive strain" and were trying to reduce it by means of simplification strategies. The processing of conceptual information is currently viewed as a serial process that is constrained by limited short-term memory and a slow storage in long-term memory (Newell & Simon, 1972).

In the study of decision making, too, the classic view of behavioral adequacy, or rationality, has been challenged on psychological grounds. For example, Simon's (1957) theory of "bounded rationality" asserts that cognitive limitations force decision makers to construct simplified models in order to deal with the world. Simon (1957) argued that the decision maker:

> . . . behaves rationally with respect to this [simplified] model, and such behavior is not even approximately optimal with respect to the real world. To predict his behavior, we must understand the way in which this simplified model is constructed, and its construction will certainly be related to his psychological properties as a perceiving, thinking, and learning animal [p. 198].

Research providing empirical support for the concept of bounded rationality is discussed next.

Recent Studies of Probabilistic Information Processing

Because of the importance of probabilistic reasoning to decision making, a great deal of recent experimental effort has been devoted to understanding how people perceive and use the probabilities of uncertain events. By and large, this research provides dramatic support for Simon's concept of bounded rationality. The experimental results indicate that people systematically violate the principles of rational decision making when judging probabilities, making predictions, or otherwise attempting to cope with probabilistic tasks. Frequently, these violations can be traced to the use of judgmental heuristics or simplification strategies. These heuristics may be valid in some circumstances but in others they lead to biases that are large, persistent, and serious in their implications for decision making. Because much of this research has been summarized elsewhere (Slovic, Kunreuther, & White, 1974; Tversky & Kahneman, 1974), coverage here is brief.

Misjudging sample implications. After questioning a large number of psychologists about their research practices and studying the designs of experiments reported in psychological journals, Tversky and Kahneman (1971) concluded that these scientists seriously underestimated the error and unreliability inherent in small samples of data. At a result, they (a) had unreasonably high expectations about the replicability of results from a single sample; (b) had undue confidence in early results from a few subjects; (c) gambled their research hypotheses on small samples without realizing the extremely high odds against detecting the effects being studied; and (d) rarely attributed any unexpected results to sampling variability because they found a causal explanation for every observed effect. Similar results in quite different contexts have been obtained by Berkson, Magath, and Hurn (1940) and Brehmer (1974). However, people are not always incautious when drawing inferences from samples of data. Under certain circumstances they become quite conservative, responding as though data are much less diagnostic than they truly are (Edwards, 1968).

In a study using Stanford undergraduates as subjects, Kahneman and Tversky (1972) found that many of these individuals did not understand the fundamental principle of sampling—that the variance of a sample decreases as the sample size becomes larger. They concluded that "For anyone who would wish to view man as a reasonable intuitive statistician, such results are discouraging" [p. 445].

Errors of prediction.   Kahneman and Tversky (1973) contrasted the rules that determined peoples' intuitive predictions with the normative principles of statistical prediction. Normatively, the prior probabilities, or base rates, which summarize what we knew before receiving evidence specific to the case at hand, are relevant even after specific evidence is obtained. In fact, however, people seem to rely almost exclusively on specific information and neglect prior probabilities. Similar results have been obtained by Hammerton (1973), Lyon and Slovic (1976), and Nisbett, Borgida, Crandall, and Reed (Chapter 8).

Another normative principle is that the variance of one's predictions should be sensitive to the validity of the information on which the predictions are based. If validity is not perfect, predictions should be regressed toward some central value. Furthermore, the lower the validity of the information on which predictions are based, the greater the regression should be. Kahneman and Tversky (1973) observed that otherwise intelligent people have little or no intuitive understanding of the concept of regression. They fail to expect regression in many situations when it is bound to occur and, when they observe it, they typically invent complex but spurious explanations. People fail to regress their predictions toward a central value even when they are using information that they themselves consider of low validity.

A third principle of prediction asserts that, given input variables of stated validity, accuracy of prediction decreases as redundancy increases. Kahneman and Tversky (1973) have found, however, that people have greater confidence in predictions based on highly redundant or correlated predictor variables. The effect of redundancy on confidence is therefore opposite what it should be.

Availability bias.   Another form of judgmental bias comes from use of the "availability" heuristic (Tversky & Kahneman, 1973). This heuristic involves judging the probability or frequency of an event by the ease with which relevant instances are imagined or by the number of such instances that are readily retrieved from memory. In life, instances of frequent events are typically easier to recall than instances of less frequent events and likely occurrences are usually easier to imagine than unlikely ones. Therefore, mental availability is often a valid cue for the assessment of frequency and probability. However, because availability is also affected by subtle factors unrelated to actual frequency, such as recency and emotional saliency, reliance on it may result in serious errors.

Availability bias is illustrated in a recent experiment we have been conducting to study people's perceptions of low-probability, high-consequence events. Our stimuli were 41 causes of death, including diseases, accidents, homicide, suicide, and natural hazards. The probability of a randomly selected United States resident's dying from one of these causes in a year ranges from about 1×10^{-8} (botulism) to 8.5×10^{-3} (heart disease). We constructed 106 pairs of these events and asked a large sample of college students to indicate, for each pair, the more likely cause of death and the ratio of the greater to the lesser frequency. We found that (a) our subjects had a consistent subjective scale of relative frequency for causes of death; (b) this subjective scale often deviated markedly from the true scale; (c) the subjects could consistently identify which of the paired events was the more frequent cause of death only when the true ratio of greater to lesser frequency was greater than 2:1. At true ratios of 2:1 or below, discrimination was poor. A subset of the detailed results is presented in Table 11.1.

TABLE 11.1

Judgments of Relative Frequency for Selected Pairs of Lethal Events

Less likely	More likely	True ratio	Correct discrimination (%)	Geometric[a] mean of judged ratios
Asthma	Firearm accident	1.20	80	11.00
Breast cancer	Diabetes	1.25	23	.13
Lung cancer	Stomach cancer	1.25	25	.31
Leukemia	Emphysema	1.49	47	.58
Stroke	All cancer	1.57	83	21.00
All accidents	Stroke	1.85	20	.04
Pregnancy	Appendicitis	2.00	17	.10
Tuberculosis	Fire and flames	2.00	81	10.50
Emphysema	All accidents	5.19	88	269.00
Polio	Tornado	5.30	71	4.26
Drowning	Suicide	9.60	70	5.50
All accidents	All diseases	15.50	57	1.62
Diabetes	Heart disease	18.90	97	127.00
Tornado	Asthma	20.90	42	.36
Syphilis	Homicide	46.00	86	31.70
Botulism	Lightning	52.00	37	.30
Flood	Homicide	92.00	91	81.70
Syphilis	Diabetes	95.00	64	2.36
Botulism	Asthma	920.00	59	1.50
Excess cold	All cancer	982.00	95	1,490.00
Botulism	Emphysema	10,600.00	86	24.00

[a]Geometric means less than 1.00 indicate that the mean ratio was higher for the less likely event. A geometric mean of .20 implies the mean was 5:1 in the wrong direction.

According to the availability hypothesis, any incident that makes the occurrence of an event easy to imagine or to recall is likely to enhance its perceived frequency. For example, one's direct experiences with a lethal event should certainly influence one's judgments. So should one's indirect exposure to the event, via movies, television, newspaper publicity, etc. Examination of events most seriously misjudged lends indirect support to this hypothesis. The frequencies of accidents, cancer, botulism, and tornadoes, all of which get heavy media coverage, were greatly overestimated; asthma and diabetes are among the events whose frequencies were most underestimated. Both of these events are relatively common in their nonfatal form and deaths are rarely attributed to them by the media. Similarly, the spectacular event, fire, which often takes multiple victims and which gets much media coverage, was perceived as considerably more frequent than the less spectacular, single-victim event, drowning, although both are about equal in terms of actual frequency.

In addition to demonstrating availability bias, this study implies that, contrary to the assumptions of some policy makers, intelligent individuals may not have valid perceptions about the frequency of hazardous events to which they are exposed.

Anchoring biases.   Bias also occurs when a judge attempts to ease the strain of processing information by following the heuristic device of "anchoring and adjustment." In this process, a natural starting point or anchor is used as a first approximation to the judgment. This anchor is then adjusted to accommodate the implications of additional information. Typically, the adjustment is crude and imprecise and fails to do justice to the importance of additional information. Recent work by Tversky and Kahneman (1974) demonstrates the tendency for adjustments to be insufficient. They asked subjects such questions as "What is the percentage of people in the United States today who are age 55 or older?" They gave the subjects starting percentages that were randomly chosen and asked them to adjust these percentages until they reached their best estimate. Because of insufficient adjustment, subjects whose starting points were high ended up with higher estimates than those who started with low values. Other biases caused by anchoring and adjustment have been described by Slovic (1972).

Hindsight biases.   A series of experiments by Fischhoff (1974, 1975; Fischhoff & Beyth, 1975) has examined the phenomenon of hindsight. Fischhoff has found that being told some event has happened increases our feeling that it was inevitable. We are unaware of this effect, however, and tend to believe that this inevitability was apparent in foresight, before we knew what happened. In retrospect, we tend to believe that we (and others) had a much better idea of what was going to happen than we actually did have. Fischhoff (1974) shows how such misperceptions can seriously prejudice the evaluation of decisions made in the past and limit what is learned from experience.

Discussion

Because these experimental results contradict our traditional image of the human intellect, it is reasonable to ask whether these inadequacies in probabilistic thinking exist outside the laboratory in situations where decision makers use familiar sources of information to make decisions that are important to themselves and others.

Much evidence suggests that the laboratory results will generalize. Cognitive limitations appear to pervade a wide variety of tasks in which intelligent individuals serve as decision makers, often under conditions that maximize motivation and involvement. For example, the subjects studied by Tversky and Kahneman (1971) were scientists, highly trained in statistics, evaluating problems similar to those they faced in their own research. Overdependence on specific evidence and neglect of base rates has been observed among psychometricians responsible for the development and use of psychological tests (Meehl & Rosen, 1955). When Lichtenstein and Slovic (1971) observed anchoring bias in subjects' evaluations of gambles, they repeated the study, with identical results, on the floor of a Las Vegas casino (Lichtenstein & Slovic, 1973).

Particularly relevant to this chapter is evidence illustrating these sorts of biases in individuals attempting to cope with natural disasters. For example, availability biases are apparent in the behavior of residents on the flood plain. Kates (1962) writes:

A major limitation to human ability to use improved flood hazard information is a basic reliance on experience. Men on flood plains appear very much to be prisoners of their experience. . . . Recently experienced floods appear to set an upward bound to the size of loss with which managers believe they ought to be concerned [p. 140].

Kates further attributes much of the difficulty in achieving better flood control to the "inability of individuals to conceptualize floods that have never occurred" (p. 88). He observes that, in making forecasts of future flood potential, individuals "are strongly conditioned by their immediate past and limit their extrapolation to simplified constructs, seeing the future as a mirror of that past" (p. 88). A more detailed linkage between psychological research, bounded rationality, and behavior in the face of natural hazards is provided by Slovic *et al.* (1974).

One additional implication of the research on people's limited ability to process probabilistic information deserves comment. Most of the discussions of "cognitive strain" and "limited capacity" that are derived from the study of problem solving and concept formation depict a person as a computer that has the right programs but cannot execute them properly because its central processor is too small. The biases from availability and anchoring certainly are congruent with this analogy. However, the misjudgment of sampling variability and the errors of prediction illustrate more serious deficiencies. Here we see that people's judgments of important probabilistic phenomena are not merely biased but are in violation of fundamental normative rules. Returning to the computer analogy, it appears that people lack the correct programs for many important judgmental tasks.

How can it be that we lack adequate programs for probabilistic thinking? Sinsheimer (1971) argues that the human brain has evolved to cope with certain very real problems in the immediate, external world and so lacks the framework with which to encompass many conceptual phenomena. Following Sinsheimer's reasoning, it may be argued that we have not had the opportunity to evolve an intellect capable of dealing conceptually with uncertainty. We are essentially trial-and-error learners, who ignore uncertainty and rely predominantly on habit or simple deterministic rules. It remains to be seen whether we can change our ways in the nuclear age when errors may be catastrophic.

WHERE DO WE GO FROM HERE?
PSYCHOLOGICAL CONSIDERATIONS
IN RISK–BENEFIT ANALYSIS

Our society has, with increasing frequency, sought help from technical experts, trained in the application of formal, analytical methods to problems of decision making. The scientific approach originated during World War II from the need to solve strategic and tactical problems in situations where experience was costly or impossible to acquire. One of the offshoots of this early work has been the technique called "cost–benefit analysis," which attempts to quantify the expected gains and losses from some proposed action, usually in monetary terms. If the calculated gain from an act or project is positive, it is said that the benefits outweight the costs and its acceptance is recommended, providing no other alternative affords a better cost–benefit ratio. A good example of this is the analysis of auto-safety features by Lave and Weber (1970). Risk–benefit analysis is a special case of cost–benefit analysis in which explicit attention is given to assessing the probabilities of hazardous events and quantifying costs from loss of life or limb, pain, and anguish.

Risk–benefit analysis, still in its early stages of development, is being counted on to provide the basic methodological tools for societal risk-taking decisions. Psychological research can contribute to this nascent methodology by identifying the major sources of error in societal risk-taking decisions and by devising techniques to minimize those errors. In the remainder of this chapter we shall speculate about some of the directions this research may take.

Evaluating Low-Probability, High-Consequence Events

The most important public hazards are events with extremely low probabilities and extremely great consequences. For example, Holmes (1961) found that 50% of the damage from major floods was caused by floods with probabilities of occurrence in any year of less than .01. The city of Skopje, Yugoslavia, was leveled by earthquakes in the years A.D. 518, 1555, and 1963, and the mudflow that took 25,000 lives in Yungay, Peru, had swept across the same valley between 1,000 and 10,000 years before. The probability of serious radiation release from a nuclear power reactor has been estimated at between 10^{-4} and 10^{-9} per reactor year. Despite the obvious significance of understanding how (and how well) experts and laymen estimate probabilities for such events, there has been little or no systematic study of this problem other than that by Selvidge (1975) and the "causes of death" study described above.

This section considers the manner in which psychological analysis may help technical experts using two sophisticated analytic techniques for assessing the probabilities of rare hazards: fault-tree analysis and scenario construction.

Fault-Tree Analysis

When frequentistic data regarding failure rates of a complex system are unavailable, estimates can be obtained analytically by means of a fault tree. Construction of the tree begins by listing all important pathways to failure, then listing all possible pathways to these pathways, and so on. When the desired degree of detail is obtained, probabilities are assigned to each of the component pathways and then combined to provide an overall failure rate. For example, major pathways in a fault tree designed to calculate the probability of a car failing to start would include defects in the battery, starting system, fuel system, ignition system, etc. Battery deficiency could then be traced to loose terminals or weak battery charge. The latter could be further analyzed into component causes, such as lights left on, cold weather, or defective generator. The likelihoods of these separate events are combined to produce an estimate of the overall probability of starting failure.

The importance of fault-tree analysis is demonstrated by its role as the primary methodological tool in a recently completed study assessing the probability of a catastrophic loss of coolant accident in a nuclear power reactor (Rasmussen, 1974). The study, sponsored by the Atomic Energy Commission at a cost of $2 million, concluded that the likelihood of such an accident ranged between 10^{-5} (for an accident causing 10 deaths) and 10^{-9} (for a 1,000-death accident) per reactor year. Fault-tree analysis, however, has recently come under attack from critics who question whether it is valid enough to be used as a basis for decisions of great consequence (e.g., Bryan, 1974).

Psychologists may be able to improve the effectiveness of fault trees by identifying biases that may afflict fault tree users and by shoring up the methodology. One methodological problem that psychologists surely can address is deciding by what technique (e.g., direct estimation, paired comparisons, Delphi methods) failure rates for component parts should be estimated. One possible source of bias worth investigating arises from the fact that one rarely has complete empirical failure rates on every component part of a complex system. The rates used are typically estimated from slightly different parts or parts that have been developed for a different purpose. Anchoring and adjustment may well play a role here, possibly leading to estimates more suitable for the original part or original context than for the one in question.

Another possible bias would arise from the omission of relevant pathways to failure or disaster. A tree used to estimate starting failure in an automobile could, for example, be seriously deficient if it failed to include problems with the seat belt system (for 1974 models), theft of vital parts, or other vandalism. The dangers of omitting relevant pathways to disaster should not be underestimated. The cartoon by Mauldin (Fig. 11.1) dramatizes this problem, reflecting the recent reports that the ozone layer, which protects the earth from solar radiation, may be damaged by the fluorocarbons released by aerosol products. In the innumerable scenarios that have been created to evaluate the major risks of technology to mankind, who has thought prior to this discovery to include hair sprays and deodorants as lethal agents?

We suspect that, in general, experts are not adequately sensitive to those avenues to disaster that they have failed to consider because of ignorance, forgetting, or lack of imagination. People who are unaware of their own omissions are likely to seriously underestimate the true failure rate. This hypothesis can surely be tested experimentally.

Even if technical experts could be helped to produce better estimates, problems with the fault tree would not be over. With most societal decisions, ultimate responsibility lies with either the general public or political policy makers. The finest analysis is of little value if it cannot be communicated to these people. Considerations of availability suggest that fault-tree analysis is a technique the results of which are particularly prone to creating misconceptions. For example, naive observers of a fault tree may be startled by the variety of possible pathways to disaster, some of which are likely to be new and surprising to them. Unless they combat the increased imaginability of disaster pathways by properly discounting the less probable paths, they may overreact, perceiving the risk to be greater than it is. Furthermore, the larger and bushier a tree is—in the detail with which specific components of each major pathway are presented—the greater the misperception may be. Therefore, analyses intended to clarify decision makers' perceptions may instead distort them.

Critics of nuclear power often appear to be playing on these proclivities. Consider this message from Alfven (1972): "Fission energy is safe only if a number of critical devices work as they should, if a number of people in key positions all follow their instructions, if there is no sabotage, no hijacking of the transports, ... No acts of God can be permitted" (p. 6).

Although Alfven's statement is an extreme position, it suggests that availability effects may make it difficult to engage in unbiased attempts at discussing low-probability hazards without, at the same time, increasing the perceived probability of those hazards. This may explain, in part, why continued discussions of nuclear power risks have led to increased resistance to this technology.

"SO **THAT'S** THE ONE MOST LIKELY TO GET US."

FIG. 11.1   Copyright © 1974 *The Chicago Sun Times.* Reproduced by permission of Wil-Jo
Associates, Inc. and Bill Mauldin.

Ultimately, public acceptance of new, high-risk technologies may be determined
more by psychological considerations than by the opinions of technical experts.

Evaluating scenarios.   Forecasts and predictions of high-consequence events
are often developed with the aid of scenarios. Some recent examples are "The
Day They Blew Up San Onofre" (Schleimer, 1974), describing the sabotage of a
nuclear reactor and its consequences, and "The Oil War of 1976" (Erdmann,
1975), describing how the world as we know it comes to an end when the Shah
of Iran decides to take it over with Western arms.

A scenario consists of a series of events linked together in narrative form.
Normatively, the probability of a multievent scenario's happening is a multiplicative function of the probabilities of the individual links. The more links there are
in the scenario, the lower the probability of the entire scenario's occurrence. The
probability of the weakest link sets an upper limit on the probability of the
entire narrative.

Human judges do not appear to evaluate scenarios according to these normative rules. We have begun to collect data suggesting that the probability of a
multilink scenario is judged on the basis of the average likelihood of all its links.

Subsequent strong links appear to "even out" or compensate for earlier weak links, making it possible to construct scenarios with perceived probabilities that increase as they become longer, more detailed, and normatively less probable. Consider the following example of such a scenario, taken from one of our experiments:

> Tom is of high intelligence, although lacking in true creativity. He has a need for order and clarity, and for neat and tidy systems in which every detail finds its appropriate place. His writing is rather dull and mechanical, occasionally enlivened by somewhat corny puns and by flashes of imagination of the sci-fi type. He has a strong drive for competence. He seems to have little feel and little sympathy for other people and does not enjoy interacting with others.
>
> In the light of these data, what is the probability that (a) Tom W. will select journalism as his college major (b) but quickly become unhappy with his choice and (c) switch to engineering?

When subjects were given the initial conditions contained in the first paragraph and asked to estimate the probability of subsequent Event a, Tom's selection of journalism as his college major, their mean estimate was .21. When they were asked to estimate the compound probability of Statements a and b, given the same initial conditions, the mean probability rose to .39. When they were asked to estimate the compound event consisting of Statements a, b, and c, the mean probability rose to .41.

These results suggest that scenarios which tell a "good story" by burying weak links in masses of coherent detail may be accorded much more credibility than they deserve.

Experiments are needed to clarify the cognitive processes that determine whether or not a scenario appears plausible, to identify biases in scenario evaluation, and to develop techniques for combatting such biases. An obvious first step toward debiasing is simply educating or warning judges about the problem. If this fails or merely adds noise and confusion to their judgments, more sophisticated techniques must be devised. For example, it may be necessary to decompose the scenario into its component events, estimate conditional probabilities for individual events given preceding developments, and then combine these conditional probabilities mathematically to produce an overall evaluation (see Edwards & Phillips, 1964, for details of a similar approach to combat a different bias). Alternatively, one could insist on the production of several alternative scenarios on any given topic and use an adversary approach to evaluation in which the merits and disadvantages of each are debated.

How Safe Is Safe Enough?

Any risk—benefit analysis must ultimately answer the question: How safe is safe enough? Starr (1969) has proposed a quantitative technique for answering this question based on the assumption that society arrives by trial and error at a reasonably optimal balance between the risks and benefits associated with any activity. Therefore one may use historical accident and fatality records to reveal patterns of "acceptable" risk–benefit ratios. Acceptable risk for a new technology becomes that level of safety associated with ongoing activities having similar benefit to society.

Starr illustrates his technique by examining the relationship between risk and benefit across a number of common activities. His measure of risk for these hazardous activities is the statistical expectation of fatalities per hour of exposure to the activity under consideration. Benefit is assumed to be equal to the average amount of money spent on an activity by an individual participant or, alternatively, to the average contribution that activity makes to an individual's annual income.

From this type of analysis, Starr concludes that (1) the acceptability of a risk is roughly proportional to the real and perceived benefits; (2) the public seems willing to accept voluntary risks (e.g., skiing) roughly 1,000 times greater than it tolerates from involuntary risks (e.g., natural disasters) that provide the same level of benefit; and (3) the acceptable level of risk is inversely related to the number of persons participating in an activity. Noting the similarity between risks accepted voluntarily and the risks of disease, Starr (1969) conjectures that: "The rate of death from disease appears to play, psychologically, a yardstick role in determining the acceptability of risk on a voluntary basis" (p. 1235).

The Starr approach provides an intuitively appealing solution to a problem facing all risk–benefit analyses and, in fact, a similar approach has already been used to develop a building code regulating earthquake risk in Long Beach, California (Wiggins, 1972). There are, however, a number of serious drawbacks to this method. First, it assumes that past behavior is a valid indicator of present preferences. Second, it ignores recent psychological research revealing systematic biases that may prevent an individual from making decisions that accurately reflect his or her "true preferences" (e.g., Lichtenstein & Slovic, 1971, 1973; Slovic & MacPhillamy, 1974). Third, the Starr approach assumes that the public has available a wide selection of alternatives from which to choose. Is it reasonable to assume, for example, that the public's automobile-buying behavior accurately reflects its preferences concerning the tradeoff between safety and other benefits? Unless the public really knows what is possible from a design standpoint, and unless the automobile industry cooperates in making available information that may not necessarily serve its own profit-maximization interests, the answer is likely to be no. Finally, the misperception of risks as observed in the "causes of death" study described above casts doubt on Starr's hypothesis regarding the "yardstick role" of disease rates. It also suggests that revealed historical preferences reflect the forces of the market place rather than the conscious weighing of risks and benefits based on full and accurate information. If so, the justification for using them as a guide for the future is not "this is what people want" but "this is what people have come to accept."

One avenue of research that might help circumvent these difficulties would be to examine risk–benefit tradeoffs via judgmental techniques. Psychological measures of perceived risk and perceived benefit could be developed for major classes of activities. Judgments of desired risk could be elicited in addition to judgments of actual risk. Analysis of these data would focus on the degree to which judged risk and benefit agreed with empirical calculations of these factors. In addition, Starr's results regarding voluntary as opposed to involuntary activities, level of perceived benefit, and number of persons participating in an activity could be reexamined by repeating his analyses within the judgmental risk–benefit space.

Perceived Risk

It is surprising that, with the exception of a few studies using simple gambles as stimuli (see, for example, Coombs & Huang, 1970; Payne, 1975), the determinants of perceived risk remain unexplored. Yet there is anecdotal and empirical evidence of a number of risk phenomena meriting serious psychological study. One is society's apparent willingness to spend more to save a known life in danger than to save a statistical life. Is this really true and, if so, why? A second is the speculation that repeated "uneventful" experience with a hazard reduces its perceived risk more than it should. Study of this question may provide insight into why the public tolerates levels of risk from some hazards (e.g., radiation from medical x rays) that they do not tolerate from nuclear power plants. A third untested notion is that hazards with delayed consequences (e.g., smoking) are discounted. Finally, perceived risk may depend greatly on the way in which the relevant information is presented. For example, risks from radiation may appear negligible when described in terms of "average reduction in life expectancy for the population within a given radius of a nuclear power plant." However, when this figure is translated into the equivalent number of "additional cancer deaths per year," risk may take on quite a different perspective.

   Research on these phenomena may also help us understand how the public responds to scientific information about risk. Growing concern over environmental risks has increased scientific research on the effects of such hazards as herbicides, fertilizers, pesticides, pollution, and radiation. It has been assumed that publication of scientific information about these hazards is sufficient to elicit appropriate public action. In fact, although scientific information sometimes leads to hasty public action, it often goes unheeded (Lawless, 1975). Although the determinants of societal response are undoubtedly complex, cognitive factors related to communication of information and perception of risk are likely to play an important role.

Value of a Life

Although the economic costs stemming from property damage, disruption of production, medical expenses, or loss of earnings can be estimated, we have no suitable scheme for evaluating the worth of a human life to society. Despite the aversiveness of thinking about life in economic terms, the fact is inescapable that by our actions we put a finite value on our lives. Decisions to install safety features, to buy life insurance, or to accept a hazardous job for extra salary all carry implicit values for a life.

Economists have long debated the question of how best to quantify the value of a life (see, for example, Hirshleifer, Bergstrom, & Rappaport, 1974; Mishan, 1971; Rice & Cooper, 1967; Schelling, 1968). The traditional economic approach has been to equate the value of a life with the value of a person's expected future earnings. Many problems with this index are readily apparent. For one, it undervalues those in society who are underpaid and places no value at all on people who are not in income earning positions. In addition, it ignores interpersonal effects wherein the loss suffered by the death of another bears no relation to the financial loss caused by the death. A second approach, equating the value of life with court awards (Holmes, 1970; Kidner & Richards, 1974), is hardly more satisfactory.

Bergstrom (1974) argues that the question "What is a life worth?" is ill formed and what we really want to know is "What is the value placed on a specified change in survival probability?" As with the Starr approach to assessing risk–benefit tradeoffs, Bergstrom argues that the best way to answer this second question is by observing the actual market behavior of people trading risks for economic benefits. For example, Thaler and Rosen (1973) studied salary as a function of occupational risk and found that a premium of about $200 per year was required to induce men in risky occupations (e.g., coal mining) to accept an annual probability of .001 of accidental death. From this, they inferred that the value of life, at the margin, is equivalent to about $200,000. Certainly, the same criticisms leveled earlier at the Starr approach apply to this method. It assumes that individuals have enough freedom of choice and perceptiveness of risks so that their preferences are valid indicators of their values.

We believe this question is too important for psychologists to ignore. They can contribute by testing the cognitive assumptions on which the economic measures rest and by providing alternative methods of assessing the value of a life, such as direct questions or other psychophysical techniques. Preliminary attempts at this by Acton (1973) and Torrance (1970) have been downgraded by economists on the grounds that "Time and again, action has been found to contradict assertion. Since surveys always elicit some degree of *strategic* behavior (What do they want me to say?), we would be better advised to observe what people choose under actual conditions" (Rappaport, 1974, p. 4). Whether attitudes or behaviors provide a more accurate reflection of people's values needs to be examined utilizing the broader perspective and expertise that psychology can provide.

Justification

Decision makers will employ the new tool of risk–benefit analysis to the extent that they believe that such a tool leads to good decisions. What are the perceived characteristics of a good decision? Tversky (1972) and Slovic (1975) have found evidence that decision makers rely on procedures that are easy to explain and easy to justify to themselves and others. If this is generally true, it may be that decisions are made by searching for or constructing a good justification, one that minimizes lingering doubts and can be defended no matter what outcome occurs. For people accustomed to relying on such justifications, risk—benefit analysis may not be satisfactory. The early steps of such techniques, which involve structuring the problem and detailing alternatives and their attributes, may be useful devices for helping the decision maker think deeply and in relevant ways about his problem. However, the latter steps, involving quantification, may be forcing people to produce information at a level of precision that does not exist.

An alternative conceptualization, possibly more in tune with people's natural predilections, would have decision makers act like debaters, marshalling thorough and convincing arguments relevant to the decision at hand, rather than like computers, making decisions on the basis of arithmetic (for a similar argument, see Mason, 1969).

These speculations lead naturally to the questions: What are the components of justifiability? What makes a good justification? Although we do not have any firm answers, we do have some hypotheses about factors that may not be viewed as adequate justifications. We think subjective factors, which are the cornerstones for sophisticated decision aids, such as tradeoff functions or probability judgments unsupported by frequentistic data, are perceived as weak justifications for decisions in the face of risk. Subjective probabilities, for example, leave one vulnerable to second guessing—imagine the designers of the Edsel explaining in 1961 that their carefully constructed opinions about the market indicated that it was likely to be a big seller. Expected value computations may also make weak justifications because of their dependence on "long-run" estimates; such estimates may not appear relevant for decisions viewed as one-shot affairs.

Will people view decisions based on shallow but nice-sounding rationales (cliches, universal truths, adages) as better than decisions based on complex, thorough decision—analytic techniques? The answer to this question obviously has important implications for understanding and predicting public decision makers' responses to information bearing on technological risk. Roback (1972) in discussing the defeat of the Supersonic Transport (SST) subsidy, provides anecdotal evidence in support of this conjecture:

> There was not . . . a nice weighing of risk and benefit . . . . What counted most in the balance, I daresay, was the question that enough congressmen put to themselves before casting a vote: "How will I explain to my constituents, the majority of whom have never even been on an airplane or traveled far from home, why we need an SST to save two or three hours' travel time between New York and Paris?" [p. 133]

If these hypotheses are true, the risk—benefit analyst may be preparing analyses merely for his own edification, as few others are likely to use them. In this event, research is vital for teaching us how to communicate risk—benefit and other valuable analytic concepts in ways that enable such material to be woven into the fabric of convincing justifications.

CONCLUDING REMARKS

We have tried to summarize, briefly and from our own perspective, the state of psychological knowledge regarding decision making under risk; we have also attempted to convey our sense of excitement regarding the potential contributions of this branch of cognitive psychology to basic knowledge and societal well-being.

Our knowledge of the psychological processes involved in risk-taking decisions has increased greatly in recent years. However, we still have only a rudimentary understanding of the ways in which bounded rationality manifests itself. We know much about certain types of deficiencies and biases, but we do not know the full extent of their generality across tasks and across individuals of varying expertise. Nor do we know how to combat these biases. We still do not understand the psychological components of value and how they determine, or depend on, decisions. We know little about perceived risk, the determinants of societal response to threat, modes of communicating information about risk, or the role of justifications in decision processes. Research in these problem areas is vital to the development of methodologies for societal decision making that can accommodate the limitations and exploit the specialties of the people who must perform and consume these analyses.

H. G. Wells once commented: "Statistical thinking will one day be as important for good citizenship as the ability to read and write." That day has arrived. Our discussion points to the need for educating both the technical experts and the public regarding the subtleties of statistical thinking. Such education should be incorporated into the curriculum of the schools, perhaps as early as in the lower grades. We need to teach people to recognize explicitly the existence of uncertainty and how to deal rationally with it. We must become accustomed to monitoring our decisions for consistency. We need to understand that the quality of a decision cannot by gauged solely by the quality of its outcome. We must recognize the distortions of hindsight when we evaluate the past.

Although the concept of bounded rationality has arisen within the mainstream of cognitive psychology (e.g., Miller's and Simon's work), research on decision processes has made little subsequent contact even with such closely related fields as the study of nonprobabilistic information processing. It should. Certainly the phenomena described here cannot be fully understood without consideration of their underlying cognitive mechanisms. Likewise, some of these phenomena may provide stimulating inputs for general theories of cognition. The hindsight results, for example, indicate one way in which semantic memory is reorganized to accommodate new information. The bias here called "availability" suggests a need to better understand the process of constrained associates production. No theory of cognitive development appears to relate to the acquisition of judgmental biases and heuristics as conceptualized here. Without such knowledge, we have no idea when it is best, or when it is even possible, to begin teaching children to think probabilistically.

Although this chapter has emphasized what psychologists can do to facilitate societal decision making, clearly a multidisciplinary approach, involving cooperative efforts with physicists, economists, engineers, geographers, and—perhaps most important—decision makers, is necessary. Only by working hand in hand with decision makers can we learn what their problems are—both those they perceive and those they do not. Only continual multidisciplinary interaction can alert us to the narrowness of our own perspective and enable us to develop practical tools for decision makers.

ACKNOWLEDGMENTS

Support for this paper was provided by the Advanced Research Projects Agency of the Department of Defense (ARPA Order No. 2449) and was monitored by ONR under Contract No. N00014-73-C-0438. (NR 197-026). We are indebted to Berndt Brehmer, Daniel Kahneman, Howard Kunreuther, and Amos Tversky for stimulating our thinking on many of the issues discussed here.

12
Studies of the Information-Seeking Behavior of Consumers

Richard Staelin
John W. Payne

Carnegie–Mellon University

Marketing is concerned with the activities of organizing, planning, and controlling a firm's resources so as to satisfy the needs and wants of chosen customer groups at a profit. In order to satisfy these needs, marketing, more than any other functional area of business, must be concerned with understanding consumer behavior. Surprisingly, only recently have marketing researchers given much attention to generalized theories or models of buyer behavior that are necessary to obtain this understanding.

The first efforts involved simple models of behavior originally developed in other disciplines such as the "rational economic man" model and the Freudian model of hidden motives or drives. Within the last decade a number of comprehensive models have been postulated that attempt to specify the interrelationships of various constructs in explaining consumer behavior. For example, the models of Howard and Sheth (1969), Nicosia (1966), and Engel, Kollet, and Blackwell (1968) all attempt to tie together such factors as motivation, perception, learning, personality, attitudes and attitude changes, social class, reference groups, dissonance, and risk taking. Each of these models has the following general framework:

1. The consumer is viewed as an adaptive problem solver, i.e., he learns from pervious experiences and his behavior is potentially understandable.

2. The consumer is a selective information processor who receives and adjusts the information so that it is more congruent with his personal wishes and needs.

3. The consumer is a social animal and consequently his behavior reflects interactions with other people.

Although a decade has passed since the first of these comprehensive models was postulated, only a few studies have attempted to determine the functional relationships between variables (e.g., Farley and Ring, 1970). Also, these models provide the marketing practitioner little insight into how the consumer actually processes information and comes to the final choice because the models are defined in terms of unobserved constructs, such as motives, drives, attitudes, and perceptual biases. Consequently, consumer behavior researchers have recently directed their attention to the actual cognitive processes involved with the task of purchasing a product, the thought being that this knowledge must be obtained before adequate models of consumer behavior can be formulated.

This chapter deals with one aspect of the cognitive process, namely how consumers seek and process information. The approach taken is to incorporate into marketing studies many of the concerns, concepts, and methodologies from research on human information processing in more traditional areas of cognitive psychology. We report three investigations of consumer information-seeking behavior. The first relates the accuracy of the consumer's decision to the amount of information provided. The second study focuses on the actual information-seeking patterns of the consumer in situations that vary in the amount of information provided. The third attempts to relate different information-seeking patterns to such factors as the circumstances surrounding the task, the prior experience of the decision maker, and the characteristics of the sources of information.

QUANTITY OF INFORMATION
AND ACCURACY OF CHOICE

Marketing managers and policy makers, such as the Federal Trade Commission, are concerned with how much information the consumer needs (or should have) to make an intelligent decision among competing consumer products. Two recent studies by Jacoby, Speller, and Berning (1974) and Jacoby, Speller, and Kohn (1974) conclude that the accuracy of judgment was greatest with moderate amounts of information (i.e., as the consumer is given too much information, the accuracy actually decreases).

Because the ramifications of this conclusion are of such great import we will review the methodology Jacoby and associates have used, reanalyze the published data, and try to tie our new results to the existing literature on information processing.

The basic design for both studies was the same. First, the consumer's ideal point for a product class was determined by asking each subject (a) to indicate how much influence each attribute associated with products within the product class had in the consumer's evaluation of a product and (b) to imagine their "ideal" brand within the product class and then to indicate how much of each attribute this ideal brand would have.

The subjects were then asked to begin their "shopping trips." Each subject was given p different brands from which to choose, each brand having k attributes. Three different product classes were studied, laundry detergent (L), rice (R), and prepared dinners (PD). For example, there might be eight brands of rice, each with four attributes (e.g., calories/serving). A 3 (number of brands) X 3 (number of attributes/brand) design with 17 college students per cell was employed for L, whereas a 4 X 4 design with 12 housewives per cell was used for the remaining two product classes. In the case of R and PD, respondents were assigned to a particular cell for both treatments. Each subject was asked to examine and evaluate all of the information provided (which depended on the cell value for p and k) and then, for L, to choose the brand they liked the most; for R and PD the subjects were asked to rank order their preference for all the brands.

The similarity of these choices to the consumer's ideal point preference measured the extent to which the consumer was able to satisfy his or her expressed desires. The dependent variable was the number of subjects who selected, from the set of p available brands, the brand most similar to their ideal point. The most similar brand was operationally defined as the brand least distant from the ideal point; distance was computed by a linear compensatory model summing the product of the individual subjects' importance scores for each of the k attributes time the absolute difference between the ideal rating for the attribute and the attribute value for the particular brand.

Table 12.1 presents the number of subjects in each cell who correctly selected their "best" brand of laundry detergent, rice, and prepared dinners. The authors then plotted these data in terms of the total amount of information available (which was defined to be the product of the number of attributes/brand and the number of brands, i.e., $k \times p$) and noted a curvilinear relationship between number of correct responses and total amount of information provided for all three product classes. They concluded "In sum, the accuracy curves from both studies suggest that providing substantial amounts of package information can result in poorer purchase decisions" (Jacoby, Speller, & Berning, 1974, p. 40).

Brands versus Attributes

The above conclusion is based on two major assumptions; that the accuracy figures for each cell can be compared across brands and that there is an equal tradeoff between brands and attributes. With regard to the first assumption it should be noted that the probability of the consumer's selecting the best brand by chance alone is 25% in the four-brand situation, but only 8.3% in, say, the 12-brand situation. Because these probabilities differ across brands it is necessary to correct for random matchups before interbrand comparisons can be made (Russo, 1974; Wilkie, 1974). One appropriate measure that takes into account these different probabilities is obtained by subtracting the expected number of

TABLE 12.1
Number of Subjects Who Correctly Selected Their "Best" Brand
for Different Number of Alternatives and Amounts of
Information for Three Product Classes[a]

Number of attributes per brand	(L)[b] Number of brands			Number of attributes per brand	(R)[c] Number of brands				Number of attributes per brand	(PD)[c] Number of brands			
	4	8	12		4	8	12	16		4	8	12	16
2	2	3	5	4	6	7	1	2	4	3	6	3	2
				8	3	5	1	4	8	2	3	0	2
4	6	6	5	12	5	9	6	4	12	7	1	0	1
6	11	8	4	16	6	10	7	5	16	10	3	1	1

[a]The source for L is Jacoby, Speller, and Kohn (1974); the source for R and PD is Jacoby, Speller and Berning (1974).
[b]The maximum number of subjects possible in each cell was 17.
[c]The maximum number of subjects possible in each cell was 12.

correct choices, assuming a random selection from the observed data. For example in R we would expect 3 (= .25 × 12) respondents in the four-brand situation to pick their best brand even if the choice process were random. Consequently, the number of correct choices after adjusting for guessing in the four-brand, 12-attribute cell for R is 2 (= 5 − 3).

The second assumption deals with the equal tradeoff between brands and attributes. Even after we correct for the different chance probabilities we note that cells with differing p and k but equal $p \times k$ values exhibit consistently more accuracy for cells with smaller brand alternatives and larger numbers of attributes. In fact, of the 15 cases having two equal $p \times k$ cells 13 show more accuracy for cells with a smaller p and larger k, a significant deviation from chance, implying the inadequacy of the $p \times k$ measure (Russo, 1974).

In order to better estimate the effects of brands and attributes on decision accuracy, the following model was postulated:

$$Y_{pkl} = \mu + C_l + B_p + A_k + BA_{pk} + \epsilon_{pkl} \qquad (12.1)$$

where Y_{pkl} = the number of subjects who selected the brand closest to their ideal brand after correcting for guessing

μ = a constant

C_l = the product class effect, $l = 1, 2, 3$

B_p = the number of brands, $p = 4, 8, 12, 16$

A_k = the number of attributes per brand, $k = 2, 4, 6, 8, 12, 16$

BA_{pk} = the interaction between brands and attributes per brand

ϵ_{pkl} = an error term

In other words adjusted decision accuracy is an additive function of a product class effect (C_l), an attribute effect (A_k), a brand effect (B_p), and an interaction effect (BA_{pk}). If, as Jacoby and associates have assumed, decision accuracy is affected by the cross-product of B_p and A_k, we may expect the interaction terms to be significant. If, however, the choice set size and number of attributes per brand influence accuracy independently, we can expect the interaction terms to be statistically insignificant.

The model was estimated using ordinary least squares after making appropriate ANOVA restrictions.[1] The interaction terms were found to be statistically insignificant $(F_{13,17} = .73)$. The model was therefore reestimated after the interaction terms were dropped, producing estimates of the contrasts within each factor. The results, displayed in Table 12.2, indicate that decision accuracy is a discontinuous monotonically increasing function with respect to the number of attributes per brand. In other words, as more information is provided the accuracy increases markedly up to and including six pieces of information. However, when the consumer is given eight pieces of information per alternative, there seems to be a sharp decrease in accuracy, after which more information seems to improve the consumers accuracy. Perhaps the added information caused the decision makers to switch their decision rules for selection from a compensatory-type rule to a rule that is easier to administer, such as satisficing. In any case, it seems that more information is associated with more accuracy at least within small ranges. However more research is needed to settle this question.

The results concerning the size of the choice set are somewhat surprising. After the correction for guessing, their seems to be little effect from moving from four, to eight, to 12, to 16 brands; the only major discrepancy occurs at eight brands and is associated with a higher degree of accuracy. However, the contrast between eight brands and the other choice set sizes is not statistically significant $(p > .10)$. It therefore seems that choice set size has little to do with accuracy after one corrects for guessing.

Measure of Decision Accuracy

It should be immediately clear that the above conclusion is influenced by the definition of decision accuracy (i.e., what is best). In order to define the ideal brand, one needs to know how consumers choose (or should like to choose) from a number of multiattribute brands. Recent empirical work indicates that the normative model of ideal points and distance measures used by Jacoby and co-workers exhibits reasonably good predictive power for brands preference (Green & Rao, 1968), although there is little evidence that consumers actually

---

[1] The reader is referred to Andrews, Morgan, and Sonquist (1967) for a discussion of the restrictions.

TABLE 12.2
Least-Square Estimates for the Effects of Different Factors
on the Adjusted Accuracy of the Decision Process

Factors	Coefficient	df	Sum of square	F
Attributes per brand[a]		5	61.8	2.62[b]
2	−3.96			
4	−1.63			
6	.38			
8	−2.88			
12	−1.25			
16	.0			
Brands[c]		3	27.8	1.96[d]
4	.21			
8	1.89			
12	−.10			
16	.0			

[a]In order to circumvent singularity the 16-attribute/brand variable was arbitrary set to zero.
[b]Significant at .05 level.
[c]In order to circumvent singularity the 16-brand variable was set to zero.
[d]Not significant at .15 level.

trade off between attributes using linear compensatory models. For example, Wright (1975) reported that decision makers, even when instructed to explicitly use a compensatory decision rule, only were able to arrive at the right choice approximately 50% of the time when selecting between six options each having four attributes with five possible values per attribute. Also, Payne (1975) reported that consumers were much more likely to use noncompensatory rules as the task became more complex.

More work is clearly needed on how the consumer selects a brand from a set of brands if studies on consumer accuracy are to be conducted. Although the ideal point model is a reasonable normative model to use as a benchmark for comparing performance accuracy, other measures should be investigated that may better reflect noncompensatory decision rules used by consumers. For example, in the case of satisficing, there is no one "ideal" decision. It would have been interesting, therefore, to see whether the brand selected in the studies by Jacoby and associates was always one of the top three brands based on the compensatory model or a brand within a given percentage of the ideal point. Although this would not prove that the consumers used a satisficing rule, it might alter the conclusions of the study (Jacoby, 1975). Finally, it is interesting to speculate that the "stochastic" behavior so often observed in marketing studies is really a result of satisficing and not the hypothesized random behavior (i.e., consumers chose stochastically only from a set of brands within a satisfactory distance from their ideal point). If this "stochastic satisficing" were the case, much of the present work in stochastic modeling would be affected.

ACTUAL INFORMATION-SEEKING BEHAVIOR

An interesting question arises from the above discussion; i.e., How much information from a $p \times k$ matrix does a consumer really process? To gain some insight into the question, 12 respondents (who were paid college students) were asked to choose among a set of p hypothetical apartments, each characterized by k attributes. The apartments were represented by "information boards" (Wilkins, 1967), which consisted of a number of envelopes containing cards labeled with the name of an attribute, e.g., "noise level." To obtain the value of that attribute for a particular alternative, the decision maker had to pull the card out of the envelope, turn it around, and place it back into the envelope. The information about the value of the attribute was on the back of the card, e.g., "noise level—low." Once a card was turned over, the value of the attribute on the particular alternative was clearly displayed for the remainder of the choice problem. Each session contained one each of a 2, 4, 8, and 12 alternative choice problem. The levels of number of attributes (4, 8, or 12) were counterbalanced across sessions and decision makers. The decision makers were told that they would be presented with a number of alternatives to choose among and a certain amount of information about each alternative. They were told that each alternative represented a furnished one-bedroom apartment and that they should chose the apartment they would prefer for themselves on the basis of the information provided about each apartment. The decision maker was not instructed on how much of the available information he or she had to use in making the decision. No time constraints were placed on the decision makers. They were instructed to work at their own pace and that they would have plenty of time to finish.

The order and amount of information sought for each $p \times k$ situation was recorded. Table 12.3 presents a summary of the amount of information sought after averaging across all respondents.

Note that as the alternatives increase (and the available information per alternative is held constant), the decision makers on the average seek more information. Likewise, as the number of attributes available increases (while the number of alternatives to consider is held constant) the total amount of information sought increases, although increases in the number of alternatives result in more information sought than an increase in the number of attributes, again pointing out the noncompensatory tradeoff between alternatives and attributes.

TABLE 12.3
The Amount of Information Available and the
Average Amount of Available Information Used for Different
Numbers of Alternatives and Attributes per Alternative

Number of available attributes per alternative	Number of alternatives			
	2	4	8	12
4	$6.76^a/8^b$	12.59/16	21.33/32	30.00/48
8	11.34/16	18.02/32	29.66/64	43.12/96
12	13.27/24	19.82/48	30.62/96	52.56/144

[a] Average amount sought.
[b] Amount available.

Finally it should be noted that even though the subjects seek more information when it has been made available, the proportion of information sought decreases monotonically as more attributes are introduced for each choice set size. This decreasing monotone relationship was also noted in general when the number of attributes available was held constant and the choice set size was increased. When choosing between p possible apartments, therefore, the subjects on the average sought more information but as a decreasing proportion of the total amount of information available.

These findings have some common-sense face validity with those presented in Table 12.2, which indicated that except for the discontinuity between six and eight pieces of information, more information resulted in more accuracy. Since we observe that consumers tend to seek more information when it is made available to them, we may infer that this added information increases the observed accuracy of their decision.

Search Strategies

Because actual information-seeking behavior was recorded, it was possible to analyze the observed behavior to determine whether the consumers spread their search evenly among alternatives or investigated only a few alternatives thoroughly. This was done by first calculating for each individual the absolute value of the difference between the percentage of information searched per alternative in the choice set and the mean percentage of information searched in the choice set for each of the 12 choice situations.

This absolute difference was defined as Y_{pkil}, where p is the choice set size, k the number of attributes per alternative, i the ith consumer, and l the particular apartment within the choice set. Then using Y_{pkil}, the sample variance was calculated as follows for an individual's search behavior across apartments, conditional on the particular choice set size and number of available attributes:

$$S^2_{pki} = \sum_{l=1}^{p} Y^2_{pkil}/(p-1)$$

The question then becomes is the person's true search variation a function of the choice set size and/or number of attributes per alternative. We postulate the following additive model:

$$\sigma^2_{pki} = \mu_i + B_p + A_k + (BA)_{pk} \qquad (12.2)$$

where

σ^2_{pki} = the ith person's true search variation for choice set p, attribute condition k

μ_i = the constant for the ith person

B_p = the effect of choice set size p

A_k = the effect of number of attributes k

$(BA)_{pk}$ = the effect of the interaction of these latter two terms

Because we do not observe σ^2_{pki} but instead the fallible but unbiased measure S^2_{pki}, Equation (12.2) becomes after substitution:

$$S^2_{pki} = \mu_i + B_p + A_k + (BA)_{pk} + \epsilon_{pki} \qquad (12.3)$$

where ϵ_{pki} is the error term associated with the fallible measure. Now note that if the original observation percentages are assumed to be normal random variables, then the variance of ϵ_{pki} is not constant but is instead a function of the choice set size, i.e., $\text{Var}(S^2_{pki}) = \sigma^2/(p-1)$. Therefore, to obtain BLUE estimates and to conduct the appropriate F tests for Equation (12.3) it is necessary to first correct for heteroscedasticity. This has been done and the results of the analysis are presented in Table 12.4.

The estimates for the levels of B_p, A_k, and $(BA)_{pk}$ indicate that as the choice set size increases the subjects are more likely to differentially search over alternatives, i.e., to obtain few pieces of information on some alternatives and many pieces on other ($p < .05$). Such a search pattern is compatible with the hypothesis that individuals are more likely to adopt noncompensatory decision rules, e.g., lexicographic, as the number of available alternatives is increased. Also, after the number of alternatives were held fixed, increases in the number of attributes per alternative led to less variation of search behavior among alternatives, again implying that alternatives and attributes acted as different cues to the individual. Finally, the interaction term was found to be insignificant.

TABLE 12.4

Least-Square Estimates for the Effects of Different Factors on the
Variation and Search Patterns in Selecting an Apartment

Factors	Coefficients	Sum of squares	df	F
Individuals specific coefficients for each respondent are not shown		24,578	12	30.4
Number of alternatives[a]		554	3	2.74
2	−271			
4	39			
8	106			
12	126			
Number of attributes/alternative[a]		348	2	2.58
4	137			
8	−61			
12	−76			
Interactions specific coefficients for each interaction not shown		346	6	.86
Error		8146	121	

[a]The sum of the variables within a factor were restricted to equal zero to obtain
estimability.

INDIVIDUAL DIFFERENCES
AND INFORMATION SEEKING

The preceding discussion and experiments have placed emphasis on treatment effects in explaining any observed differences with respect to the information-seeking behavior between groups of individuals. However, it is unreasonable to believe that all consumers exhibit the same behavior even when they are in the same situation. Individual differences can be attributed to a number of factors besides the task environment, the factors being such things as experience, motivation, and ability. In this section we investigate, at a more macrolevel, individual differences in the information-seeking behavior for consumers of major durable goods.

The purchase of a major durable represents a significant cash outlay and so offers a purchase situation where the consumer may exhibit substantial problem-solving behavior. It should be pointed out, however, that many buying "deci-sions" may not involve complex problem solving. For example, most repeat purchases for nondurable goods (i.e., canned juice, rice) probably do not involve any problem-solving activity, and even if there is some activity, this activity may be reduced by using brand names (i.e., chunking information), considering only a few alternatives, referring to a small number of sources of information, etc. In fact most current marketing models characterize these nondurable situations as stochastic and ignore the actual information-seeking and decision-making aspects of the choice process.

The data reported here were obtained from personal interviews in 653 households that purchased one or more of the following durable products in a 19-month period prior to interview: automobile, color television set, black and white television set, refrigerator or freezer, washing machine, kitchen stove, or air conditioner. Because these data are based on recall and not direct observation, they suffer from the normal problems of forgetting and other measurement error. However, they do represent a probability sample of households in the continental United States, excluding Alaska, and can be hoped to provide some indication of the information-seeking behavior of typical consumers.

Several different kinds of questions were employed to obtain relative measures of information seeking and receiving.

Two open-response questions relied on unaided recall and emphasized buyer initiative. The questions were: "Where did you look for information or advice? I mean what were the sources of information?" and "What kinds of information did you seek?"

An aided recall approach also was employed. The following questions were asked about sources from which information was received, whether or not the buyer sought out the sources:

"Did you talk with friends or neighbors about different brands of . . . ?"

"Did you consult any books, pamphlets, magazine or newspaper articles on the product?"

"Did you study newspaper or magazine advertisements?"

"Did you watch TV commercials on the product more carefully than, say, a year earlier?"

Immediately afterwards, the respondent was asked: "From which of these sources did you get any useful information or advice?" For each source named, the respondent was asked: "What kind of information was this?"

The number of types of information sources a buyer used was measured by counting each type mentioned in answer to either the aided or unaided recall questions. The retail outlet was counted if named in response to the unaided recall question or, in the absence of such mention, if the buyer had visited more than one dealer or store.

The results for both car and appliance buyers were very similar; 14% of the buyers did not report using any sources, 30% reported using only one source, 44% used either two or three types of sources, whereas 12% used four.

Some variation in number of sources was observed according to the type used. The number tended to be lower when source use included friends and neighbors and retail outlets than when it included advertising or books, pamphlets, and articles. When only one type of source was consulted, that type was the retail outlet in 60% of the cases and friends and neighbors in 22%.

The data did not permit measures of the number of individual sources used within a given type or measures of frequency of use, except for visits to retail outlets. The findings therefore understate to an unknown extent consumer usage of information sources. Even so, they clearly show that the majority of buyers of major durables consult more than one type of source before buying, even though there is indication that a substantial minority may not engage in extensive external search activity. (The latter point is reinforced by the fact that 40% of the total sample reported initially considered just one brand and ended up by purchasing this brand. Even for major durable goods, therefore, we note consumers reporting limited or nonexistent information seeking, which may indicate that the decision maker does little information processing other than searching memory.)

In order to investigate individual differences in the total amount of information sought, an index of information seeking was constructed for each purchaser, taking into consideration (a) different types of information sought (i.e., performance, quality, prices, service), (b) different sources used (i.e., friends or neighbors, books or pamphlets, newspapers or magazine advertisements, TV commercials), and (c) the number of outlets visited. The index was constructed by giving points each time the respondent mentioned seeking specific types of information, sources of information, or visiting a retail outlet. Although the construction of this index is arbitrary in that there is little justification for the particular weighting scheme used (which gave equal weight to sources, types of information, and number of retail outlets visited) it is somewhat analogous to the total number of attributes considered before a purchase. This measure is hoped to roughly approximate the total information-seeking activity of the purchase.

An automatic interaction detector (AID) analysis (Sonquist & Morgan, 1969; Staelin, 1971) was conducted to determine the possible strategies used by consumers that were related to this measure of the consumer's information-seeking behavior. For instance, consumers could limit their choice set to the previously owned brand and so reduce their amount of information seeking and processing. In contrast, consumers might spend considerable effort locating the best price on a particular brand or the lowest priced brand that met certain quality standards. In this situation one would expect considerable information-seeking activity.

Figure 12.1 shows the tree diagram produced by the AID run. The average information-seeking score for the total sample was 9.08, with a standard deviation of 5.19. The large standard deviation indicates substantial variation in the total amount of information-seeking activity reported by the different households.

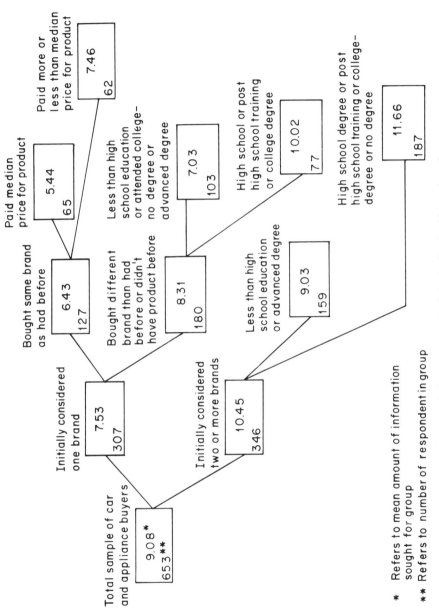

FIG. 12.1   AID analysis of information-seeking behavior for durable good purchasers.

* Refers to mean amount of information sought for group
** Refers to number of respondent in group

197

Number of Brands Considered

The sample split that produced the greatest reduction in variation in the total amount of information-seeking activity was the number of brands initially considered. Households that initially considered just one brand were less likely to seek information (average score = 7.53) than were those that initially considered two or more brands (average score = 10.45). Therefore, one strategy for reducing the information processing required was to limit the number of alternatives considered.

The next question may logically be: What factors are associated with a household considering only one brand? Although it is not the aim of this chapter to thoroughly investigate this question, some exploration is possible. To get some insight as to when, if ever, in the process a consumer opens up his search to consider more than one branch, a sample of 217 consumers who were in the process of purchasing a major durable were asked (a) the number of brands now being considered and (b) the degree to which they had completed the purchase decision process.[2]

The analysis of the data indicates that when these potential purchasers are classified by the percent of the purchase decision process completed, there is a definite tendency for households in the early stages of the decision process to report that they are either open minded or considering only one brand, whereas households further along in the decision process show less of a tendency to consider just one brand and more of a tendency to consider a number of brands. Finally, those households which were classified as having completed 80% or more of the process were much less likely to report that they were open minded. (26% compared to 48% earlier in the process) and much more likely to report that they were considering only one brand (46% compared to 30% earlier in the process).

We hypothesize that initially households either use the strategy of limiting their attention to one brand or are quite open about the brand choice. Some of the purchasers who initially limit their attention to one brand broaden the number of brands under consideration (i.e., increase their evoked set) as they start to collect information. Our analysis has been cross-sectional, not longitudinal, and so we do not know what sorts of information have caused the potential purchaser to broaden the set of alternatives. This would seem to be a fruitful area for research. In any case our data suggest the hypothesis that as purchasers get further along in the decision process they first broaden their choice set and then, as they near the termination of the decision process, they simplify the decision by reducing the number of alternatives down at least to a few brands no matter how many brands they initially have considered.

---

[2] The percentage of the process completed was determined by asking the respondent when they first thought of buying the product and when they intended to actually purchase the product.

Effects of Previous Experience

One reason for a consumer to limit the number of brands considered would be favorable previous experience with the product. In fact, just over one-half of the purchasers who were satisfied with their previous product reported initially limiting their attention to one brand. This figure dropped to 36% for dissatisfied previous users. However, previous experience with the product was not the only factor that caused the purchasers to limit their brand selection, because 38% of the purchasers who did not have use of the product before purchasing it also reported initially considering just one brand. We must therefore assume that these purchasers were influenced by factors other than previous experience with the product.

Another related question is: Are the purchasers with previous experience limiting their attention to the same brand they have had before or some other brand? The degree of satisfaction with the old product seems to have only a minor influence on the brand initially considered. Of the previous users who initially considered only one brand, 56% of the satisfied users report initially considering their previous brand, compared to 47% for the dissatisfied previous users. However, previous experience seems to have a greater effect on the actual purchase decision, for 40% of the satisfied previous users repurchase the same brand, whereas the percentage is only 21 for previous users who have expressed some dissatisfaction with their old product. The above results lend credence to the hypothesis that purchasers initially consider brands with which they are most familiar (i.e., their former brand) but are more receptive to information concerning other brands if they have had a poor experience with their former product. Perhaps the reason dissatisfied previous users initially consider the old brand is that they find their old product to be a convenient anchor point about which to evaluate any new information.

In summary, we noted that approximately 46% of the purchasers reported initially considering one brand and that this brand decision seemed to limit the amount of information they sought during the purchase decision process. The strategy to limit one's attention to one brand was associated with previous experience with the product, although other factors came into play, because some households that did not have use of the brand prior to the purchase also initially considered just one brand.

This leads us to believe that consumers are gathering information consciously or unconsciously even before they explicitly consider purchasing a product. The information seeking and processing is therefore going on all the time, even though the explicit purchase decision evaluation may be of limited duration. This implies that durable good purchasers are likely to be brand conscious even before they are in the market for a product. Also, information that is received either consciously or unconsciously prior to the start of the decision process (i.e., prior to the first conscious thought of buying the product) has major influence on the amount of information a consumer seeks during the process as well as on the actual brand choice he makes at the end of the process.

Future studies in information seeking should attempt to estimate the influences of each type of information source both before and after the first active consideration. For instance, advertising is a constantly available source of information that can be tapped by the consumer with a minimum level of effort. This source could therefore have its major effect prior to the first conscious thought of the decision. Unfortunately, our survey method precluded our determining any search activity other than previous experience prior to the beginning of the decision process.

Final Choice

The previous discussion has centered on the initial size of the choice set. A similar strategy for lowering the amount of information needed is to buy the same brand as before. However, this strategy was associated with reduced information seeking only for those purchasers who initially considered just one brand, with the average information seeking being reduced by 24% compared to those who bought a different brand. For purchasers who considered two or more brands initially, buying the same brand as used before did not reduce the average amount of information-seeking activity. It therefore seems that the decision to consider more than one brand requires the purchasers to obtain enough information to make a valid comparison of the brands. In other words, irrespective of their final decision, they were required to seek the same amount of information in order to make the desired comparisons.

The Effects of Price

All of the products purchased in our study cost over $100, with the average noncar purchase being approximately $260. One might therefore expect that consumers purchasing the more expensive products would seek more information because these higher priced products represented a greater risk. However, consumers purchasing cars and color televisions (i.e., the high-priced items) on the average reported seeking no more information than any other group of durable purchasers. The only time price came into effect was for those purchasers who initially considered one brand, this effect being most pronounced for the subset of purchasers who also bought the same brand as used before. For this subset of purchasers, the consumers who purchased a product much more expensive than the average price within the product class, tended to seek more information. However, the consumers within this set who paid a price much less than the average price also tended to seek more information than did those who paid an average price. Perhaps this group of low-priced consumers were collecting extra price information so as to obtain the "best price deal."

Education

The educational level of the consumer might reflect the purchaser's willingness and capability to seek and comprehend information. Consequently, we would expect the higher educated consumers to seek more information than those with less education. This monotone relationship was not found for the groups in our sample, the groups being ordered as less than high-school degree, high-school degree, post-high-school training, some college, college degree, advanced degree. In fact, the advanced degree consumers, who were primarily lawyers and doctors, were among the lowest information seekers. Excluding this group, however, a monotone relationship was observed for consumers who initially decided to consider two or more brands. For those considering only one brand initially, college dropouts joined the high-school dropouts (and advanced degree consumers) as seeking on average less information than the high-school or college graduate.

Education level also seemed to have an interactive effect on the direct relationship between previous satisfaction with the product and information-seeking activity. Purchasers with a high-school education or greater, excluding the college dropout and the advanced degree households, on the average altered their behavior depending on their previous exposure to the product. Thus, if they were not fully satisfied or were dissatisfied with the old product, they were much more likely to extensively seek information before purchasing a replacement. However, purchasers with less than a high-school education or those who dropped out from college (also those with advanced degrees) reported little difference in average behavior according to previous levels of satisfaction, again indicating that the factors influencing behavior were not simple linear combinations of variables but were interactive.

SUMMARY

We have noted many individual differences in the ways consumers seek information. The diversity of behavior is related to the consumer's individual needs, experiences, abilities, and task environment, although considerable dispersion was observed even after we controlled for these variables. This dispersion is typical of consumer behavior studies, indicating the marketing researcher's inability to explain (predict) individual behavior as opposed to group tendencies. This last point merits attention because if, in fact, there exists a wide dispersion of behavior that is caused by events not known or predictable to the manager or events not under the manager's control, then there is no need for the manager to know exactly why or how any one given individual behaves; instead, he need only know how consumers behave in general. If, however, there exist some underlying theories of choice behavior that can lead one to understand how and why people behave as they do, and these theories involve variables that can be influenced by the market manager or at least forecasted by him, then this new knowledge can have great value to the marketing decision maker.

The above implies that if cognitive psychologists are to have any major impact on the marketing practitioner, they must develop general theories that involve actionable variables. Such constructs as motives and drives, although useful in understanding behavior, provide little assistance to the marketing manager who must decide such things as the appropriate price to charge or the content of an advertising message. This does not mean that cognitive psychology should ignore the field of marketing. In fact, it means just the opposite. Marketing offers an extremely rich field of study and the payoffs are tremendous. The purchase decision process is a complex task that requires much information processing. Right now marketing managers make multimillion dollar decisions with only limited knowledge of how the consumer is going to react. Until better understanding of the consumer's information-processing capabilities and purchase decision strategies is obtained, marketing managers are forced to engage in the art of twirling some dials (i.e., setting price, advertising messages) and hoping the black box (i.e., the consumers) responds favorably so that the firm makes a profit.

ACKNOWLEDGMENTS

The authors would like to thank John Carroll and Dave Klahr for their comments on previous drafts and Terry Gleason and Timothy McGuire for their comments on formulating the ANOVA-type analyses.

13

Applying Models of Choice to the Problem of College Selection

Janet Berl
Gordon Lewis
Rebecca Sue Morrison

Carnegie–Mellon University

Several years ago Edwards and Tversky (1967) pointed out that in the literature on riskless choice there was virtually only one model, that of additive weighting. Additive weighting still dominates the literature of riskless choice, but it is not the only model. Several other models purport to describe how decision makers go about making choices. Chief among these are satisficing (Simon, 1955) and lexicography (Coombs, 1964; Luce, 1956; Tversky, 1969). The evidence for these models, however, is scant (for a review see Russ, 1971; MacCrimmon, 1973). Using data from a study of college selection we present here a comparison of several models of riskless choice.

College selection provides an interesting context in which to compare models of riskless choice. The problem is one in which the outcome is of considerable importance to the decision maker, the criteria for a "good" decision appear exceptionally vague, and information about alternatives is received sequentially—over an extended period of time—and even then is often incomplete. These characteristics set this problem apart, certainly in degree and sometimes in kind, from the types of tasks typically discussed in the mainstream of decision literature (cf. Edwards, 1954, 1961; Slovic & Lichtenstein, 1971; Taylor, 1965). The college selection problem possesses few of those characteristics of the experimental situation that enable one to control most of the relevant variables, and hence it is a challenging problem.

Although college selection in its entirety contains both risky and riskless elements, we have focused on the latter, on the aspects of evaluation and selection among alternatives. We begin by outlining the various proposed models, describing the problems in applying the models to the data, and detailing the various assumptions and changes that have had to be made to allow a comparison of the models. The final sections present a comparison of the predictions of the interpreted models and comments on the use of such models as these in static analyses of nonexperimental data.

THE BASIC MODELS

In addition to the additive weighting, satisficing, and lexicographic models, we consider two others: dominance and a composite model. To clarify the discussion we introduce the following notation: let $\{A_i\}$ be the set of alternatives, $\{F_i\}$ the set of factors, and s_{ij} the value or score of A_i on F_j.

Additive Weighting

The additive weighting model assumes that a weight, w_j, can be attached to each factor F_j. The value of alternative A_i is given by

$$V(A_i) = \sum_j w_j s_{ij},$$

with the highest score, Max $\{V(A_i)\}$, being the most preferred.

Dominance

In contrast to the standard additive model (but not to the additive difference model; cf. Tversky, 1969) the dominance model assumes that comparisons are made factor by factor across each factor and that an alternative is picked if it dominates all other alternatives. An alternative A_i is dominant if $s_{ij} \geq s_{kj} \; \forall j, k$ and if $s_{ij} > s_{kj} \; \forall k \neq i$ and for some j, where "$\geq$" and "$>$" stand for "is equal to or better than" and "is strictly better than," respectively. Because there may be no dominant alternative, people have found it convenient also to introduce the concept of an undominated alternative: A_i is undominated if for each $k \; (k \neq i)$ there exists some j such that $s_{ij} > s_{kj}$.

Dominance relations are commonly represented by partial orderings of the following type:

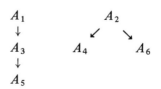

where $A_i \rightarrow A_j$ means A_i dominates A_j. The set of undominated alternatives then consists of each alternative at the "top" of an unconnected partial order, in our example, A_1 and A_2.

Lexicography

In addition to comparing alternatives across factors, the lexicographic model assumes the factors can be strongly ordered. Letting F_1 be the most important factor, A_i is the most preferred alternative if $s_{i1} > s_{k1}$, $\forall\ k \neq i$. If there are ties, they are broken, if possible, by consulting successively the next most important factor(s).

Satisficing

Satisficing was advanced by Simon (1955) as an alternative to the classical notion of rationality. He argues that decision makers do not and cannot maximize in most situations, that they settle for alternatives that are satisfactory, even though a better alternative might be found if the decision maker were to exhaust the set of all alternatives. In particular, if we let $\{T_i\}$ be the set of thresholds or minimally satisfactory scores on $\{F_i\}$, A_i is satisfactory if $s_{ij} \geq T_j$, $\forall\ j$.

A Composite Model

Finally, a composite model for college selection has been proposed by Lewis, Morrison, Penz, and Wicinas (1974), adapted from the work of Soelberg (1967). This model distinguishes between factors of primary and secondary importance. It assumes that a decision maker will (1) place in a set of second priority any alternative that is "unacceptable" on a factor of primary importance; (2) rank the alternatives in each set according to the number of primary factors on which each alternative is "outstanding"; and (3) if there are any ties, attempt to break them by considering the number of primary factors for which each alternative is at least "satisfactory" (i.e., not unsatisfactory and not lacking information).

RESEARCH SETTING

During the 1972–1973 academic year, Pittsburgh area high-school seniors who were taking college preparatory courses were invited to participate in a longitudinal study of college selection. One hundred forty-four students from six area high schools who indicated that they were at least thinking about going to college were selected. The students were enlisted during the first week of October, and they were told that they would be interviewed individually for about an hour periodically from then until sometime in the spring. On average each student had eight interviews. They were interviewed until they made a final decision about where to attend, until they changed their minds about college, or until they dropped out of contact. Of the 144 students who had an initial interview, complete data were obtained for 127. The final sample contained 21 black females, 26 black males, 33 white females, and 47 white males. The present report concerns 63 of the students selected at random from the longitudinal study. (See Lewis & Morrison, 1975, for description of the schools and for details about the selection of the students for the present analyses.)

Data

In the interviews we sought information about actions by the student or others that provided information, criteria for judgment, alternatives, or additional sources of information. The interviews themselves were as nondirective as possible, although still they attempted to elicit this type of information. In the present analysis we are concerned solely with evaluations of schools, of factors, and of information that a student received about a school on a given factor.

The partial history shown in Table 13.1 illustrates the type of information obtained. In this partial history we have included only statements that contain evaluations about the schools to which the student was eventually admitted, the members of his or her choice set. Two things should be noted. First, there is less than total information about all school—factor combinations. This point becomes more obvious when we represent the above information in matrix form as the student's "memory." Second, the set of evaluations consists of both rankings and ratings.

Ratings are absolute statements that implicitly compare an entity (i.e., the alternative, factor, or alternative—factor combination) to some fixed standard rather than to another entity. A statement such as "X has an excellent football team" would be judged a rating (assuming that "quality of football team" was a factor for that student), because no comparison was made to any other specific school. Ratings were classified into the following categories:

Rating	Code
Outstanding, excellent	α
OK, satisfactory, good	β
Not satisfactory, unacceptable, bad	γ

Rankings, in contrast, are explicit comparisons among two or more entities, for example, "In quality of faculty, X is better than Y, which is better than Z." Rankings were coded ordinally from 9 to 1 (none of the relative judgments received ever required more than nine levels of discrimination), with 9 the best alternative.

TABLE 13.1
Partial History of Evaluations by Student X

Date	Statement[a]
Oct. 18	Miami University: Not too many people from Pittsburgh (15)
	George Washington University: Likes Washington, D.C. (4)
Dec. 13	Syracuse: Applying to drama (6) because it will be easier to get in there (7) and will then transfer to liberal arts (6); "beautiful school" (3) with a campus not in the middle of a city (4)
	Miami: Easier to get into (7); beautiful campus (3); friend goes there (11)
	George Washington: Right in middle of city (4) but more to do there than at Syracuse (10)
Jan. 17	Syracuse: Knows people who love it (11)
Feb. 22	Syracuse: Friend's going there might not be in its favor (14)

[Had been accepted at all of these schools by Feb. 22. Stated she would not rank schools or evaluate them until she has seen the rest of them. She had also applied at one other school but had not yet heard; subsequently rejected at that school.]

April 11	Syracuse: Father prefers it because she would have so many close friends there (11)
	Miami: Visited; people very friendly (10); campus beautiful (3); good size (9); good academically (8); drama department (6); friend going there loves it (11); concerned that town may be a little small (4)

[Has decided to attend Miami.]

[a]Numbers in parentheses refer to factor numbers for this student. They are used as labels in Table 13.2.

There is a third kind of evaluation, which we have called an "anchored ranking," that combines a ranking and a rating. This includes such statements as "X and Y are both outstanding, but X is better." Anchored rankings are represented by a letter–number combination, e.g., α–9. The statement "X and Y are both outstanding but X is better" would be coded α–9 for school X and α–8 for school Y. The anchoring may occur for only one school and at the bottom of the ranking rather than at the top. For example, the anchored ranking (9, 8, γ–7) implies that the first alternative is preferred to the second, which in turn is preferred to the third, and in addition the third is unacceptable. In this example one cannot infer anything about the absolute level of the first or the second alternatives.

These coded evaluations were then entered into an $m \times n$ matrix, the "memory," representing the m schools to which the student had been admitted and the n factors that the student had mentioned as being important to him or her in selecting a school. If during the 8 months of interviews the student never evaluated a given school on a particular factor (even with probing by the interviewer) a ϕ was entered in that cell of the matrix. As far as we knew, the student had no information on how good or bad that school was with respect to that factor.

Table 13.2 presents the coded version of the information in Table 13.1. As mentioned previously, the extent to which information is missing is much more readily seen. In addition, the reader will notice that some factors (1, 2, 5, 12, and 13) are missing in this example. We omitted factors that the student said were important but for which no information at all was ever obtained and factors for which there was no information concerning the schools to which the student was finally admitted.

EXTENDING THE MODELS

When one attempts to apply these models in nonexperimental situations a variety of problems appear. One of the first is missing information, which creates a major problem for each of the models. Dominance assumes that one can compare each pair of alternatives across all factors; satisficing assumes that one can compare each alternative to threshold values across all factors; lexicography assumes that one can compare all alternatives across a given factor of known relative importance; the composite model assumes one can compare the factors on importance; and the additive model assumes that both the factor weights and the factor scores are known. None of the models specifies what one is to do if information is missing when a comparison is called for.

Slovic and MacPhillamy (1974) have worked on the problem of missing data with respect to the additive weighting model. Their results indicate that a dimension on which information is not missing receives higher weight than that dimension receives when information is missing for one of a pair of alternatives. The results by Dawes and Corrigan (1974) and Einhorn and Hogarth (1975), however, indicate that the effort to "fine tune" the weights in the additive model may outweigh the benefits. In any case, it would be difficult to apply the Slovic and MacPhillamy results in such a situation as that depicted in Table 13.2, in which the "common dimensions and the "unique" dimensions depend on the particular pair of alternatives being considered.

The extent of the problem of missing data was illustrated in Table 13.2, where 37% of the entries showed missing information. For the 63 students, approximately 47% of the possible pieces of information that might have been used to make a decision was missing. This figure refers only to information on schools to which the student was actually admitted and factors that were still of some importance at the time of the final decision. The percent of missing information would be higher if all the schools that the student had ever considered and all the factors that had ever been mentioned had been included.

TABLE 13.2
Matrix of Evaluations by Student X

School	Factor[a]									
	3	4	6	7	8	9	10	11	14	15
Miami	α	γ	β	β	β	β	α	α	ϕ	β
George Washington	8	γ	ϕ	ϕ	ϕ	ϕ	9	ϕ	ϕ	ϕ
Syracuse	α–9	β	β	β	ϕ	ϕ	β–8	β	γ	ϕ

[a]Factors: 3, campus; 4, near (but not in) a city; 6, curriculum—including dram; 7, possibility of acceptance; 8, quality of school; 9, size: not too small but not over 15,000; 10, social life—including people; 11, other's opinions; 14, distance—not too far; 15, not too many people from Pittsburgh.

In evaluating ratings we have assumed (for all but the additive weighting model, which will be taken up later) that $\alpha > \phi > \gamma$ and $\alpha > \beta > \gamma$. The assumption $\alpha > \beta > \gamma$ seems reasonable. The relation between ϕ and γ asserts that it is better to know nothing about an alternative than to know it is "unacceptable" or "bad," and the lack of a relation between ϕ and β implies that knowing nothing and knowing that an alternative is merely satisfactory are not comparable. Obviously, given priors about the state of the world, one could construct examples in which either of these latter assumptions would be unreasonable.

Unfortunately, missing information is not the only problem. Additional problems exist for each of the models when one attempts to apply them to data such as those in Table 13.2. We again consider each of the models in turn, together with the assumptions that we have made to utilize the models for the present analysis.

Dominance

When considering dominance we defined two concepts: the dominant alternative and the set of undominated alternatives. The problem with a choice model that produces a set of best alternatives is that it does not specify what the decision maker would do with such a set. Soelberg's (1967) findings suggest that decision makers either adapt thresholds in order to make finer distinctions among the alternatives until one alternative emerges as better or search for additional criteria on which the alternatives can be ranked.

In applying a decision rule to a matrix, such as Table 13.2, however, neither possibility is open to the analyst. The matrix contains all of the information and all of the discriminations that the decision maker had reported at the time the decision was to be made. The matrix is undoubtedly not a perfect representation of the decision maker's information, but it is the best representation available to the analyst. Given two or more undominated alternatives, the only apparent option is to predict the decision maker to pick with equal probabilities from that set.

Lexicography

In applying the lexicographic model there are two kinds of problems that arise. There is the question of missing evaluations of alternatives as discussed above—how to compare a ϕ with an α, β, or γ. There is also the problem that the decision makers do not always give an unambiguous and complete ordering of the importance of the factors themselves.

If it is possible to identify some factor as most important and if there are comparable evaluations for all of the alternatives on the most important factor, the standard lexicographic model can be applied in a straightforward manner; if ties occur in the evaluations of two or more alternatives one attempts to break the tie by moving to the next most important factor. In some cases, however, there is a missing evaluation for one or more of the alternatives on the most important factor, or some of the evaluations may not be comparable (e.g., if two alternatives are evaluated relative to each other and a third is evaluated absolutely). We assume the student to treat these cases of noncomparability of alternatives as if they are ties and so attempts to resolve the ties and noncomparabilities by moving successively to the next most important factors.

In some instances factors are tied in importance. In such a case, if the tied factors identify the same alternative as best, the decision maker's problem is solved. If, however, the alternative that is best on one of the tied factors is not the same as the alternative best on the other, we assume that decision maker to attempt resolving the problem by moving to the next most important factor(s). It is also possible to have three or more factors tied in importance. We would assume in that case that if the majority of most important factors produced the same best alternative that alternative would be chosen, but if there were no majority winner, the decision maker would attempt to resolve the conflict by moving successively to the next most important factor(s) to find a best alternative.

Finally, in some cases the information given to us by a student produces only multiple, unconnected, partial orders of factors. For example if the decision maker had announced that F_1 was more important than F_3, F_2 was extremely important, F_4 and F_5 were only of a minor consideration, and that he could not compare F_4 and F_5, the following partial order would result:

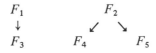

In a case such as this, we assume the decision maker to process the alternatives lexicographically with regard to each separate branch. For example, if there were ties or noncomparable alternatives on the left hand branch (F_1 most important factor) he would attempt to break the ties or noncomparabilities by moving to F_3; if there were ties or noncomparabilities on the right hand branch he would move down the branch F_2-F_4 and separately down the branch F_2-F_5. Finally, we assume he compares results from F_2-F_4 with those from F_2-F_5, obtaining the set of best alternatives from this partial order. Having done this, we assume he compares the set of best alternatives from each unconnected partial order to obtain the final set of best alternatives. As in the case with dominance, if the final set contains more than one best alternative we assume that the decision maker chooses among them with equal probability.

Satisficing

One problem for the satisficing model is that there may be several alternatives that are at least minimally satisfactory. Simon's discussion of satisficing suggests that in some contexts one stops searching when one has found a "satisfactory" alternative. Because students cannot assume that they are necessarily going to be admitted at a given school, however, they are motivated to identify (and apply to) more alternatives than if admission were under their control, and this can lead to multiple satisfactory (or partially satisfactory) alternatives if more than one application is accepted.

We assume that students seek to order the alternatives in a manner consistent with the threshold notion of satisficing. First, the alternatives are categorized as "satisfactory" (not unsatisfactory on any criterion and satisfactory on at least one) or "unsatisfactory" (unsatisfactory on one or more criteria or not satisfactory on any). By defining a "satisfactory" alternative in this way we permit inclusion, in the set of satisfactory schools, of schools for which there may be missing information, as long as it is not all missing. Second, if there is more than one satisfactory alternative, the set is ordered according to the number of factors for which each alternative is satisfactory (as opposed to no information). That is, we assume the decision maker prefers positive evidence to no evidence. If there are no satisfactory alternatives, we assume that the student first orders the set according to the number of factors for which each alternative is unsatisfactory and, among those unsatisfactory on the fewest factors, orders them according to the amount of positive information that exists.

Composite Model

The problems encountered in using the composite model stem primarily from the identification of "primary factors." If the student has specifically indicated that some subset of the factors is of primary importance there is no problem, but this is not always the case. Where no subset of factors has been evaluated as primary we assume that those indicated as being "somewhat important" or "moderately important" are the most important factors. In the absence of any coded as "somewhat important" or "moderately important," those not specified are assumed to be more important than those factors specifically indicated as being "of little importance."

Additive Weighting

The major problem in applying the additive model is the apparent need for interval level values for the scores and for the factor weights, but intervally measured scores and weights may not be necessary. In their analysis of why the additive weighting model does so well, Dawes and Corrigan (1974) point to three characteristics of the situations in which the additive weighting model has been so successful: (a) typically each input variable has a conditionally monotonic relationship with the output; (b) there is error in measurement; and (c) deviations from optimal weighting do not make much practical difference.

In the data on college selection, most of the evaluations are provided as deviations from an ideal point ("I want to be away from home, and school X is just the right distance, school Y is OK but a little too close, and school Z is totally unacceptable—it's halfway across the country"), and given the nature of the coding there is a monotonic relation between the numbers we have used and the evaluations. With regard to factor weights, both Dawes and Corrigan (1974) and Einhorn and Hogarth (1975) demonstrate that equal weighting of factors in the linear model does as well in most cases (and sometimes even better) than "optimal" weights determined by regression procedures. In short, arbitrary numbers assigned monotonically to the ratings and equal factor weights should provide reasonably good inputs for the additive model.

The remaining problem is what to do about missing data. We have already assumed for the other models that knowing an alternative is outstanding on a factor is undoubtedly more favorable for the alternative than knowing nothing, but the latter is probably more favorable for the alternative than knowing that it is unacceptable. We also pointed out that whether knowing that an alternative is merely satisfactory or acceptable on some factor is better or worse than knowing nothing at all about the alternative on that factor probably depends on one's prior expectation about the unknown information. Nevertheless, the additive model requires some response to the question of the relative importance of knowing something versus knowing nothing. To test the impact of assigning different numbers to missing information, three methods of scoring were used. The first method assumed that "acceptable" was better than "no information" and that "no information" was better than information that labeled a school as "unacceptable." This was scored $\alpha = 3$; $\beta = 2$; $\phi = 1$; $\gamma = 0$. A second scoring method assumed that "no information" had the same value as knowing that an evaluation was "acceptable": $\alpha = 3$; $\beta = \phi = 2$; and $\gamma = 1$. The third scoring method ignored ϕ and simply averaged over the s_{ij} for which information was available: α = 3; β = 2; γ = 1. The results of these three methods were virtually identical. In the next section the results from only the last method are reported.

RESULTS

Of the 63 students, 17 were admitted to only one school and one was rejected at the only school to which she applied. This leaves 45 cases with two or more acceptances to which all of the models can be applied. In the case of a single acceptance, dominance, lexicographic, and additive models are essentially irrelevant.

Both the satisficing and the composite models make strong predictions: if a school, even a single acceptance, is not satisfactory on some factor (the satisficing model) or not satisfactory on a primary factor (the composite model) the models predict the student to not attend. In five of the 17 single-acceptance cases, the single alternative was in fact unsatisfactory on at least one factor. Two cases involved factors of primary importance. In one of these two cases the student said he would attend, contrary to the composite and to the satisficing models. In the three other cases the students all said that they would attend, contrary to the satisficing model. There is some negative evidence for both satisficing and composite models, therefore, in the case of single acceptances.

The 45 cases in which students have two or more acceptances are shown in Table 13.3. Column 2 shows the number of schools to which the student has been admitted; Columns 3–7 show the performance of the five substantive models.

If the model predicted a set of alternatives and this set included the alternative actually chosen by the student, the score would be equal to the number of schools to which the student was admitted minus the number of schools in the set predicted by the model. (If the model predicted a tie among all alternatives, and if the student attended one of them, therefore, the model would score 0.) If the set did not include the alternative chosen by the student the score would be simply the negative of the number of alternatives predicted by the model.

For a given student, the maximum score for any model is the number of acceptances the student has had minus 1. The sum of these maximum possible scores over all students is 87. The score for a null model choosing the alternatives in the predicted set randomly would have an expected value of 0 (regardless of the number of alternatives selected). Summing the scores over all students for each model, dominance scored 40, lexicography and the composite model each 47, satisficing 57, and additive weighting 67. Each of the five models scores significantly better than the expected value of the null model ($p < 10^{-4}$, using a two-tailed sign test).

The most noticeable characteristic of the dominance model is that it was never clearly wrong, but at the same time it often "can't make up its mind." In 33 of

TABLE 13.3
Success of Each Model in Predicting Final Choice[a]

Student	Number of acceptances	Model				
		DOM	LEX	COM	SAT	ADD
1	3	1	0	−1	2	2
2	3	1	−1	1	2	2
3	3	2	2	2	2	2
4	2	1	1	1	1	1
5	2	0	−1	1	1	1
6	5	2	−1	−1	3	−1
7	2	0	−1	1	1	1
8	2	0	0	1	−1	1
9	2	1	1	1	1	1
10	2	1	1	0	1	1
11	2	1	0	1	1	1
12	3	1	0	1	2	2
13	2	0	1	1	1	1
14	2	1	1	1	1	1
15	4	2	2	3	3	3
16	2	0	1	1	1	1
17	2	0	1	0	−1	−1
18	2	0	1	0	1	1
19	2	0	0	1	−1	1
20	3	1	2	−1	2	2
21	4	1	−1	3	3	3
22	5	4	3	−1	−1	3
23	2	1	0	0	0	0
24	4	0	2	3	3	3
25	2	0	0	1	1	1
26	2	1	1	1	1	1
27	2	0	1	1	1	1
28	3	1	2	2	2	2
29	2	0	1	1	1	1
30	7	4	6	6	6	6
31	7	1	5	6	−1	−1
32	3	2	1	−1	2	2
33	3	0	1	1	0	1
34	2	1	1	1	1	1
35	5	3	4	−1	−1	3
36	4	2	3	3	3	3
37	2	1	1	0	1	1
38	2	0	−1	1	1	1
39	2	0	1	0	−1	−1
40	4	1	−1	1	2	3

(continued)

TABLE 13.3 (*cont'd*)

Student	Number of acceptances	Model				
		DOM	LEX	COM	SAT	ADD
41	4	1	2	1	3	3
42	3	1	2	2	2	2
43	3	0	0	−1	2	2
44	3	0	2	2	2	2
45	2	1	1	1	1	1
Totals		40	47	47	57	67

[a]Score = $n - k$ if correct and $-k$ if incorrect, where n is the number of acceptances and k is the number of alternatives predicted by the model.

the 45 cases the model predicts two or more alternatives, instead of a single one. It does, however, succeed in narrowing the selection in 16 of these cases (e.g., picking two out of four possible alternatives). In the other 12 cases it predicted a single alternative and was right in every instance.

The lexicographic model is intermediate between dominance and either satisficing or the composite model in the number of single-choice predictions. The reason for this appears, at least in part, to be the occurrence of multiple partial orders of factors and our rules for processing multiple candidates for "most important factor." In the present data, there were multiple candidates for "most important factor" in 18 of the 45 cases. Three of these involved ties, and in the other 15 cases the candidates for "most important factor" contained at least two candidates that were undominated and not directly comparable.

The most notable difference between the satisficing and the composite model is the number of nonsingular predictions. Only four ties were produced by the satisficing model. However, the more significant comparison lies in the closeness of the results compared to the difference in the amount of information used. The composite model assumes that all one really needs to know is information on the subset of primary factors. On the average, 9.2 factors were used in the satisficing model and 2.5 factors in the composite, and the latter figure is probably an overestimation of the number of primary factors, because in cases where no factors were explicitly rated all factors for that student were treated as if they were primary. Although the satisficing model has a higher score, the composite model does reasonably well for the amount of information that it uses.

Consistent with the existing literature, the additive model shows the most impressive performance. This model failed to predict the correct alternative only four times and predicted ties in only four cases.

Comparison of the five models against each other, again using a two-tailed sign test, shows that the additive model scores significantly better than the dominance, Lexicographic, and composite models ($p < .02$). There is not a significant difference, however, between the performance of the additive weighting model and that of the satisficing model. Nor is there a significant difference between satisficing and either the composite or the lexicographic model.

The data reported in Table 13.3 include the information obtained during the "last interview," the interview in which the student announced his or her decision. Because it is reasonable to expect that there might be rationalization (cf. Festinger, 1957; Soelberg, 1967), we replicated the analysis, exlcuding the information from the last interview. The scores for the models were substantially lower: dominance 26, lexicography 23, satisficing 17, composite 23, and additive weighting 27. This appears to support the hypothesis that the last interview contains substantial rationalization; case by case examination, however, does not support this interpretation.

In the case of the additive weighting model, for example, there were 12 cases for which the score improved between the next to last and the last interview. Nine of these cases clearly appeared to be the result of external, intervening events: receipt of information about financial aid (four instances); conditional acceptance, admission only to a branch campus or contingent on starting in the summer (three instances); the discovery of a new alternative apparently unsolicited; and breaking up with a boyfriend (previously the student had planned to attend the school the boyfriend attended). In each of these cases the intervening event was sufficient to account for the change in preferred school. In some cases there were also changes in other evaluations concerning the newly preferred school, but these were not "necessary"; the model would have predicted the change in preference from the intervening event alone.

The three cases not accounted for by intervening events include one in which the model initially predicted the backup school, one in which a student did not decide between two different careers (business and nursing) until the last interview, and one in which in the final interview the student reversed his preference for "size of school," choosing a small liberal arts college over the previous first choice, a large midwestern university. This last case appears to be the only reasonably clear case of rationalization in all the cases examined.

DISCUSSION

Although the additive weighting model predicts final choices better than any other model, there is general agreement that it is not plausible as a description of decision making at the information-processing level. Dawes and Corrigan (1974) have discussed reasons for the robustness of the additive weighting model as a predictor of final choices, but neither they nor most others see it as more than a "black box" that predicts final choices quite well. There is evidence, for example, that even when the decision maker believes himself to be using an additive weighting model, he appears to overestimate the number of factors he uses (Shepard, 1964) and to give poor estimates of the factor weights (Dawes & Corrigan, 1974; Slovic & MacPhillamy, 1974) relative to the weights that best reproduce his decisions.

Even if other models that have been proposed are intuitively more plausible, this alone does not make a good model. If these models are good describers of the process then one can expect them to predict well also, but they do not and the question of why remains. Several possibilities exist:

1. Sensitivity to errors. One of the more obvious possibilities is the sensitivity of model to errors. If true scores are close on any dimension, so that errors in measurement may reverse the true order, both dominance and lexicography can produce highly erroneous predictions (for lexicography only if the dimension is actually used on which the reversal has occurred). Moreover, for lexicography there is the additional problem of knowing whether one has obtained the true order of the factors.

In the case of satisficing, errors in measuring the thresholds (or errors in measuring scores close to the threshold) can lead to a disposition of an alternative contrary to the disposition by the decision maker himself. Furthermore, the model assumes constant thresholds (for a dynamic model of aspiration change, cf. Starbuck, 1963). Even if the analyst picks up a threshold change, the decision maker may fail to inform the analyst that previous evaluations of different alternatives should also be revised. Finally, the composite model, incorporating parts of the various models, inherits most of their liabilities as well.

Another type of error is caused by missing data. What looks like missing data to the analyst may not really be missing to the decision maker. Some data (e.g., that the University of Pennsylvania is located in the East) may be so obvious to the decision maker that they are never mentioned, but always to assume that the decision maker knows such things runs the risk of assuming too much.

2. Categorization. A related problem is errors introduced through the grossness of the categories used in coding rating statements (outstanding, acceptable, unacceptable). In defense of the present procedures it should be noted that the students themselves typically have used gross categories and sometimes even have refused to evaluate alternatives at all. Nevertheless, any categorization scheme creates some distortion of the data.

3. Recall. The analysis undoubtedly also produces errors in the assumption that the student remembers and uses everything stored in the "memory." The process for constructing the memory was to enter all evaluations and to change them only when the student indicated that the evaluation had changed. There were no changes or deletions unless reported by the student. This is equivalent to assuming total recall. One could analyze only those items that had been

reported or repeated within the last k weeks, but this would ignore the differential importance of items of information.

4. Subject differences. Because it is reasonable that different people may pursue different strategies in decision making, one might have expected the students to be partitioned such that for some students the lexicographic model (but no others) predicted their choices, for others the satisficing model (but no others) predicted their choices, and so on. The data in Table 13.3 show no such partitioning, but this does not mean that there are not individual differences in the use of decision rules. It would require a rather careful experimental design to demonstrate this phenomenon, if it exists, and it would be surprising indeed if the data obtained in an uncontrolled setting were to have provided precisely the required natural experiment.

5. Special assumptions. One of the main messages in this chapter has been the necessity of making additional assumptions in order to apply the various models. The results of any analysis, however, depend on the specific assumptions made. In one case (the conversion of ordinal data for use in the additive weighting model) we tried four different possibilities and found them virtually equivalent, but this was not a definitive solution to that problem and in no way touched on the numerous alternative assumptions one could make there or elsewhere.

CONCLUSIONS

The problem of high-school seniors deciding where to attend college was selected as a context in which to test alternative models of riskless choice. College selection is a situation in which decision makers are faced with a problem of a type not previously encountered and one of some importance, at least for most of the decision makers. In order to apply the models, however, a number of assumptions had to be made. In making these assumptions we attempted to retain the spirit of the basic model, although in some cases (such as satisficing) the assumptions resulted in procedures that looked almost as much like additive weighting as like the original model. In the case of lexicography, the lack of evidence of a strong ordering of factors, together with incomplete information about alternatives, leads to an extraordinarily complex version of what is usually considered a simple model.

The need for special assumptions arose because of the static nature of the analysis and because the data were gathered in a setting in which the investigators attempted to minimize their interference with the way in which the students structured the decision task. The former problem is fairly easily corrected. A dynamic or process analysis should help in assessing how the students were structuring the problem and what kinds of decision rules they might have been using. Even so, one can anticipate the picture to be less clear than that obtaining in a setting in which one can control access to information (at least for the large part) and where one can record more of the relevant steps taken by the decision maker in processing information.

The other problem, the tension between uncontaminated data concerning decision making in important situations and the amount of information and detail that one would like to have, is not as easily resolved. The less one interferes, the less one is likely to know and the more assumptions one is likely to have to make. Until more is known about how decision makers deal with missing and contradictory information under a variety of different circumstances, static analyses must continue to require that the analyst make numerous assumptions about the manner in which decision makers handle such matters.

As to the different models that were examined, the additive weighting model once again showed its predictive power. Dawes and Corrigan (1974) have discussed the robustness of the linear model vis-à-vis multiplicative and other nonadditive models. Although the original study of college selection has not been designed to answer the question, there is still little good evidence about why the additive model—which is not taken by most people to be descriptive of the decision-making process—does as well or better than the other models that allegedly are more descriptive of the decision-making process. Several suggestions about the failures of these models have been offered here, but there is still a good deal to learn.

ACKNOWLEDGMENTS

The data analyzed in this chapter were gathered under ONR Contract N00014-67-A-0314-0015.

14

Decisions Made about Other People: A Human Judgment Analysis of Dating Choice

James Shanteau
Geraldine Nagy

Kansas State University

INTRODUCTION AND BACKGROUND

How do we make decisions about other people? How do we choose a doctor, decide between prospective employees, or choose a date? The purpose of this chapter is to illustrate a novel approach to the study of decisions made about other people. The approach incorporates features of three widely used techniques in the study of human judgment and decision making: information integration, multiple regression, and binary choices. Although these techniques have been extensively applied in previous judgment research, they have not been applied jointly before. As demonstrated in the studies reported here, however, when used in a complimentary fashion these techniques have considerable potential for understanding complex social judgments.

The approach is illustrated through a series of studies on dating judgments. We choose dating for several reasons. First, we wanted to study an area representative of the complexity of typical social judgments. Second, we sought a task in which our subjects (introductory psychology students) would be interested and in which they would have considerable experience. Finally, we found the topic fascinating but little understood and felt out approach could contribute to the understanding of several long-standing issues in this area.

One issue raised by previous investigators and that seemed particularly fruitful to examine here involves the joint influence of physical attractiveness and expectancy of rejection. Walster, Aronson, Abrahams, and Rottman (1966) hypothesized that when making a dating choice people attempt to maximize the social desirability of their date (as measured by physical attractiveness) and minimize their chances of rejection. If expectancy of rejection is related to an individual's own physical attractiveness, then he or she should choose a date of similar attractiveness to him- or herself. This leads to the commonly held belief that people should match up with each other.

Several studies have examined matching at a group level (e.g., Berscheid, Dion, Walster, & Walster, 1971; Huston, 1973; Walster *et al.,* 1966). The results, however, have unexpectedly revealed little or no difference between the preferences of attractive and unattractive subjects. Although one study (Huston, 1973) has provided evidence that judged probability of rejection is related to physical attractiveness, there is no evidence that probability of rejection has any influence on dating choices. Furthermore, the cognitive processes used by subjects to integrate physical attractiveness and probability have not been analyzed at all. A major goal of this research, therefore, is to study the cognitive processing mechanisms underlying the influence of attractiveness and probability on dating judgment.

There are, however, several major problems to be overcome. A crucial problem is how probability of rejection is to be defined for the subject. One possibility is to define the probability *explicitly.* Another more realistic possibility is to let subjects *implicitly* infer the probability from information such as the date's photograph. Whereas explicit definition of probability causes no analytic problems, implicit definition does present problems because a *subjective inference* is involved. The techniques proposed here were specifically designed to allow analysis of combination rules involving such inferences. Furthermore, it is of some interest to compare the rules used with explicit and implicit probabilities.

Another major problem is that most dating studies are based on group analyses. Many of the predictions regarding matching, however, revolve around individual differences, e.g., in physical attractiveness. Yet, previous analyses have generally been insensitive to such differences. Our approach, in contrast, examines dating judgments at the single-subject level. This allows maximum sensitiviity to issues involving individual differences. For instance, the question of whether subjects match on physical attractiveness as well as other characteristics (e.g., personality, interests) is analyzed below.

In addition, we were also concerned with the relative importance of physical attractiveness in dating. The available evidence suggests that physical attractiveness dominates dating judgments (Kleck & Rubenstein, 1975). Although this notion may be personally unappealing, there are other reasons for reexamining this conclusion. For one thing, physical attractiveness has been the only salient cue in much of this research; other information has generally not been explicitly provided (e.g., Walster *et al.,* 1966). In cases where other information was provided, either (1) appropriate techniques were not used to isolate its influence (e.g., Kleck & Rubenstein, 1975) or (2) the information was not representative of what is typically available in dating (e.g., Lampel & Anderson, 1968). The importance of physical attractiveness has therefore not been adequately determined.

Perhaps the easiest way to summarize our approach is by reference to the cartoon dilemma of Les, Funky Winkerbean's friend, in Fig. 14.1. Les' problem is how to handle both physical attractiveness and probability of rejection. This typifies the kind of problem we have given our subjects. We were specifically interested in the role that subjective inferences, such as probability of rejection, play in the cognitive processes of dating. In doing this, we hope to clarify several unresolved issues in dating. Finally, although our approach has been specifically aimed toward dating, we feel that the techniques may also have applications to other complex social judgments.

PROPOSED APPROACH

The basic goal is to provide a quantitative description of each subject's dating strategy. Toward this goal, three discrete steps are involved. The first is to specify the *integration function* or combination rule by which explicit pieces of information about a date are integrated into a single judgment. The second involves determination of the *subjective inference function* used to combine inferences into a dating judgment. The final step is a *choice validation* of the accuracy of each subject's inference function. Although the procedures for each step are well documented and require little discussion, the present approach contains several novel features that need some elaboration before considering applications to dating studies.

FIG. 14.1 Cartoon showing cognitive-processing dilemma of trying to take both physical attractiveness and probability of rejection into account in making a dating choice. (Funky Winkerbean by Tom Batiuk, May 20, 1975. Courtesy of Field Newspaper Syndicate.)

Integration Function

The integration function can best be evaluated using the theory of information integration developed by Anderson (1974a, b). These procedures have been successfully applied in a variety of decision-making tasks, ranging from gambling and utility judgments (Shanteau, 1974; Shanteau & Phelps, 1975) to inference judgments (Shanteau, 1970, 1972, 1975a). Beyond this, the approach has been widely used in a number of other psychological tasks, including personality impression formation (Anderson, 1974a).

Information integration theory. The basic elements of integration theory are shown in Fig. 14.2a (adapted from Anderson, 1974b). According to the theory, a set of stimuli can be viewed as multiple pieces of information (S_1, S_2, S_3, . . .). Each piece is represented psychologically by both a scale value (s) and a weight value (w). The scale value defines the psychological location of the information along the dimension of judgment. The weight value, in contrast, is concerned with the salience or importance of the information.

The weight and scale values are then combined by an integration function into an overall response, R. In general, this can be specified as

$$R = \sum ws \qquad (14.1)$$

The contribution of any single piece of information is therefore equal to its weight times its scale value; and this product is then summed over all stimuli. Although the application of this formula varies from task to task, a few simple algebraic models derived from Equation (14.1) have been found to be widely useful. Three simple models deserve comment.

The adding model is probably the simplest and most frequently used algebraic model in psychological research. This model states that information combines to form a judgment by simple addition so that "the more, the better." The overall judgment is the sum of the various individual components. Although such a model has been widely assumed to hold in many settings (Edwards & Tversky, 1967), evidence for adding is scarce (Shanteau & Phelps, 1975).

A frequently considered alternative to adding has been the averaging model. According to this model, information is combined by averaging, which is analogous to a "center of gravity" notion. A comparison of adding and averaging models is central to the present research because the two models imply quite divergent psychological processing mechanisms. These models can be compared in pivotal tests (Anderson, 1965) which, in essence, boil down to comparing "the more, the better" with a "center of gravity" process; the actual steps are illustrated below.

Probably the single most important model in previous decision-making research has been the multiplying model. For instance, multiplying was consistently found in a variety of situations involving the combination of risk with payoffs (Shanteau, 1975b). The central characteristic of multiplying is that one

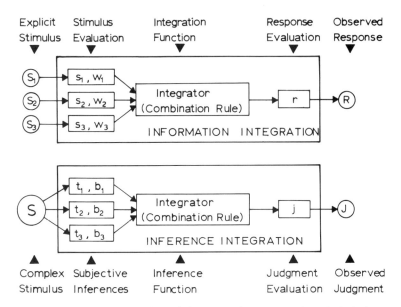

FIG. 14.2 Schematic representation of the assumed sequence of psychological processes; mental operations are shown inside the boxes. (a) Information integration analysis going from a set of explicit stimuli (S_1, S_2, S_3) to an observed response. (b) Inference integration analysis going from one complex stimulus (S) to an observed judgment. Note that the observed response (judgment) may be some nonlinear transformation of the "true" internal response (judgment); although procedures are available for the removal of nonlinear transformations (Anderson, 1974b), they were not necessary in the present research.

variable or dimension acts by modulating or magnifying the effect of another variable. Although the tests for this model are more involved than for adding or averaging, the results, as seen below, are easy to visualize.

Functional measurement. Parallel to the development of information integration theory, a set of procedures called "functional measurement" were introduced to test and evaluate integration models (Anderson, 1974b). Although these procedures vary somewhat from model to model, they all share a common logic. That is, testing models and estimating parameter values must go hand in hand. Whereas the testing of models is clearly important and has often dominated previous research, the estimated values are of equal concern here. As should become apparent, the weight and scale values are a vital and distinguishing part of each subject's approach to dating.

Two particular advantages of functional measurement are worth emphasizing. The first is that whereas precise goodness of fit tests have been developed (e.g., Shanteau & Anderson, 1969, 1972), functional measurement readily lends itself to simple graphical analyses. Accordingly, results will be graphically presented here to allow for direct visual inspection. In the same spirit, the results using other techniques (e.g., multiple regression) have also been translated into visual terms. In all cases, however, supportive statistical analyses were performed and are available. The second advantage of functional measurement is its ability to analyze single-subject data. As noted previously, individual differences are crucial for understanding dating, and so it is important to work at the level of each individual. Therefore, most of the results reported here are for single subjects; when group data are presented, they reflect the individual data.

Inference Integration

The techniques described above allow identification and analysis of the integration function when all information is explicitly defined by the experimenter. However, this is unreasonable in many naturalistic settings, such as dating, where subjects draw their own subjective inferences about what information to use and how to use it. To deal with this situation, analyses based on multiple-regression techniques were employed.

Subjective inference function. Before describing our use of multiple regression techniques, it is essential that the distinction between the integration function and the inference function be clearly understood. As seen in Fig. 14.2a, the integration function is based on the combination of explicit dating information, represented by scale values s_1, s_2, and s_3. The experimenter provides the information (such as an explicit statement of probability), therefore, and the subject puts it together using an integration function. In comparison, Figure 14.2b illustrates the situation where subjects draw their own inferences. In this case, a single complex stimulus S (such as a photo of a date) can lead to a number of subjective inferences, represented by t_1, t_2, and t_3. Probability is therefore inferred by the subject rather than specified by the experimenter. These inferences, in turn, are used to form dating judgments.

There are several advantages to deriving both the integration function in Fig. 14.2a and the inference function in Fig. 14.2b. For one thing, the two functions can be used to compare the psychological difference in receiving implicit and explicit information. Probability of rejection, for instance, may be used more when it is explicitly defined than when it is implicitly inferred. Second, the integration function provides a starting point from which to explore various types of inference functions. Techniques for determining combination rules are well developed for information integration but relatively undeveloped for inference integration. Finally, the two procedures shown in Fig. 14.2 have not been compared before. The differences and similarities in the two approaches are therefore of interest in their own right.

Multiple regression. The inference function can be determined using a standard multiple-regression equation:

$$Y = \sum bX \tag{14.2}$$

The judgment (Y) is the sum of the products of the beta weights (b) and the predictor values or cues (X); the sum is over all predictor dimensions. In previous applications, the cues have usually been specified directly from the stimulus values; they can then be used to derive a set of weights that "best" predict the judgments. In addition to simple linear terms, more complex models can be constructed through the use of predictor cross-products. This is seldom done, however, because it adds little in the way of predictive accuracy (Slovic & Lichtenstein, 1971).

As can be seen, Equations (14.1) and (14.2) are formally equivalent. The techniques applied here attempt to take advantage of this equivalence by using the strengths of each. For instance, the integration function provides possible combination rules to be considered in the subjective inference function. As a result, specific forms of the regression equation are tested that, contrary to past applications, usually contain configural cross-product terms. Also, whereas previous work has focused on the predictive accuracy of regression models (see Birnbaum, 1973), our interest is in describing combination rules and in estimating psychological vaules. Accordingly, model testing and scaling techniques more in line with functional measurement are used.

Another difference from the usual multiple-regression research is in the interpretation of the parameters. Typically, the cue values represent an objective specification of the stimuli. In the present view, an objective value has little psychological relevance, and instead subjective values are used throughout (represented by t's in Fig. 14.2). These subjective values can be determined in several ways, although functional measurement procedures are probably the best. A good approximation to such values can be obtained from direct ratings (Shanteau, 1974), and so these are used in the present studies. The weight values, in contrast, are directly interpretable in terms of psychological importance.

In all, the present use of multiple-regression techniques is aimed at answering questions about combination rules normally dealt with by information integration. This novel extension allows a direct comparison of rules used to combine implicit and explicit information. Furthermore, the redefinition of parameters in the regression equation allows for a more meaningful psychological interpretation.

Choice Validation

Once each subject's inference function has been derived, it still must be tested and validated. The usual evaluation of regression equations has been by split-half or other reliability checks. A rather different approach is advocated here. The accuracy of each subject's inference function was first checked by goodness of fit tests. These statistical tests were based on examination of the discrepancies between observed judgments and those derived from the inference function.

Significant discrepancies may possibly suggest that some variables or dimensions have been omitted.

Even if the subjective inference function passes the goodness of fit tests, it is of little interest if it is not predictive of the individual's dating preferences. The crucial criterion then is to be able to predict a subject's actual dating choices. Choice procedures, of course, have been widely used in studies of decision making (Luce & Suppes, 1965) and in the measurement of psychological values (Krantz, Luce, Suppes, & Tversky, 1971). In contrast, choices were used here to validate models derived using other techniques.

The importance of the choice validation should not be overlooked. If we really understand how subjects make dating judgments (or any other complex social judgment), then we should be able to predict new behavior as well as describe past behavior. Although such a criterion is much stricter than usual, we feel it essential in furthering our understanding of dating. Indeed, finding out what we cannot predict is probably as important as finding out what we can predict. By examining the nature of incorrect predictions, it is possible to improve subsequent judgment descriptions in later studies. While doing this, we can learn something more about the processes involved. Therefore, the use of a stringent choice criterion provides a self-correcting mechanism whereby the inference functions can be made more accurate and more inclusive.

To summarize, the present approach to dating is based on three steps. The first is to test and evaluate the integration function used to combine explicit dating information. At this level, the problem becomes a study in information integration (see Fig. 14.2a). The next step is to derive the inference function for the combination of subjective inferences. This is done using some modified multiple-regression techniques (see Fig. 14.2b). The final step is to validate the derived inference function against actual dating choices.

DATING JUDGMENTS IN WOMEN

The proposed approach was used originally by Shanteau and Nagy (1974) to examine the influence of attractiveness and probability on women's dating judgments. These variables were selected for two reasons. First, they played a central role in much of the previous dating research. Despite numerous studies, however, the role of these variables is little understood. A second reason is that the two variables are parallel to those used in gambling research. The combination of probability and outcome in gambling has been extensively studied, using both information integration (Anderson & Shanteau, 1970) and multiple-regression analyses (Slovic & Lichtenstein, 1968). In dating, the chances of rejection parallel the probability of a gamble, and the attractiveness of a date parallels the desirability of the gambling outcome. Although this parallel should not be carried too far, it has provided a starting point.

Integration Function

The first part of the study was devoted to analysis of the integration function for the combination of attractiveness and probability. To do this, 15 female undergraduates made preferences between two dates. Each date was described by a photo and a verbal statement of probability. For example, subjects were given such alternatives as these:

Fairly likely   Unlikely

Tom   Joe

The names uniquely identified photographs selected in pilot work to cover a broad range of attractiveness. The probabilities defined the chances that the date would go out with the subject.

Procedurally, the photos and probabilities were varied in a factorial design; the stimuli are shown in Fig. 14.3. These hypothetical dates were factorially compared to a set of alternative dates. Preference responses were made by sliding a pointer along an unmarked bar; the endpoints were defined by anchor stimuli more extreme than any of the experimental stimuli. The preference judgements were recorded by the experimenter using a meter stick mounted on the rear of the response scale. Each subject was run individually on 4 successive days. Instructions and practice were given in the initial session; the subject was then run through four replications of the design over the next 2 days (the final day is discussed below). The stimuli were presented in random order.

Based on previous studies of risky decision making (Shanteau, 1975b), a multiplying model was expected for the combination of photo and probability information. That is, the attractiveness of the date was thought to be magnified or modulated by the probability level. Formally, this can be written as

$$R = w \times s \qquad (14.3)$$

The desirability of the date, R, was thus expected to equal the product of the subjective probability, w, and the perceived attractiveness, s.

If a multiplying model holds, then the results should plot as a diverging fan of straight lines. As seen in Fig. 14.3, the curves for a set of dates do diverge and are very nearly linear; the mean preferences have been collapsed across the alternative dates. In addition to this graphical test, the multiplying model was also supported by statistical tests at the single-subject level; these tests were based on bilinear trend analyses (see Anderson & Shanteau, 1970).

Not only does this method of graphical analysis allow a visual inspection of fit, it also allows direct assessment of the psychological values of the stimuli. For instance, the curves show that both Tom and Bob are well liked, whereas John and Jim are intermediate and Bill is less well liked. Of perhaps more interest are the subjective probability values spaced along the horizontal. As can be seen, the probability phrases order themselves as expected. One surprise, however, was the

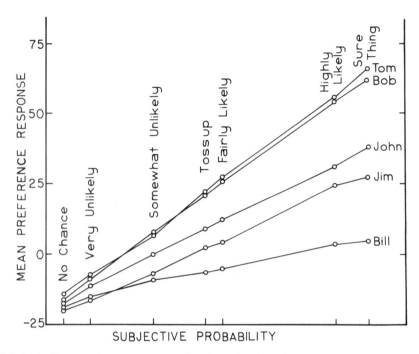

FIG. 14.3 Mean preference responses for dates described by a photo and an explicit statement of probability. Points are averaged over alternative dates. High-positive values indicate a strong preference for the listed date; zero indicates no preference; negative values indicate a preference for the alternative data. Probabilities are spaced along the horizontal according to their subjective spacing; photograph names are listed as curve parameters. Multiplying model predicts that curves should form a fan of diverging straight lines; both graphical and statistical analyses support the model. (From Shanteau & Nagy, 1974.)

large spacing between highly likely and fairly likely. This apparently indicates that subjects perceive these phrases as being psychologically quite different.

Subjective Inference Function

In the first part of the study, probability was explicitly defined. In a second part, probability was left up to each subject to infer; i.e., the photo was the only stimulus provided. Our goal was to derive the inference function used to combine inferred probability and attractiveness. Based on the integration analyses, probability and attractiveness might be expected to combine by multiplying. Different rules, however, may be used because probability is implicitly inferred rather than explicitly defined. Subjects may use different strategies, therefore, depending on what they feel is important; for instance some subjects may feel that only attractiveness is important. Therefore, in addition to a multiplicative combination, the present analysis was also sensitive to the influence to each variable alone.

Procedurally, subjects made choices and stated their degree of preference between all possible pairs of seven photos in a triangular design. They were told to base their choices on any and all factors they considered important in actually choosing a date. At a separate time, subjects rated the physical attractiveness of each photo and also estimated the probability that they (the subject) would be accepted by the pictured date. Each subject was run through four replications of the design on the final day of the study. In addition, background information and a photo was taken for each subject; each was also interviewed in depth about her strategies in the study and in dating generally.

The basic analytic approach was to try to describe the pattern of preferences for each subject from their ratings of attractiveness and probability. The method is illustrated for three subjects in Fig. 14.4. The spacing along the horizontal reflects the rated attractiveness of the photos. The probability estimates are represented by stars. The filled circles give the relative preference values for each date compared to all others. As can be seen, there were wide individual differences in both the preference values and the attractiveness and probability ratings. It is noteworthy that the preference curves for most subjects were markedly nonlinear with physical attractiveness (Subject 13 is an exception). This indicates that the preferences were related to more than the attractiveness of the date.

More detailed analyses of the preference curves revealed a number of dating strategies. Of particular interest, 11 of the 15 subjects preferred dates that they rated as intermediate in attractiveness. Plots for two such subjects are shown in Fig. 14.4a and b. Such subjects shared several general characteristics. First, the shape of the preference curves reflects the probability values. There seems therefore to be a definite connection between probability ratings and dating preferences. Second, an inverse relation was observed between probability and attractiveness: the greater the attractiveness, the smaller the probability. Such a relationship had been predicted by the matching hypothesis but not confirmed (Walster *et al.*, 1966). These two unresolved issues were therefore addressed by this study.

The subject in Fig. 14.4c exemplifies a rather different approach to dating. This subject (and three others) based her preferences solely on attractiveness. Such subjects seemed to be "shooting for the moon" in that their preferences are closely related to attractiveness but unrelated to probability.

A quantitative description of each subject's inference function was determined through multiple-regression analysis. Three terms were used in the regression equation: attractiveness, probability and the attractiveness × probability cross-

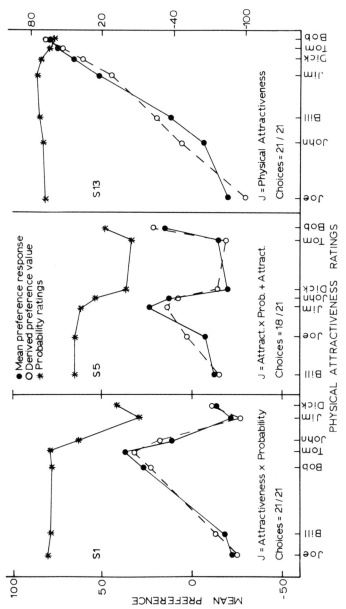

FIG. 14.4 Each panel depicts one subject's judgment strategy. The spacing along the horizontal axis reflects the subject's attractiveness ratings for the photos. The probability ratings (stars) are plotted as a function of attractiveness. The filled circles show the mean preference values for each date compared to all other dates. The dotted line represents the derived values from a regression analysis of the probability and attractiveness ratings. Also included within each panel are (a) the terms of the subject's inference function, and (b) the number of choices correctly predicted. These subjects reflect the general pattern of results for the remaining subjects. A few subjects showed inference functions similar in form to (c); however, most subjects revealed an inference function as in (a) or (b). Although discrepancies between observed and derived values appear small, they were statistically significant for Subjects 5 and 13.

232

product. The general judgment (J) equation can then be stated as

$$J = b_1 \text{ (Attractiveness)} + b_2 \text{ (Probability)}$$
$$+ b_3 \text{(Attractiveness} \times \text{Probability)} \qquad (14.4)$$

The values in parentheses represent the attractiveness and probability ratings for each photo. The beta weights (b) were determined from a multiple-regression analysis. These weights were then used in Equation (14.4) to obtain the derived preference values shown by open circles in Fig. 14.4.

Inspection of the subjective inference functions derived from Equation (14.4) revealed several interesting trends. As expected, subjects showing the "shooting for the moon" strategy essentially ignored probability (and the cross-product) and keyed entirely on attractiveness. In contrast, the remaining 11 subjects had large cross-product terms: in fact, the cross-product was dominant for most of these subjects. A few subjects, as exemplified by Fig. 14.4a, seemed to adopt a "playing it safe" strategy of preferring dates of intermediate attractiveness but high probability of acceptance. A somewhat different strategy of "having your cake and eating it too" was followed by several other subjects, as shown in Fig. 14.4b. Such subjects seemed to be "playing it safe" with preferences for dates of intermediate attractiveness, but at the same time still having some preference for a highly attractive date.

Choice Validation

To evaluate the validity of the inference functions, the first step was to examine the discrepancies between derived and observed preference values. Although the deviations in Fig. 14.4 appear minimal, significant discrepancies were found for 10 subjects (including Subjects 5 and 13 in Fig. 14.4). The locus of the discrepancies was not always obvious, but it did appear that some other variable(s) might be influencing the judgments (see below).

The ultimate criterion is the ability of the inference function to predict the subject's actual choices. Out of a total of 21 choices, an average of 19.0 choices were correctly predicted. This ranged from a low of 16 correct up to a high of all 21 correct. More detailed analyses revealed few errors of any large magnitude and most errors occurred when subjects had little or no preference between the two dates. The inference functions therefore seemed to be fairly accurate in predicting choices. On the whole, then, this study seemed to provide a particularly encouraging start.

DATING JUDGMENTS IN MEN

Because the previous study used women as subjects, it seems obvious to ask about the dating judgments of men. Accordingly, a reduced version of the original study was run on 14 male undergraduates by Nagy, Jewett, and

Shanteau (1976). On the first of 2 days, each subject made preference judgments between two dates described by a photo and an explicit probability. On the second day, subjects made choices between pairs of dates described by photos alone and also rated the attractiveness and probability for each photo.

The results for the integration function were quite similar to those in Fig. 14.3. The diverging fan of straight lines characteristic of multiplying was quite apparent. One notable difference from the women was that the set of photos produced a much greater range of slopes. There was even a hint of a negative slope for the least attractive photo (indicating that higher probabilities were viewed as worse than lower probabilities for that photo). Because there was an effort to equalize the range of photos for men and women, this suggests that men may differentiate more on the basis of attractiveness.

The inference functions for men, in contrast to women, revealed much greater uniformity. In almost all cases, dates seen as more attractive were preferred, i.e., the curves were monotonic. This means that implicit probabilities were largely ignored; in comparison, explicit probabilities as reported above were combined multiplicatively with attractiveness. One possible explanation for this seeming conflict is that men may mistrust their own inferred probabilities but place greater importance on external probabilities. Another common finding for men was an "elbow" in their preference curves, i.e., subjects had little preference between unattractive dates but had strong preferences between attractive dates. The nonlinear shape of these curves suggest that, although preferences do depend on attractiveness, there is a relatively complex relation between preference and attractiveness (see the Discussion).

The validity checks revealed good fits for the derived inference values. Furthermore, the average number of correctly predicted choices was 19.5 out of 21. The overall implication of these results is that men place much greater importance on physical attractiveness than women, but do so in a relatively complex way.

INFLUENCE OF COMPATIBILITY

As noted on several occasions, there seemed to be other factors influencing women's dating judgments beyond attractiveness and probability. This evidence came from three sources. First, roughly half the women in earlier studies showed significant discrepancies between observed and derived preferences. Although these discrepancies were generally small, their overall consistency is striking. Second, several subjects revealed irregular preference curves, which suggested the influence of other factors. Finally, interviews with subjects produced a number of comments of this sort: "I don't think he would ask me out—he's not my type," "We just wouldn't get along together," or "He's a blond and I'm a brunette and so we wouldn't fit well." All this implies that subjects may be making an inference of compatibility and that this may play an important part in their judgments.

To examine this further, Nagy, Ruggles, and Shanteau (1976) studied the joint influence of attractiveness, probability, and compatibility. Using procedures similar to before, 15 female undergraduates were run for 2 days. On one day, a three-factor integration function of attractiveness X probability X compatibility was analyzed. On the other day, subjects made separate ratings of attractiveness, probability, and compatibility (compatibility was defined as "how well you would expect to get along with this person"). Finally, subjects made preferences based on the photos alone.

The results for the integration function revealed a three-dimensional diverging fan of straight lines. This means that the integration function can be described by a three-factor multiplying model of probability X attractiveness X compatibility. An interesting feature of this model is that it is noncompensatory: a zero (or low) value for any one of the factors can produce a low judgment regardless of the values for the other factors. To be desirable, therefore, a date must be simultaneously in the middle or high range on each of the factors; having high values on just one or two factors is not enough.

Analyses of the preference curves revealed wide individual differences. Whereas attractiveness played a role in most subjects judgments, some subjects also relied on compatibility while others relied on probability. Several subjects, however, showed more complex preference curves, such as using compatibility at low attractiveness and probability at high attractiveness. In any case, it was clear that compatibility did play some role in most subjects' dating judgments. In the validity checks, the inclusion of compatibility provided a noticeable increase in the fit. For instance, the average number of correct choices was over 20 out of 21. Compatibility is therefore an important addition to attractiveness and probability as a fundamental determinant of dating judgments for women.

INFLUENCE OF OTHER INFORMATION

In the previous studies, photos were the primary source of information. Although there is much that can be drawn out of a photograph, this is obviously not the only type of dating information normally available. The importance of other information was emphasized in an informal study in which women were asked to describe how they "made up their minds about a date." Subjects reported using such factors as "how friendly he is," "whether we have a good time together," or "having things in common." It was clear, therefore, that information other than photos needs to be considered to understand dating.

Based on such considerations, Nagy (1975) extended the present approach to investigate the influence of other types of information on dating. Twenty-five female subjects rated the desirability of dates such as

Very sexually aggressive
Bill

The names corresponded to photos that varied in attractiveness. The dating characteristics were selected on the basis of high importance ratings from pilot subjects; each characteristic was then modified by an adverb (the stimuli are listed below). The general experimental procedure was similar to before.

The dating judgments were therefore based on three pieces of information: (1) an adverb modifying (2) a dating characteristic paired with (3) a photo. The combination of adverb and characteristic was expected to follow a multiplying model (Cliff, 1959). This combination was in turn thought to combine with the photo by averaging (Lampel & Anderson, 1968). There were therefore two integration functions of interest in this study.

Integration Functions

Both graphical and statistical tests supported a multiplicative combination rule for the adverb and dating characteristics; this implies that characteristics were modulated by the adverbs. The multiplicative rule, however, was not followed for the combination of adverbs and "Sexually Aggressive." Although the reasons for this difference are not entirely clear, one possibility is that there is an intermediate ideal or most preferred point for sexually aggressive (Coombs, Dawes, & Tversky, 1970); in contrast, the other characteristics appear to have extreme ideal points.

The analyses of averaging in the combination of adverb–characteristic and photo are shown in Fig. 14.5. The left panel shows the adverb and photo interaction (averaged over characteristics), and the right panel shows the characteristic and photo interaction (averaged over adverbs). In both cases, the solid lines are very nearly parallel; this implies additivity for the two factors in each panel. As can be shown, additivity is a common property of both simple adding and averaging models. A pivotal test between the models is provided by the filled points. In the upper part of the right panel, for instance, the filled square (dotted line) is the mean response to an attractive photo (Bill) alone. If an adding model holds, then combining Bill with a high-valued characteristic (wealthy) should increase the response. As seen in the filled circle, however, the mean response actually showed a decrease. This is precisely what is predicted by a simple averaging model. Similar results can be seen for other corresponding points in the two panels. In addition, averaging predicts that the slope of the dotted lines should be steeper than the solid lines; the results also support this prediction.

In all, subjects apparently had a two-step integration function in which they (1) multiplied the adverb and characteristic together, and then (2) averaged this combination with the photo. Psychologically, this implies that subjects modified or modulated the characteristic by the adverb and then balanced this result against the photo.

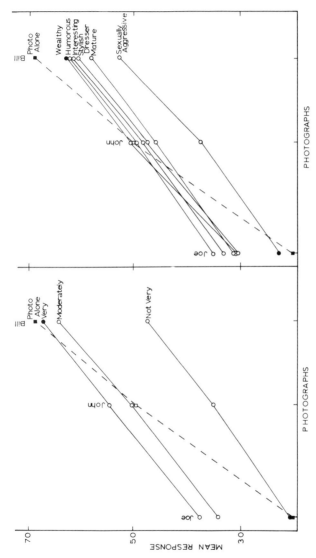

FIG. 14.5 Mean judgments of dates described by a photo and adverb–modified characteristic (Nagy, 1975). The left panel represents the adverb × photo interaction (averaged over characteristics); the three solid lines correspond to adverbs and are plotted against the subjective values for photos spaced along the horizontal. The right panel represents the characteristic × photo interaction (averaged over adverbs) with the six characteristics plotted against the photos. Both plots are close to parallel and support additivity. The dotted lines represent the mean response to the photos alone. In both panels the dotted line is steeper than the other curves and supports a simple averaging model.

237

Subjective Inference Function

A simple regression model was used to examine the inference function for the combination of photo and adverb–characteristic. The primary interest here was on the weights attached to photo and adverb–characteristic. It has been widely reported that physical attractiveness is the primary determinant of dating choice (e.g., Walster *et al.,* 1966). Although this contention has been inadequately tested in previous studies, it can be directly evaluated here.

As predicted, the regression analyses revealed that the mean percent of variance accounted for by photos was rather high (39%). The dating characteristics, however, accounted for an even higher percent variance (42%); the difference is nonsignificant. When other information is available, therefore, attractiveness does not dominate dating judgments.

It was also informative to compare the relative importance of the various dating characteristics. For most subjects, the personality traits (interesting, humorous, and mature) were most important. In contrast, material assets (wealthy and stylish dresser) were least important, with sexually aggressive intermediate in importance.

One cautionary note of a technical nature is needed when weights are used as indication of importance. This interpretation assumes that the subjective ranges of the stimuli are consistent; otherwise, the weights become confounded with the range of the scale values. Fortunately, a comparison of scale values revealed a consistent range across characteristics. Therefore, these weights can indeed be interpreted to reflect importance.

Choice Validation

The validational analyses proceeded somewhat differently in this study. The analysis of the choice predictions, in contrast to before, involved combinations of stimuli different from those used to get the derived functions. Despite this difference, the choice predictions were quite accurate. Excluding "no preference" responses, an average of 87% of the choices were correctly predicted. Overall, the results of this study seemed to have been successful, in first, analyzing a two-part integration function and, second, deriving inference functions that were quite accurate in some stringent tests.

DISCUSSION

The key to this series of studies on dating has been the ability to handle subjective inferences. This discussion is therefore organized around the role of subjective inferences in our research. We first discuss the importance of subjective inferences. Second are some comments on how the ability to deal with inferences has allowed us to answer several unresolved questions in dating. We next point out some possible uses of the present techniques in both future dating research and other areas of social judgment. Finally, we have some concluding comments on both the advantages and the disadvantages of the approach.

Subjective Inferences

A basic assumption underlying the present research is that subjects do in fact make subjective inferences and that these inferences are used in their judgments. This assumption appears viable for two reasons. First subjects reported in interviews that they often draw inferences about probability of rejection. Further analyses also revealed that many subjects used compatibility inferences; this was a factor we had not initially anticipated. Second, the overall success of the approach in predicting choices also supports the basic assumption. This is shown most clearly for subjects who preferred dates of intermediate attractiveness. Without probability inferences, the choices of such subjects would be almost impossible to describe analytically. It seems clear to us that subjects do draw inferences and that these inferences play a vital role in their dating judgments.

Unresolved Issues in Dating

By quantitatively describing each subject's inference function, the present approach was able to clarify several unanswered issues in dating research. The most important concerns the joint role of physical attractiveness and expectancy of rejection. Although previous investigators hypothesized that expectancy of rejection will coact with physical attractiveness leading subjects to "match," evidence for this notion is meager. Additionally, there has been little evidence that probability of rejection has any influence at all on dating judgments.

In contrast, the studies reported in this chapter provide direct evidence that subjects' probability inferences are reflected in their dating judgments. For most women subjects, these inferences were combined with the judged physical attractiveness of the date following a multiplicative combination rule. Psychologically, this implies that the subject's feelings about physical attractiveness are modulated by inferences of probability of rejection. Therefore, the most preferred date was not necessarily the most attractive (from the subject's point of view). Indeed, the majority of subjects chose dates of intermediate physical attractiveness.

Beyond matching on physical attractiveness, there is also the question of matching on other characteristics, e.g., personality traits or interests. This issue was directly examined as part of a supplementary design in Nagy (1975). Female subjects evaluated dates described by a photo and a characteristic modified by an adverb. Two characteristics were selected that on the basis of pilot work were likely to show matching (intelligent and affectionate); these were then modified by a broad range of adverbs (maximally, very, fairly, moderately, slightly, not very, and minimally). The use of seven adverbs allowed determination of each subject's ideal point on the two characteristics. This was then compared to each subject's self-preceived standing on those characteristics.

Results showed that most subjects preferred dates either equal to or slightly more intelligent or affectionate than themselves. These results suggest that, whereas subjects do not always precisely match their own standing, their preferences are at least somewhat related to their own self-perceptions. Therefore, although a strict version of matching was not supported, there was evidence of a tendency toward matching on characteristics other than physical attractiveness.

In addition to matching, the present techniques also proved useful in delineating a number of individual differences in dating judgments. For women, several types of judgment strategies were observed. A few subjects revealed the "shooting for the moon" strategy (as in Fig. 14.4c). However, the majority of subjects revealed either the "playing it safe" strategy (Fig. 14.4a) or, the "having your cake and eating it too" strategy (Fig. 14.4b). One might expect, based on the matching hypothesis, that these strategies would be related to the subject's own physical attractiveness. For example, a subject using the "shooting for the moon" strategy might be more physically attractive than a subject using the "playing it safe" strategy. However, both informal observation and formal ratings of each subject's photo revealed little relationship between physical attractiveness and the strategy employed.

Several interesting differences in the approach of men and women to dating were also observed. First, most women used inferences of probability and attractiveness to arrive at their judgments, whereas men keyed almost entirely on physical attractiveness. This seemingly supports the stereotype that men are more concerned with physical attractiveness than women. This may be an oversimplification, however, because a more detailed examination revealed a strategy for men that is more complex than it looks. Most men showed an "elbow"-shaped preference function, which indicates that they had little preference until dates were at least moderately attractive; above that, they had large preferences based on physical attractiveness. Men therefore appeared to be using a two-stage or two-part processing strategy that depended on the attractiveness of the date.

A second difference between men and women occurred in the way explicit and implicit probabilities were incorporated into preferences. Most women appeared to multiply both implicit and explicit forms of probability with attractiveness. Men, in contrast, combined explicit probabilities multiplicatively but generally did not reflect inferred probabilities in their preferences.

Another relevant issue concerns the importance of physical attractiveness. Contrary to previous conclusions, results in Nagy (1975) show that whereas physical attractiveness is important it by no means dominates the subject's dating judgments. For most subjects, it was roughly of equal importance to other characteristics. When other information was provided, therefore, physical attractiveness did not play any larger role than other information. This suggests that previous conclusions may be incorrect, especially as other information has seldom been provided.

Future Research

In addition to clarifying several issues raised by previous investigators, the present approach leads to several possibilities for future dating research. One possibility is to provide information sequentially about dates as subjects ask for it. This would allow analysis of the buildup of the subject's judgments (e.g., see Payne & Carroll, Chapter 2). The major benefit of such a task is that it more closely represents the gradual acquisition of information in the actual dating situation. Another possibility for extending the present approach is the use of protocol analyses (e.g., see Berl, Lewis, & Morrison, Chapter 13). We have extensively used interviews in interpreting our data, and this may be further extended to give a more complete verbal account of the decision-making process.

In addition, this approach might also be employed in the study of consumer decisions (e.g., see Staelin & Payne, Chapter 12). Many consumer decisions involve services provided by people, e.g., choosing a doctor or a TV repair man. However, little is known about consumer decisions regarding services (Schneider, 1973). Consumer evaluations are known to be influenced by subjective inferences; for example, quality is often inferred from price (McConnell, 1968). By using the present approach, the influence of subjective inferences on consumer choices could be specifically examined.

Concluding Comments

Our intention has been to illustrate the value of a human judgment approach to the study of decisions made about other people. We have attempted to demonstrate the utility of this approach by showing how these judgment techniques have allowed us to clarify several long-standing issues in dating. More specifically, the approach allowed us to examine the cognitive processes used by each subject to combine subjective inferences into a dating judgment.

There are general limitations of the approach that deserve discussion. For example, the approach does not deal with interpersonal interactions between persons in the dating situation. This, however, was a self-imposed limitation; our goal as stated initially was to examine the cognitive processes of individual subjects. However, knowledge of an individual's cognitive processes can be informative as to their interactions with a date. In all, the approach has been very helpful in our understanding of dating, and we feel that a similar understanding can be achieved in many other areas through use of these human judgment techniques.

ACKNOWLEDGMENTS

This research was supported in part by Public Health Service Grants MH 22610 and M26002 from the National Institute of Mental Health. Preparation of this chapter was supported in part by NSF Grant BMS 20504. We wish to thank John Carroll, David Klahr, and John Payne for their helpful comments on the manuscript. The authors also wish to thank Susan Ellingboe, Randy Jewett, and Barbara Ruggles for their assistance in running subjects and analyzing data in the studies reported here.

15
The Social Psychologist as Troll

David Klahr

Carnegie–Mellon University

> Once on a time there were three billy goats who were to go up to the hillside to make themselves fat, and the name of all three was "Gruff."

So starts the well-known folk tale (Asbjörnsen & Moe, 1957) of the Great Ugly Troll who kept threatening to devour successively larger and fatter Billy Goats as they crossed his bridge. However, each goat managed to convince the Troll that deferred gratification held greater rewards than immediate consumption.

> "Oh, no! pray don't take me. I'm too little, that I am," said the Billy Goat. "Wait a bit till the second Billy Goat Gruff comes. He's much bigger."

> "Well, be off with you," said the Troll.

And he waited for a bigger Billy Goat.

In attempting to create a framework in which to place the chapters presented in this volume, it occurred to me that over the past two decades, social psychology has been behaving a bit like our Troll, waiting to dispatch increasingly formidable problems but readily convinced that the next problem, the really big one, was the one to aim for and thus letting the present one slip away.

What does it mean to imply that the early problems were the easy ones? Let me give a few examples. Some of the most famous social psychological investigations of the 1950s were Asch's studies of group pressures toward conformity in decision making (Asch, 1956). What decision faced the subject? He had to decide which of three lines was the longest. Recall that Asch varied many things in his studies, such as the discriminability of the lines, the unanimity of the other "judges" (actually stooges giving the wrong answers), but the basic decision remained the same. What were the consequences of this decision for the decision maker or for others? Precisely nil. Other studies of the time had a similarly minor effect on the subsequent fate of the decision maker. For example, a major effort in social psychology was directed toward the study of

243

attitudes. Almost everything that social psychology discovered about attitudes came from choice situations in which the decision maker had to decide which of several statements best fitted his own view of the world.

Now consider the decisions facing the various subjects studied in the papers presented here. Staelin and Payne (Chapter 12) describe real consumers deciding how to spend their money on real products, products with which they must live after they make their choice. Shanteau and Nagy (Chapter 14) describe college students attempting to decide with whom to try to get a date. They report that their subjects took the game quite seriously, not surprisingly, as dating choices loom so large in the life of college students. Berl, Lewis, and Morrison (Chapter 13) report on data collected during what was probably the most important decision yet made in the life of their subjects: college choice. And Slovic, Fischhoff, and Lichtenstein (Chapter 11) describe some of the difficulties that face those attempting to make profoundly important decisions involving such public policy issues as nuclear energy development, disaster insurance, and auto-safety standards. (Other chapters in this volume continue the list of important and tough problems, e.g., Dawes on clinical judgement and Carroll and Payne on parole decisions, but I shall confine my specific comments to the four chapters in this section of the book.)

What are some of the characteristics of these problems that make them much harder—for both the decision maker and the social psychologist—than the kinds of problems studied earlier? What makes them bigger Billy Goats? I shall attempt to sketch an answer along three dimensions: the processing requirements of the tasks, the analytic tools used by the social psychologist to understand the phenomena, and the consequences of the decision for the decision maker.

PROCESSING REQUIREMENTS

Current cognitive theories of human problem solving place much of the explanation for the problem solver's behavior on the characteristics of the task environment. The more complex that environment is, then the more complex must be the behavior of the problem solver. For example, if the task environment includes as one of its central elements other complex problem solvers—e.g., humans—then the problem increases greatly in complexity. We have several ways to model the behavior of humans in these kinds of complex situations. If the other complex entity in the decision maker's task behaves with any regularity at all, then we can invoke probabilistic models. If the other entity is also directly involved in the decision, then we can utilize the tools of game theory. However, these are the analyst's tools, not those utilized by the decision maker. Indeed, the main point of the chapter by Slovic and co-workers (and Dawes', too) is that humans are unable to correctly utilize these tools in dealing with complex problems.

What do they do? Slovic and associates say they use a variety of heuristics: availability, representativeness, hindsight, coherence, justification. Citing their own work, and that of others, they demonstrate some of the remarkably incorrect ways that people go about making decisions. Unfortunately, we do not yet know much about how these heuristics are supposed to combine or interact. It is still hard to decide, a priori, whether people are going to over- or underadjust to sample information. Similarly, we do not know whether they use "anchoring and adjustment" as Lichtenstein and Slovic (1971, 1973) have found, or whether they become conservative Bayesians, as Edwards (1968) appears to consistently find. Does the gambler's fallacy prevail, after a flood, so that people, believing that the worst is unlikely to recur in the immediate future, return to the flood plain? Or do they invoke availability, and, conjuring up a flood equivalent to the one that has just receeded, take to the hills?

The difficulty here is that these heuristics do not appear to be the same kind of thing as the heuristics found in other studies of problem solving. Simon (1957) proposed satisficing as one such heuristic in decision-making tasks, and Newell and Simon (1972) listed such things as means–end analysis, depth–first search, and factorization as strategies subjects used to deal with their limited capacity. However, the heuristics of Slovic and others in his lab seem more like labels for paradigms intentionally concocted to elicit maladaptive behavior. They do not seem like shortcuts with a reasonably high probability of success. Instead, they are "cognitive illusions" similar to perceptual illusions; compelling even when we know of their existence and can explain their source. Furthermore, with respect to the cases where there is an optimal statistical procedure for reaching a decision, there is no a priori reason to expect people to know it. As one of my students (Henrion, 1975) commented in his written reaction to this symposium:

> It seems somewhat ingenuous to find people's ignorance of these laws at all surprising.[1] Quite the contrary, it should be more surprising if it were found that people had a precise intuitive grasp of a body of mathematics which was only formally developed in recent centuries and whose principles are only communicated with difficulty at institutions of higher learning [p. 9].

How does a high-school senior choose a college? This task also places great demands on the processor, but not at all in the way that Berl, Lewis, and Morrison (Chapter 13) characterize it. Their focus is on "nonroutine" decision making, but their analysis, based on which of several models is the best, tells us nothing about why nonroutine decisions should differ from routine ones. Is limited capacity really a problem here? After all, their subjects had over 30

---

[1] Perhaps "ingenuous" is too strong. I believe that Slovic and his colleagues at Oregon are truly puzzled by human stupidity. It probably derives from their observation that many of the world's people choose to live in places other than Oregon, a fact that Oregoniods seem at a loss to explain.

weeks to compute some decision function. I believe that the difficulty of this decision—and I do not deny its difficulty—lies at a higher level, in the choice of a decision rule. This seems to be the most important characteristic of nonroutine problems: We do not know which programs to invoke to solve them. In some cases the problem then becomes the construction of a solution procedure. In the college choice case, that does not appear problematic. Indeed, the high-school students probably could have been taught about each of the models considered by the authors, and they could have been trained in how to crank alternative colleges through several different decision models. However, there is no obvious way to decide which of those models apply to the data. That is, there is no higher level decision rule about how to choose decision rules. Although Berl and co-workers are reluctant to accept their own results, it appears that in the end their subjects chose the conceptually simplest model—linear additive—and used that to make their choices.

One of the initial requirements for a problem solver is the creation of a problem representation. Once constructed, this representation profoundly affects subsequent performance. The creation of a problem representation is itself a major subproblem to be solved in many decision situations. Cognitive psychologists have been studying this aspect of problem solving for many years (remember functional fixedness [Duncker, 1945]?) recently utilizing some sophisticated approaches (Simon & Hayes, 1975). The chapters in this volume show that social psychologists have begun to directly address this issue, but in other guises. For example, Shanteau and Nagy (Chapter 14) have added to our knowledge of problem representations in their dating study. The only difference between what they call integration functions and inference functions is that in one case the experimenter gets further into the act by explicitly defining probabilities of rejection, whereas in the other it is the subject who makes such estimates ("inference" seems an inappropriate term). Similarly, Slovic's discussion of anchoring and adjustment, and the inequivalence of preference vs. bidding, are examples of the effect of initial representation on problem-solving performance.

ANALYTIC TOOLS

We know little about the weaponry of the Troll in our tale. In fact, all we know about him is that he had "eyes as big as saucers and a nose as long as a poker." Not really very potent, but then neither were the tools of the early social psychologists. However, in the past several years we have seen a progression of increasingly sophisticated and powerful analytic tools in the use of social psychologists. Multivariate statistical analysis and game-theoretic approaches have become widespread in the attempt to build models that capture the complexity of the phenomena under investigation. In the chapters in this volume, we see the beginnings of the utilization of perhaps the most powerful and complex technology yet developed in the behavioral sciences: the use of what can be broadly classified as an "information-processing approach."

There are many variants of this approach in the area of cognitive psychology, but they all share some common characteristics. First, they postulate a basic system architecture for the human information processor, or at least the part of it under investigation. This architecture is constrained by the parameter estimates obtained from the experimental labs concerned with basic processes. Next, in dealing with any task environment, they attempt to explicitly account for the internal task representation with which the problem solver must deal. In some cases, this representation is the sole focus of investigation, e.g., in studies of semantic memory (Anderson & Bower, 1973; Bobrow & Collins, 1975; Norman, Rumelhart, et al., 1975). As noted above, this task representation can often be the major determinant of behavior. Then, the theories of performance in any task domain are stated. Because these theories are typically rule systems, the implications of which require many inferential steps, the models are stated in a formal language that can be interpreted by a computer program, in order to precisely set forth the predictions of the model.

If social psychology is to benefit as much from this paradigm as cognitive psychology has, it must do more than import the information-processing terminology and metaphor. It must also import, and creatively adapt to its needs, the powerful technology to which it often just alludes.

CONSEQUENCES OF DECIDING

What happens after the decision? In particular, what happens to the people and the things with which the decision maker is subsequently to interact? This is the third factor that I think justifies the view that social psychology is currently concerned about much harder problems than those studied in the past.

No Consequences

It is hard to imagine that Asch's subjects ever encountered any consequences subsequent to their decisions. Similarly, for all of its purported predictive validity with respect to actual behavior, the immense amount of attitude testing that obsessed social psychology for many years had no immediate or obvious interactional consequence for the decision maker.

Consequences for Others

Many decisions made by one person have direct and intentional consequences for others, but not for the decision maker. The best example in this book is the parole decision, but many personnel, clinical, and admissions decisions have this property. The decision maker in these kinds of situations is attempting to make some kind of optimal allocation of people to situations, but he need not involve himself in the consequences of the decision. Although the alternatives being considered are extremely complex and dynamic systems, they may for purposes of the desicion be considered in the same way as any complex object. The important point is not whether decisions are "about people," as Shanteau and Nagy describe their focus, but whether the decisions are about future interaction with those people.

Consequences for the Decision Maker

When I choose a date, I must live with the consequences of that choice. When I buy a car, or a house, or a box of rice, I must deal with what I have chosen. When I choose a college, I must go there. The bearing of consequence is a fundamental aspect of many of the problems now being studied by social psychologists and it gives the problems a character that is completely lacking from simpler situations.

The public policy issues addressed by Slovic provide the best example of the subsequent consequences of decision making for the decision maker. The issues at stake are so pervasive that no one can escape their consequences, whether for good or evil. The policy makers must ultimately lie in the bed they make. If nuclear power can harm us, it can harm them; if regulatory agencies waste our money, they waste theirs also. If price controls help or hurt us, they help or hurt them as well.

Slovic and associates present an alarmingly lucid summary of the kinds of decisions that policy makers are being asked to explicitly make. It may have escaped the reader's notice, but the closing sections of their chapter ask: 'What are the cognitive processes whereby a person decides the value of a human life, either his own or others'? Clearly, such decisions have always been made in less explicit forms, but now social psychology is beginning to investigate precisely how. What question could be more central to the survival of the human race?

CONCLUSION

As the research in this volume attests, the Great Troll of social psychology now stands ready to deftly dispatch the Biggest Billy Goat of All: "Real Problems." He is armed with an array of formidable tools, ranging from multivariate statistical analysis to computer simulation. Being no great friend of Billy Goats, I admit that I am on the side of the Troll (although my children may be horrified to discover my true allegiance). However, I must remind the reader of two things about our tale. First of all, the Troll let the little ones get away in his lust for the big payoff. That was a shame, for the little goats would have been easily conquered. Instead they got off scot free, and to what avail? The story, as you may recall, ends like this (Asbjörnsen & Moe, 1957):

> "Now, I'm coming to gobble you up!" roared the Troll [to the biggest Billy Goat of
> all.]
> "Well, come along!" [said Big Bill.] "I've got two spears,
> And I'll poke your eyeballs out at your ears.
> I've got besides two great big stones,
> And I'll crush you to bits, body and bones" [p. 25].

That is what the Billy Goat said, and that was what he did. He finished off the
Troll, and tossed him into the river. Of course, that was just a fable.

ACKNOWLEDGMENTS

This work was supported by a grant from the Spencer Foundation.

Part IV

THE UNITY OF COGNITIVE AND SOCIAL PSYCHOLOGY

Simon (Chapter 16) offers a discussion of these chapters as a whole. He provides the argument that cognitive psychology and social psychology are fundamentally the same. He further explores the themes of these chapters and the requirements of a cognitive social psychology.

16
Discussion:
Cognition and Social Behavior

Herbert A. Simon

Carnegie–Mellon University

The lot of a symposium summarizer is often not a happy one. The very idea of such a summary implies not only that the symposium has had definite central themes, but that the symposiasts actually have addressed themselves to those themes. My role as a summarizer of this symposium has been made easy by the fact that both conditions have been met: there are central themes, and the speakers have concerned themselves with them. I should like to devote most of my comments to accenting these themes, and to saying what I think we have learned about them from the papers that have been presented.

A number of remarks have been made here, particularly in Shelley Taylor's (Chapter 5) discussion of the first group of chapters, about the history of cognitive social psychology. Those remarks prompted me to take off my shelf the first (1954) edition of the Lindzey *Handbook of Social Psychology* to see how the topic was handled there. Of course, I could have gone even further back, to Newcomb's (1950) postwar textbook or the still earlier Murphy and Murphy (1931) readings book; but I judged that even 1954 would seem more like prehistory than history to many of our symposiasts.

At any rate, I found in Lindzey that the cognitive side of social psychology was represented mainly by a chapter by William Lambert (1954), which emphasized learning, taking a Hullian, S–R, position; and a chapter by Martin Sheerer, which was written almost exclusively from a Gestalt viewpoint. The present conference owes very little to S–R learning theory, for a reason stated well by Taylor: Except for notions of "mediational processes," which have never been more than vague, S–R theory leaves little room for psychological processes to occur between stimulus and response. And it is precisely with such processes that most of the chapters of this volume have been concerned. They have been concerned with cognitive processes in social behavior, and more precisely, with information processes in social behavior.

The Sheerer (1954) chapter of Lindzey (1954), on the other hand, after its Gestalt language has been translated into the more precise diction of informa- tion-processing psychology, has much relevance for this volume; for person perception, to which we have devoted so much attention here, is one of its central topics. What I found most interesting about Sheerer's account, however, was that it rested heavily, for its empirical evidence, upon research in individual psychology. He interposed no curtain—neither iron, nor bamboo, nor any other opacity—between social and individual psychology but wrote on the assumption that the same human being carries on both social and individual cognitive processes and uses the same basic mental equipment for both.

By way of contrast, the corresponding chapter (Zajonc, 1964) in the second edition of the *Handbook* is largely devoted to cognitive dissonance and balance theories and, what is more significant, makes almost no reference to the literature of cognition outside social psychology. A quick perusal of the list of journals referenced at the ends of the two chapters dramatizes the difference: the earlier unity with general cognitive psychology is replaced by nearly com- plete isolation. The point of view of Sheerer's chapter has been disappointingly muted in the social psychology of the past 20 years, and its revival seems to me perhaps the most significant theme of the discussion in this symposium. That brings me to the first of the series of propositions that run as common themes through this volume.

COGNITIVE SOCIAL PSYCHOLOGY IS COGNITIVE PSYCHOLOGY

Social choices are choices; attributions of human agency are causal inferences; perceptions of other persons are perceptions. When the processes underlying these social phenomena are identified, as they are in the chapters of this book, particularly those of the second and third parts, they turn out to be the very same information processes we encounter in nonsocial cognition. Information is extracted from a complex stimulus situation; it is subjected to the kinds of information processes we call "thinking," "judging," "problem solving," or "inferring"; during the course of that processing, there is brought to bear on it a wide range and variety of information already stored in memory. We neither need nor want separate theories of social thinking and other (antisocial?) thinking. We simply need a theory of thinking.

Now particular social situations define particular task environments. Con- versing with a new acquaintance is different from solving an algebra problem. That is to say, the substances of the situations are different, as are the scripts, in Abelson's terms, that are relevant to them. This does not imply that they are handled by different processors. The point is illustrated by GPS, the General Problem Solver (Newell & Simon, 1972) computer program devised to simulate human problem solving. GPS is "general" in that its processes make no reference to any specific problem domain. It is a perfectly general scheme for taking a starting situation and trying to transform it into a goal situation. GPS is, in principle, as willing to judge a new acquaintance as it is to tackle an algebra problem—providing that the problems are specified for it in a form it understands.

Defining the problem for GPS means characterizing the goal situation, the starting situation, and the actions that are admissible for transforming one situation into another. The problem-solving methods of GPS are general; the problem specification is specific to the task domain. In the parole decision process discussed by Carroll and Payne (Chapter 2), for example, they define risk and punishment as the dimensions relevant to the decision. Their decision maker draws on information or beliefs about the characteristics of an offender or his crime that are associated with the risk of recidivism and on beliefs about the seriousness or "punishability" of the crime. Starting with those premises, which define the social problem, judgmental processes go to work that are presumably the same ones that are used in any other many-factor decision.

This commonality of social and other thinking is reflected in a number of the empirical phenomena that are reviewed in this volume. Hamilton (Chapter 6) argues, for example, that stereotyping can arise from the normal cognitive processes of attention, discrimination, and selective perception, without the need to postulate any special mechanisms of social stereotyping. He introduces into evidence the experiment by Tajfel and Wilkes (1963), where subjects misjudge systematically the lengths of lines after they have been induced by a simple naming procedure to stereotype the lines as "long" or "short." He then cites other experiments to show that the same experimental manipulation induces stereotyping behavior in social situations. Hamilton goes on to show, by reference to his own experiments and those by Chapman, how identical manipulations can produce illusory perceptions of correlation between uncorrelated variables in social and nonsocial task situations.

Nisbett and co-workers (Chapter 8) document the fact that human inductive processes exhibit similar biases and pathologies in making social and nonsocial inferences. These authors review a considerable body of evidence showing that people generally do not use consensus information in making causal attributions in social situations; they then draw a close parallel between this phenomenon and the demonstration by Kahneman and Tversky (1973) that base-rate information fails to affect predictions. Their explanation for these results rests on the hypothesis that concrete information (information about specific instances) has far more impact on judgment than abstract information. Clearly, there is nothing peculiarly "social" about this explanatory mechanism, and indeed the empirical evidence argues for its generality.

At a more general level, Dawes (Chapter 1) argues that man's "bounded rationality"—the limits of his information-processing capabilities in the face of complex situations—can be adduced to explain a variety of phenomena in social as well as individual behavior. In particular, he proposes that the limits of man's ability to reach decisions in the face of a multiplicity of incommensurable criteria are a principal reason for the generally observed superiority of simple linear decision rules over the judgments of experienced clinicians.

The many empirical studies that are introduced into evidence in these chapters point away from the idea of separate theories of social causation or social semantic memory; they point toward the idea of a general theory of causal inference and semantic memory, which gets its application to particular social situations by adding to it the task-specific semantic content of those situations.

The chapters by Abelson (Chapter 3) and Schmidt (Chapter 4) take important steps toward the construction of a formal theory of the processes involved, although I could wish that they had made the generality of their proposals more explicit instead of emphasizing the social content of their models. Abelson hypothesizes a semantic memory containing numerous scripts applicable to different social situations. "By a script," he says, "I mean a coherent sequence of events expected by the individual, involving him either as a participant or as an observer" (p. 33). The sequence of events expected by a physicist when he lobs a rocket off into space seems to fit this definition of script, as does the sequence of events expected by President Ford when he threatens a Congressional bill with a veto. If memory is indeed organized as a set of scripts, as Abelson hypothesizes, then social scripts only differentiate themselves from others by their specific content. Testing the script hypothesis is, as Abelson is well aware, a large undertaking, involving among other things the construction of large-scale simulations of human semantic memory. Because gratifying progress has been made in this direction over the past decade, it may not be too long before we can test alternative theories about how that memory is actually organized.

Schmidt's chapter, describing the BELIEVER program, is a concrete example of how one component of such a memory can be constructed—a system for making causal inferences. Schmidt does, however, specifically limit the BELIEVER system to attribution of causality to human actors. As basis for his system he uses Heider's (1958) reasoning that its actions are understood or explained when an observer can identify a plan and motive that caused the actor to decide to perform the observed action. The key terms here are "actions," "actor," "plan," and "motive."

There is an alternate way of putting the matter, however, that brings out more clearly the relation of social causation to causation in general. I should like to outline this alternative briefly (Simon, 1953; Simon & Rescher, 1966). We might say, for example, "The drop in wheat prices was caused by the ample winter rains, which produced a bumper crop." Two causal mechanisms are implied by these statements: the causal effect of the amount of rain upon the size of the wheat crop and the causal effect of the supply of wheat upon the price of wheat. Both mechanisms seem to be of the same general kind, resting on a lawful connection between a pair of phenomena, whereby a change in the one induces a change in the other. The first mechanism certainly does not fit Schmidt's definition, however, for the weather is not (save metaphorically) an actor, nor does it have plans or motives. What about the second? If we asked an economist to elaborate upon the second mechanism, he would introduce two actors (the wheat farmer and the consumer of wheat), motives for each (to maximize net return and to maximize utility, respectively), and plans for each. The wheat farmer's plan would be to so adjust his selling price that he could dispose of his entire harvest; the consumer's plan would be to adjust the amount of wheat consumed to the price, so as to allocate his total fixed budget in the optimum way among different objects of consumption. Hence, the second, but not the first, mechanism fits the Heider–Schmidt definition of causal explanation.

What is peculiar about the causal explanation of the social situation that does not fit the physical phenomenon? There seem to me to be two differences. First, in the Heider–Schmidt scheme, causation is traced back specifically to the human agent. We say that the lower price at which wheat is offered is caused by the farmer's desire to realize a profit, and his plan to do so by setting the price at a level at which the wheat can be sold. We leave aside the equally true statement that the cause of the lower price was the bountiful winter rain.

The second, and more fundamental, difference between the social and physical causation is that a decision maker is an essential component of the former but not of the latter. The terms "motive" and "plan" are peculiar to the processes that go on in the systems we call "decision makers." There is no reason, of course, why the decision maker has to be human. There are many cases today (e.g., in making inventory restocking decisions for a business concern) where the decision maker is a computer. The computer has motives (to achieve an optimal balance between the costs of stockouts and of excess inventories) and plans (for example, to employ the order points and order quantities found by solving a cost-minimization equation). Schmidt's BELIEVER could be used, without essential alteration, to attribute causal agency to the automated decision maker, as readily as to the human.

The distinction we should make, therefore, is not between social causation and nonsocial causation, but between causation involving a decision-making agent, and causation not involving such an agent. A general system for making causal attributions would have as a particular component a system for attributing cause to actors. I would find BELIEVER more compatible with the general thesis that cognitive social processes are cognitive processes if the program were factored in this way—and would argue also that it would then be a better simulation of the human causal attribution process. However, I do not think that any fundamental change is required in the system to achieve this factorization.

I have introduced numerous pieces of evidence to show that most of the contributors to this volume subscribe to the thesis that cognitive social psychology is cognitive psychology. That thesis is, of course, an empirical hypothesis and hence subject to empirical test. It is perfectly conceivable, although it is not plausible, that the processes of the human brain that handle social situations are quite distinct from the processes that handle other situations. Several of the experiments from the chapters that I have already mentioned indicate that there is no such separation of processes. These experiments also provide a general experimental paradigm that can be used to test the commonality of cognitive processes over a wider range of task domains. The paradigm is simple. We find two tasks that have the same formal structure (e.g., they are both tasks of multidimensional judgment), one of which is drawn from a social situation and the other is not. If common processes are implicated in both tasks, then we should be able to produce in each task environment phenomena that give evidence of workings of the same basic cognitive mechanisms that appear in the other.

Let me conclude my discussion of this topic by mentioning a situation where this paradigm has apparently not yet been applied, but could be. Schulz (Chapter 9) demonstrates by his field experiment that a person's feeling of control over events in his life is an important determinant of his attitudes and affect. As he points out, the control exercised by the subjects in his experiment is control over another person. If the same cognitive processes are at work in both social and nonsocial situations, then we can expect the same effect to be produced by giving the subjects control over inanimate aspects of their environments (menus for meals, room temperature, and so on). Experimental activity along such lines should help to tell us how far we can expect to go in building a common theory for social and general cognitive psychology.

COGNITIVE PSYCHOLOGY IS COGNITIVE SOCIAL PSYCHOLOGY

If it can be claimed, as has been argued in the last section, that cognitive social psychology is simple a special branch of cognitive psychology, a strong case can also be made for a converse proposition: that virtually all cognitive psychology is also social psychology. The contributors to this book, social psychologists all, were singularly unimperialistic, for they hardly raised the latter claim. It was raised, however, by Greene (Chapter 10) in his discussion of Part II. He suggests that if we wish to understand individual differences in problem solving—particularly when the problems to be solved are ill structured and hence afford maximum opportunity for alternative approaches—we must look to the social and learning experiences of the subjects who exhibit the differences.

I should like both to applaud and to enlarge Greene's suggestion. Human behavior can be regarded as genuinely nonsocial only to the extent that it is determined by some combination of the physiological characteristics of the central nervous system and sensory organs with the structure of the task environment. If we notice differences among human subjects placed in the same task environment, and if those differences are not explainable in physiological terms, then we must find something in their previous lives, produced presumably by the culture in which they have lived and the other persons with whom they have interacted, to account for the differences in task performance. For behavior to be social, therefore, it is not necessary for persons other than the behaving subject to be present; persons with whom he has interacted in the past make it equally social.

A number of the chapters in this book concern themselves with individual differences. Frieze (Chapter 7) shows how factor analytic methods can be used to identify individual differences in making causal attributions. Shanteau and Nagy (Chapter 14) have examined the differences in the ways in which individuals make dating decisions. Staelin and Payne (Chapter 12) have identified different styles for processing information in making market brand decisions. Finally, Carroll and Payne (Chapter 2) examine individual differences in making parole decisions.

In none of these four cases is there any reason to believe that the observed differences in cognitive style have anything to do with the fact that the inference or choice being made by the subjects is a social inference or choice. If these findings on differences among subjects have anything social about them, it is much more likely to refer to the "inputs" to the cognitive processes than to their "outputs."

In Greene's argument and its extension stated above are correct, then cognitive social psychology needs to stake out broader territories for exploration than it has in the past. In particular, it needs to pay attention to the social component of problem solving and reasoning styles. Let me cite an example from one chapter that will illustrate my meaning, and then a few other examples from my own research. Dawes (Chapter 1) expresses hopes that more decision makers can be induced to use linear decision rules instead of the less valid clinical procedures they now employ in making judgments. However, this hope is meaningful only if human beings are educable in this respect, if the processes of clinical judgment are not innate but are learnable and unlearnable. If these processes are not innate, then we should not be surprised to find differences among them from one individual to another and also, of more interest, from one culture or subculture to another.

The discipline of management science or operations research, which has grown up since the World War II, is devoted largely to discovering new methods for making management decisions of various kinds; replacing "intuition" and "judgment" with such esoteric formal techniques as linear programming, queuing theory, and Bayesian decision theory. The conditions under which such techniques (in this discipline or any other) are or are not adopted, do or do not diffuse throughout the application culture, are a topic of concern to cognitive social psychology, but a topic that has not been represented at this symposium.

Although none of the previous symposia in this Carnegie series has been devoted to social psychology, it is easy to find examples of cognitive research in those volumes that can be treated from a social psychological standpoint. Chase and Simon (1973) described differences between chess amateurs and chess masters in what could be seen and retained in a few second's exposure to a chess position and demonstrated that those differences had to be ascribed to experience and not to physiological differences in memory or imagery. It appears that we cannot have a cognitive psychology of chess without understanding the social psychology and sociology of chess knowledge.

Paige and Simon (1966) discovered three quite distinct cognitive styles among students confronted with identical sets of algebra word problems. Some of the students tackled the problems syntactically, others tackled them semantically, and a few made extensive use of both syntactic and semantic information. There are hints, at least, in their data that a student coming from a mathematics subculture is likely to approach such problems differently from a student coming from an engineering subculture. In some recent research, Gerritson, Gregg, and Simon (1975) have induced large differences in the speed of performance of subjects in a sequence extrapolation task by instructing them in different strategies for performing the task.

From all of these pieces of evidence, and from many others, we are drawn toward the conclusion that to explain human performance in most cognitive tasks it is necessary to introduce subject strategies as intervening variables that are likely to produce or to account for individual differences of large magnitude. If we follow that path, then we shall want, in turn, to know how the differences in strategy have come about—why one college sophomore employs one particular strategy, another sophomore another. Such an inquiry is bound to involve the social determinants of such differences.

Interest attaches not only to individual differences among members of ostensibly homogeneous groups (e.g., college sophomores), but even more to differences between subgroups in a society who have had different social and educational experiences. At a commonsense level, most of us believe that there are differences in cognitive style among lawyers, physicists, economists, accountants, and historians. Yet there has been almost no careful work on the nature of those differences or their consequences for performance in various cognitive tasks. Here is an arena of work in cognitive social psychology that appears to have great importance, both for basic psychology and for applications.

THE NEW CONCERN WITH PROCESS

Perhaps the most prominent theme, then, of this volume has been its emphasis upon the assimilation of cognitive social psychology to cognitive psychology, and vice versa. A second theme, however, has been almost equally prominent: the concern for the explanation of cognition in terms of organizations of information processes.

Taylor (Chapter 5), in commenting on this new interest in process in social psychology, points out that it is inimical to two established folkways. First, as mentioned earlier, it is not especially compatible with S–R ways of thinking, always wary of intervening variables that are not directly observable. Second, it is incompatible with the use of variance analysis as a principal analytic tool. The variance analysis paradigm, designed to test whether particular stimulus variables do or do not have an effect upon response variables, is largely useless for discovering and testing process models to explain what goes on between appearance of stimulus and performance of response. These traditional methods are particularly inappropriate when both stimulus and response are complex, as in problem-solving tasks, so that a long interval or processing time separates them.

Consequently, if we are to study process, we are going to have to employ research methods and research designs that are appropriate to that kind of investigation, and these are going to be different from the methods and designs we have used to study simple stimulus–response connections. The shift from S–R formulations of theory to information-processing formulations is a fundamental shift in paradigm, and it is bringing with it fundamental shifts in method also.

As Klahr (Chapter 15) and Taylor (Chapter 5) warn us, it is not enough to take over into cognitive social psychology the language of information processing, bounded rationality, and satisficing. What is needed is more than a set of suggestive metaphors. There now exists in information-processing psychology a whole collection of technical research tools, including formal languages for building and stating theories, observational techniques, and the computer used as a means for simulating behavior. Approaching social cognition from an information-processing point of view means using these tools, not simply using the information-processing metaphors. Let me spell out a little more specifically just what are the methodological requisites for approaching cognitive social psychology from an information-processing point of view.

Density of Observations

If we are to understand a system whose elementary processes have durations of the order of tens or hundreds of milliseconds, then we must have means for observing the system's behavior at comparable intervals. A high temporal density of observations is essential for gathering data to test information processing theories.

We are still far short of having the range of methods we need to make observations with adequate frequency, but several techniques have proved themselves useful to this end. In tasks where varying numbers of repetitions of a single process can be postulated, chronometric techniques have been used effectively (as in the Sternberg paradigm, for example) to estimate process times as short as 25 or 50 milliseconds. Recordings of eye movements provide temporal data with resolutions down to a few hundreds of milliseconds. They can only be used in tasks or parts of tasks, however, where a visual display constitutes an important part of the stimulus. Finally, verbal protocols provide a rich source of data at densities comparable to the densities of eye movement records, and containing far more information per data point than the latter.

Some progress has been made in devising methods for encoding verbal protocols objectively and subjecting them to systematic analysis (Newell & Simon, 1972; Waterman & Newell, 1971).

In the research reported in this volume, Berl and her co-authors (Chapter 13) have made some use of verbal protocols. None of the other studies employ chronometry, eye movements, or protocols. It might be argued from this observation that the methodology of cognitive social psychology has not yet caught up with the important substantive shift that is occurring.

Formalism for Stating Theories

Progress in information-processing psychology requires adequate formal languages for describing the organization of processes and of semantic memory. The so-called list-processing languages for computers have now been used widely and successfully for this purpose. Abelson's script proposal and Schmidt's BELIEVER system are examples in the area of social psychology of this approach to formalism.

Formalization in terms of computer programs, expressed in list-processing languages, is something quite different from using flow charts as a kind of metaphor to describe processes and their organization. Flow charting, however, can serve as a useful first step toward the full formalization, and we see that step taken, for example, in the chapters by Frieze (Chapter 7) and Carroll and Payne (Chapter 2).

Individual Differences

A prominent characteristic of information-processing psychology has been its reluctance to lose information about individual differences by averaging data over subjects. This attention to the behavior of individual subjects, and consequently to individual differences, is encouraged and reinforced by the methodologies mentioned in the previous section—particularly the use of verbal protocols as data and the formalization of theory in computer programs that permit the behavior of individual subjects to be simulated.

As has already been remarked, this concern with individual differences is well represented in this volume, specifically by Frieze (Chapter 7), Shanteau and Nagy (Chapter 14), Staelin and Payne (Chapter 12), and Carroll and Payne (Chapter 2).

LINEAR DECISION RULES

Three of the chapters here, those by Dawes, Berl *et al.*, and Shanteau and Nagy, have a good deal to say about linear (additive) decision rules in multiple-criterion situations. Linear decision rules can be introduced in at least two ways: as a special case of maximizing subjective expected utility or simply as a pragmatic device (weighted average) for aggregating over numerous dimensions.

Consider a situation where we have a number of alternatives from which we wish to choose a "best" one. Each alternative can be characterized along a number of different dimensions. If we can assign to each dimension of each alternative a real number that measures the degree of goodness of that alternative on that dimension and, to each dimension, another number that measures the weight, or importance, of that dimension, then we can multiply weight by value for each dimension of an alternative and sum over all dimensions to obtain the total value or utility of that alternative. Obviously, the rational rule of choice under these circumstances is to select the alternative with the highest total value.

The linear decision rule is the special cast of utility maximization in which the weighted values along individual dimensions represent expected utilities, the dimensions do not interact with each other, and the total utility is an additive function of the component utilities.

The three chapters I have mentioned all treat linear decision rules in quite different terms, but in a curious way they all end up at the same point. Dawes (Chapter 1) reviews the evidence comparing the accuracy of linear decision rules with the accuracy of clinical judgments in situations where that accuracy can be checked against an objective external criterion. The studies he cites are virtually unanimous in showing that linear decision rules are always as accurate as, or more accurate then, skilled human clinical judgment. From these findings, Dawes draws one conclusion explicitly, and another implicitly. The implicit conclusion is that people generally do not use linear decision rules in making their clinical judgments, for if they did, the judgments would be more accurate than they actually are. The conclusion Dawes draws explicitly is a normative one: that we would all be better off if clinical judgment in a wide range of practical choice situations were replaced by linear decision rules. (This proposal supports the argument I have made that cognitive psychology is social psychology. For if many people read Dawes' paper and are convinced by it, then in fact we shall find linear decision rules being used widely in the actual process of human choice—something that Dawes says does not often happen now.)

Shanteau and Nagy (Chapter 14) are concerned with the description of behavior. They show that the behavior of subjects expressing preferences among alternative partners for a date can be described *as if* the subjects are maximizing expected utility. Their study does not include data on the choice process that would allow us to conclude that the subjects are actually maximizing utility; what is shown is simply that the behavior is not inconsistent with the maximization hypothesis. Note that in this study there is no question of whether the decision rule is valid, for there is no objectively correct choice. Instead, the question is whether people behave as utility maximizers.

The interest of Berl and her co-authors (Chapter 13) is similar to that of Shanteau and Nagy: they wish to describe how a student makes a choice among colleges. They find that a satisficing model gives reasonably good predictions of choice (better than two other models they test); but a simple unweighted linear decision rule gives even better predictions. Again, the information available on the actual process the students have gone through in making their choices does not provide any indication that they have used numerical values or averages of them—what is shown is that a linear decision rule makes good predictions of behavior. This study, as reported, only dealt with the students' final choices among colleges that had already accepted them for admission; quite a different model might be needed to account for their initial search behavior in deciding to which colleges they would apply.

What shall we make of all this? On the descriptive side, I must emphasize how little direct evidence is available about the second-by-second, or even hour-by-hour, course of the decision process. Nevertheless, if we do not believe that people actually maximize utility, or approach such a maximization by using a linear decision rule, we must explain why the human processes mimic such a rule so closely. Some hints as to the direction in which an explanation may lie can be found in a paper by Feldman and Newell (1961) on event-matching behavior. It is well known that if subjects are faced repeatedly with a choice between alternative A, which pays off 70% of the time, and alternative B, which pays off 30% of the time, in most circumstances they pick A in slightly more than 70% of the trials, and B in slightly less than 30% of the trials. This behavior is known as "event matching," and it is clearly suboptimal, for the best strategy is to choose A on every trial. The event-matching strategy would be rewarded, on average, on 58% of the trials, whereas the consistent choice of A would be rewarded on 70% of the trials.

Feldman and Newell showed the important result that event-matching behavior could be the byproduct of a wide range of subject strategies—most of them not involving explicit or intended event matching at all. In particular, if subjects were actually trying to find pattern in recent trials and to extrapolate that pattern to succeeding trials, their behavior would result in event matching.

The result found by Feldman and Newell for predictive behavior raises the possibility that some similar artifact may account for the frequent appearance of behavior mimicking the linear decision rule. For example, many of the experiments from which the evidence for the linear decision rule is drawn involve averaging over subjects. (This is not the case for the study by Shanteau and Nagy, however.) This averaging may tend to linearize the relations among the variables. Another, more interesting, possibility is that choice may involve successive attention to different dimensions of the alternatives, with the result that the alternative that is most often noted favorably is chosen.

Scepticism that the linear decision rule really describes the choice process, and not simply its outcome, is reinforced by the other studies reported here by Nisbett *et al.* (Chapter 8) and Hamilton (Chapter 6) showing that people are poor statisticians—that they do not handle successive pieces of evidence in the way that a Bayesian inference process would require. It is not plausible that subjects who exhibit grossly suboptimal behavior in using base data should suddenly become good utility maximizers when faced with multidimensional choices.

SOCIAL PSYCHOLOGY OF THE ONE AND THE MANY

In his comment, Klahr (Chapter 15) called attention to the fact that none of the chapters in this volume concerned themselves with social groups or interactions among people. Instead, they have all dealt with the social psychology of individual persons. The psychology is "social" only in the sense that the choices, judgments, or attributions being made have to do with other people.

The absence from the symposium of studies of group interaction cannot be because such interaction lacks cognitive content. There is no lack of intended, if bounded, rationality in the decision making that takes place in business concerns. I should conjecture that the emphasis on the individual to the exclusion of the group is more likely a consequence of the greater facility with which experiments can be carried out on individuals, combined with a reductionist belief that the behavior of groups is, after all, simply the aggregated behavior of the individuals who compose them.

I find myself warmly sympathetic with both arguments. In my previous incarnation as a social psychologist, I carried out or participated in a number of experiments on group behavior, several of them large-scale field experiments. They were full of grief and travail, from the moment I began the arduous task of negotiating access to a field situation to the final winnowing of enormous masses of data. I am in no position to cast the first, or even the second, stone at social psychologists who have retreated to the "social psychology of one," for I have retreated even a step further into individual cognitive psychology. I have rationalized that retreat with the same two arguments suggested above: the greater cost–effectiveness of individual studies and the reductionist argument that nothing more may be needed.

The reductionist argument must, however, be used with care. In particular, we must distinguish between in-principle reduction and in-practice reduction. It is very easy to say that all chemical reactions in nature are simply special cases of the behavior predicted by the Schrödinger equation. Most physical scientists would accept that proposition. It is another thing to say that only the simplest molecules and reactions need be studied in the laboratory, because the behavior of the others is merely an elaboration of the simplest cases. Such a strategy would have left us in ignorance of insulin, and of DNA, and of all the other great structures of molecular biology. In practice, we are not clever enough to infer the more complex phenomena from the laws we have extracted by study of the simpler. However devout our faith in in-principle reduction, that faith is no substitute for the empirical study of reality in all its complexity.

Moreover, even when we are able to explain complex behavior in terms of principles and mechanisms derived from the study of simpler components, establishing the relationships—both empirical and theoretical—between the component and composite phenomena is seldom a trivial task. It is certainly not one that should be neglected by social psychologists.

Let me mention one example of "emergent" phenomena, drawn from the dissertation of Kenneth Friend (1973). Friend studied three-man groups in a competitive bargaining situation. His interest was in predicting when each member of the group would speak and what he would say; what response he would make to an offer, or what new offer he would put forth. The experimental evidence showed definite regularities of response, and Friend was able to capture the principal regularities in a computer program that simulated the interaction. The program contained, of course, components designed to simulate the behavior rules of the individual participants, but it is not clear how the evidence for inferring or testing such rules could have been derived without running the group experiment. One could contemplate an experiment with one human subject and two computer-simulated partners, but this alternative would require enough to be known about the appropriate behavior of the simulated participants to write the simulation programs. The required knowledge, moreover, is essentially equivalent to the theory of interaction that is the object of the investigation.

No single symposium can cover a whole large topic without selection or omission. The intent of my comment is not to object to the particular way in which the boundaries of this one have been drawn, but to emphasize that we have only dealt with one of several important aspects of cognitive social psychology. There is room for another symposium in the future to look at cognition in the context of group interaction and human behavior in large organizations or even in social systems.

IMPLICATIONS FOR SOCIETY

This book has addressed itself to a considerable range of important human choice behaviors, including dating, buying, choosing a college, getting out of jail, and dying. This assortment of decisions will not quite carry us from the cradle to the grave, but it will very nearly do so. The chapters have been concerned with several central cognitive mechanisms, in particular, processes of decision making, person perception, and causal attribution. These are basic mechanisms for determining man's relationship to man. Understanding them and improving their operation is an important route toward the improvement of the quality of the personal and organizational lives of all of us.

However as Dawes (Chapter 1), Nisbett *et al.* (Chapter 8), and Slovic *et al.* (Chapter 11) show us, these mechanisms are important not only on a microlevel of interpersonal interactions, but also on a societal level. Dawes observes that it is one thing for social disasters to be caused by human malevolence and quite another thing for them to be caused by human stupidity. Making sound prescriptions for social problems requires that distinction to be made with accuracy; the cures for the two diseases will be very different.

Nisbett and his co-workers call attention to a bias in human information processing—the vastly greater influence of concrete as compared with abstract information upon our views and attitudes—that has serious, but largely unexplored, implications for social communication. Television, for example, is a medium that is almost exclusively adapted to communicating the concrete example rather than the abstract generalization. It has grave limitations as a means for drawing balanced samples from a complex reality. What are the consequences for opinion formation in a society that relies heavily upon a mass communication medium possessing these characteristics?

Finally, Slovic and his associates survey the numerous decisions made in our society that involve the balancing of risks against benefits. Some of these decisions are unprecedented in the scale of their consequences, if not the depth of uncertainty that surrounds them. We must balance, for example, our needs for economically priced energy against the environmental dangers of available energy sources, resource limitations, and the risks of nuclear accidents. The policy decisions our society makes in these and other risky situations must depend heavily on human decision-making processes and on the ways in which risks are treated by those processes.

Many of the problems of this kind have a large social psychological component. Moreover, they tend to be problems in the "psychology of one" instead of "many," hence amenable to the kinds of experimental techniques that have flourished in social psychology during the past decade and that have been exemplified in the material presented here. There is no lack of research opportunities here that combine social relevance of the most basic kind with deep scientific interest.

ACKNOWLEDGMENTS

This research has been supported by Public Health Service Grant MH-07722 from the National Institute of Mental Health.

References

Abelson, R. P. Simulation of social behavior. In G. Lindzey & E. Aronson (Eds.), *Handbook of social psychology*, Vol. 2. Reading, Mass.: Addison-Wesley, 1968. Pp. 274–356.

Abelson, R. P. Are attitudes necessary? In B. T. King & E. McGinnies (Eds.), *Attitudes, conflict, and social change*. New York: Academic Press, 1972. Pp. 19–32.

Abelson, R. P. Sentence figurality. Paper presented at the Eastern Psychological Association meeting, Philadelphia, 1974. (a)

Abelson, R. P. Social psychology's rational man. In G. W. Mortimore & S. I. Benn (Eds.), *The concept of rationality in the social sciences*. Boston: Routledge & Kegan Paul, 1974. (b)

Abelson, R. P. Concepts for representing mundane reality in plans. In D. G. Bobrow & A. M. Collins (Eds.), *Representation and understanding: Studies in cognitive science*. New York: Academic Press, 1975. Pp. 273–309. (a)

Abelson, R. P. The reasoner and the inferencer don't talk much to each other. Paper presented at the Workshop on Theoretical Issues in Natural Language Understanding, Massachusetts Institute of Technology, 1975. (b)

Abelson, R. P., & Kanouse, D. E. The acceptance of generic assertions. In S. Feldman (Ed.), *The consistency postulate in attitude theory and research*. New York: Academic Press, 1966. Pp. 173–197.

Acton, J. P. *Evaluating public programs to save lives: The case of heart attacks.* (Report No. R-950-RC) Santa Monica, Calif.: Rand Corporation, 1973.

Ajzen, I. Attribution of dispositions to an actor: Effects of perceived decision freedom and behavioral utilities. *Journal of Personality and Social Psychology,* 1971, *18,* 144–156.

Ajzen, I., & Fishbein, M. Attitudinal and normative variables as predictors of specific behaviors. *Journal of Personality and Social Psychology,* 1973, *27,* 41–57.

Alfven, H. Energy and environment. *Bulletin of the Atomic Scientists,* 1972, *28*(5), 5–8.

Allport, G. W. *The nature of prejudice.* Cambridge, Mass.: Addison-Wesley, 1954.

Anderson, J. R. *Language, memory, and thought.* Hillsdale, N. J.: Lawrence Erlbaum Assoc., 1976.

Anderson, J. R., & Bower, G. H. *Human associative memory.* Washington: Winston, 1973.

Anderson, N. H. Averaging versus adding as a stimulus-combination rule in impression formation. *Journal of Experimental Psychology,* 1965, *70,* 394–400.

Anderson, N. H. A simple model for information integration. In R. P. Abelson, E. Aronson,

W. J. McGuire, T. M. Newcomb, M. J. Rosenberg, & P. H. Tannenbaum (Eds.), *Theories of cognitive consistency: A sourcebook.* Chicago: Rand McNally, 1968. Pp. 731–743.

Anderson, N. H. Looking for configurality in clinical judgment. *Psychological Bulletin,* 1972, *78,* 93–102.

Anderson, N. H. Cognitive algebra: Integration theory applied to social attribution. In L. Berkowitz (Ed.), *Advances in experimental social psychology,* Vol. 7. New York: Academic Press, 1973. Pp. 1–192.

Anderson, N. H. Information integration theory: A brief survey. In D. H. Krantz, R. C. Atkinson, R. D. Luce, & P. Suppes (Eds.), *Contemporary developments in mathematical psychology,* Vol. 2. San Francisco: Freeman, 1974. Pp. 236–305. (a)

Anderson, N. H. Algebraic models in perception. In E. C. Carterette & M. P. Friedman (Eds.), *Handbook of perception,* Vol. 2. New York: Academic Press, 1974. (b)

Anderson, N. H., & Shanteau, J. Information integration in risky decision making. *Journal of Experimental Psychology,* 1970, *84,* 441–451.

Andrews, F. M., Morgan, J. N., & Sonquist, J. A. *Multiple classification analysis.* Ann Arbor: University of Michigan, Institute for Social Research, Survey Research Center, 1967.

Aristotle. *Prior analytics.* (H. Trendennick, translator) Cambridge, Mass.: Harvard University Press, 1938.

Asbjörnsen, P. C., & Moe, J. E. *[The three billy goats gruff].* (G. W. Desent, translator) New York: Harcourt, Brace, 1957.

Asch, S. E. Studies of independence and conformity: I. A minority of one against an unanimous majority. *Psychological Monographs,* 1956, *70*(9, Whole No. 416).

Attneave, F. *Applications of information theory to psychology: A summary of basic concepts, methods, and results.* New York: Holt, Rinehart and Winston, 1959.

Attneave, F. How do you know? *American Psychologist,* 1974, *29,* 493–499.

Averill, J. R. Personal control over aversive stimuli and its relationship to stress. *Psychological Bulletin,* 1973, *80,* 286–303.

Bainbridge, P. L. Learning in the rat: Effect of early experience with an unsolvable problem. *Journal of Comparative and Physiological Psychology,* 1973, *82,* 301–307.

Bales, R. F. *Interaction process analysis.* Cambridge, Mass.: Addison-Wesley, 1950.

Bandura, A. Vicarious processes: A case of no-trial learning. In L. Berkowitz (Ed.), *Advances in experimental social psychology,* Vol. 2. New York: Academic Press, 1965. Pp. 1–55.

Bar-Tal, D., & Frieze, I. Attributions of success and failure for actors and observers. *Journal of Research in Personality,* in press.

Beard, B. H. Fear of death and fear of life. *Archives of General Psychiatry,* 1969, *21,* 373–380.

Becker, H. *Outsiders.* New York: Free Press, 1963.

Beckman, L. J. Effects of students' performance on teachers' and observers' attributions of causality. *Journal of Educational Psychology,* 1970, *61,* 76–82.

Bem, D. J. Self-perception: An alternative interpretation of cognitive dissonance phenomena. *Psychological Review,* 1967, *74,* 183–200.

Berkson, J., Magath, T. B., & Hurn, M. The error of estimate of the blood cell count as made with the hemocytometer. *American Journal of Physiology,* 1940, *128,* 309–323.

Berscheid, E., Dion, K., Walster, E., & Walster, G. W. Physical attractiveness and dating choice: A test of the matching hypothesis. *Journal of Experimental Social Psychology,* 1971, *7,* 173–189.

Billig, M. Normative communication in a minimal intergroup situation. *European Journal of Social Psychology,* 1973, *3,* 339–343.

Billig, M., & Tajfel, H. Social categorization and similarity in intergroup behavior. *European Journal of Social Psychology,* 1973, *3,* 27–52.

Birnbaum, M. H. The devil rides again: Correlation as an index of fit. *Psychological Bulletin,* 1973, *79,* 239–242.

Bobrow, D. G., & Collins, A. M. (Eds.). *Representation and understanding: Studies in cognitive science.* New York: Academic Press, 1975.

Borgida, E., & Nisbett, R. The differential impact of abstract vs. concrete information on decisions. *Journal of Applied Social Psychology,* in press.

Bowman, E. H. Consistency and optimality in managerial decision making. *Management Science,* 1963, *9,* 310–321.

Brand, E. S., Ruiz, R. A., & Padilla, A. M. Ethnic identification and preference: A review. *Psychological Bulletin,* 1974, *81,* 860–890.

Braunstein, M. L. Perception of rotation in depth: A process model. *Psychological Review,* 1972, *79,* 510–524.

Brehmer, B. Hypotheses about relations between scaled variables in the learning of probabilistic inference tasks. *Organizational Behavior and Human Performance,* 1974, *11,* 1–27.

Brigham, J. C. Ethnic stereotypes. *Psychological Bulletin,* 1971, *76,* 15–38.

Brill, S. The secrecy behind the college boards. *New York Magazine,* 1974, *7*(40), 67–83.

Brody, E. Seeking appropriate options for living arrangements. In E. Pfeiffer (Ed.), *Alternatives to institutional care for older Americans: Practice and planning.* Durham. N. C.: Duke University, Center for Study of Aging and Human Development, 1973. Pp. 64–72.

Brown, G. *The BELIEVER system.* (NIH Report CBM-TR-33) New Brunswick, N. J.: Rutgers University, Computer Science Department, 1974.

Bruce, B. C. *Belief systems and language understanding.* (NIH Report CEM-TR-41) New Brunswick, N. J.: Rutgers University, Computer Science Department, 1975.

Bruce, B. C. & Schmidt, C. F. Episode understanding and belief guided parsing. Paper presented at the Association for Computational Linguistics Meeting, Amherst, Mass., July, 1974.

Bruner, J. S., Goodnow, J. J., & Austin, G. A. *A study of thinking.* New York: John Wiley, 1956.

Bryan, W. B. Testimony before the subcommittee on state energy policy. California State Assembly, Committee on Planning, Land Use, and Energy, February 1, 1974.

Burton, I., Kates, R. W., & White, G. F. *The human ecology of extreme geophysical events.* (Natural Hazard Working Paper No. 1) Toronto: University of Toronto, Department of Geography, 1968.

Carder, B., & Berkowitz, K. Rats' preference for earned in comparison with free food. *Science,* 1970, *167,* 1273–1274.

Carroll, J. S., Payne, J. W., Frieze, I., & Girard, D. L. Attribution theory: An information processing approach. Unpublished manuscript, Carnegie–Mellon University, 1975.

Carter, R. M. The presentence report and decision making process. *Journal of Research in Crime and Delinquency,* 1967, *4,* 203–211.

Chaikin, A. L. The effects of four outcome schedules on persistence, liking for the task and attributions of causality. *Journal of Psychology,* 1971, *39,* 512–526.

Chapman, L. J. Illusory correlation in observational report. *Journal of Verbal Learning and Verbal Behavior,* 1967, *6,* 151–155.

Chapman, L. J., & Chapman, J. P. Genesis of popular but erroneous psychodiagnostic observations. *Journal of Abnormal Psychology,* 1967, *72,* 193–204.

Chapman, L. J., & Chapman, J. P. Illusory correlation as an obstacle to the use of valid psychodiagnostic signs. *Journal of Abnormal Psychology,* 1969, *74,* 271–280.

Chase, W. G., & Simon, H. A. The mind's eye in chess. In W. G. Chase (Ed.), *Visual information processing.* New York: Academic Press, 1973.

Cleary, T. A. Test bias: Prediction of grades of Negro and white students in integrated colleges. *Journal of Educational Measurement,* 1968, *5,* 115–124.

Cliff, N. Adverbs as multipliers. *Psychological Review,* 1959, *66,* 27–44.

Cole, N. S. Bias in selection. *Journal of Educational Measurement,* 1973, *10,* 237–255.

Coombs, C. H. *A theory of data.* New York: Wiley, 1964.

Coombs, C. H., & Huang, L. Tests of a portfolio theory of risk preference. *Journal of Experimental Psychology,* 1970, *85,* 23–29.

Coombs, C. H., Dawes, R. M., & Tversky, A. *Mathematical psychology: An elementary introduction.* Englewood Cliffs, N. J.: Prentice-Hall, 1970.

Cooper, J., Jones, E. E., & Tuller, S. M. Attribution, dissonance, and the illusion of uniqueness. *Journal of Experimental Social Psychology,* 1972, *8,* 45–57.

Crespi, I. What kinds of attitude measures are predictive of behavior? *Public Opinion Quarterly,* 1971, *35,* 327–334.

Cunningham, J. D., & Kelley, H. Causal attributions for interpersonal events of varying magnitude. *Journal of Personality,* 1975, *43,* 74–93.

Dalrymple, W. Letters: Medical school admissions. *Science,* 1974, *186,* 93.

Darley, J. M., & Latane, B. Bystander intervention in emergencies: Diffusion of responsibility. *Journal of Personality and Social Psychology,* 1968, *8,* 377–383.

Darlington, R. B. Another look at "cultural fairness." *Journal of Educational Measurement,* 1971, *8,* 71–82.

Davis, W. L., & Phares, E. J. Internal-external control as a determinant of information-seeking in a social influence situation. *Journal of Personality,* 1967, *35,* 547–561.

Dawes, R. M. Cognitive distortion. *Psychological Reports,* 1964, *14,* 443–459.

Dawes, R. M. A case study of graduate admissions: Application of three principles of human decision making. *American Psychologist,* 1971, *26,* 180–188. (a)

Dawes, R. M. The effects of repeating on test scores of the graduate record examination are overwhelmingly significant. *ORI Technical Report,* 1971, *11*(3). (b)

Dawes, R. M. An inequality concerning correlation of composites vs. composites of correlation. *Methodological Note,* 1971, *1*(1). (c)

Dawes, R. M. The role of the expert in constructing predictive systems. *Proceedings of the 1974 Conference on IEEE Systems, Man and Cybernetics.* Dallas, Texas: IEEE Systems, Man and Cybernetics Society, 1974.

Dawes, R. M. Graduate admission variables and future success. *Science,* 1975, *187,* 721–723. (a)

Dawes, R. M. The mind, the model, and the task. In F. Restle, R. M. Shiffrin, N. J. Castellan, H. R. Lindman, & D. P. Pisoni (Eds.), *Cognitive theory,* Vol. 1. Hillsdale, N. J.: Lawrence Erlbaum Assoc., 1975. Pp. 119–129. (b)

Dawes, R. M., & Corrigan, B. Linear models in decision making. *Psychological Bulletin,* 1974, *81,* 95–106.

deGroot, A. D. *Het Denken van den Schaker.* The Hague: Mouton, 1965. (translated as *Thought and Choice in Chess.*)

Denenberg, H. S. Nuclear power: Uninsurable. *Congressional Record,* November 25. Washington, D.C.: U. S. Government Printing Office, 1974.

Dillehay, R. C. On the irrelevance of the classical negative evidence concerning the effect of attitude on behavior. *American Psychologist,* 1973, *28,* 887–891.

Dion, K. L. Cohesiveness as a determinant of ingroup-outgroup bias. *Journal of Personality and Social Psychology,* 1973, *28,* 163–171.

Doise, W., Csepeli, G., Dann, H. D., Gouge, C., Larsen, K., & Ostell, A. An experimental investigation into the formation of intergroup representations. *European Journal of Social Psychology,* 1972, *2,* 202–204.

Doise, W., & Sinclair, A. The categorisation process in intergroup relations. *European Journal of Social Psychology,* 1973, *3,* 145–157.

Dunker, K. On problem solving. *Psychological Monographs,* 1945, *58*(5, Whole No. 270).

Edwards, W. The theory of decision making. *Psychological Bulletin,* 1954, *41,* 380–418.

Edwards, W. Behavioral decision theory. *Annual Review of Psychology*, 1961, *12*, 473–498.

Edwards, W. Conservatism in human information processing. In B. Kleinmuntz (Ed.), *Formal representation of human judgment*. New York: John Wiley, 1968. Pp. 17–52.

Edwards, W., & Phillips, L. D. Man as transducer for probabilities in Bayesian command and control systems. In M. W. Shelley, II, & G. L. Bryan (Eds.), *Human judgments and optimality*. New York: John Wiley, 1964. Pp. 360–401.

Edwards, W., & Tversky, A. (Eds.) *Decision making*. Baltimore: Penguin Books, 1967.

Ehrlich, H. J. *The social psychology of prejudice*. New York: John Wiley, 1973.

Einhorn, H. J. The use of nonlinear, noncompensatory models as a function of task and amount of information. *Organizational Behavior and Human Performance*, 1971, *6*, 1–27.

Einhorn, H. J. Expert measurement and mechanical combination. *Organizational Behavior and Human Performance*, 1972, *7*, 86–106.

Einhorn, H. J. Expert judgment: Some necessary conditions and an example. *Journal of Applied Psychology*, 1974, *59*, 562–571.

Einhorn, H. J., & Bass, A. R. Methodological considerations relevant to discrimination in employment testing. *Psychological Bulletin*, 1971, *75*, 261–269.

Einhorn, H. J., & Hogarth, R. M. Unit weighting schemes for decision making. *Organizational Behavior and Human Performance*, 1975, *13*, 171–192.

Eisdorfer, C. Background and theories of aging. In G. L. Maddox (Ed.), *The future of aging and the aged*. Atlanta, Ga.: Southern Newspapers Publishers Association Foundation, 1971.

Eisendrath, R. M. The role of grief and fear in the death of kidney transplant patients. *American Journal of Psychiatry*, 1969, *126*, 381–387.

Elig, T. W., & Frieze, I. A multi-dimensional scheme for coding and interpreting perceived causality for success and failure events: The CSPC. *JSAS: Catalog of Selected Documents in Psychology*, 1975.

Engel, J. F., Kollat, D. T., & Blackwell, R. D. *Consumer behavior*. New York: Holt, Rinehart and Winston, 1968.

Erdmann, P. The Oil War of 1976: How the Shah won the world. *New York Magazine*, 7(48), 39–51.

Farley, J. V., & Ring, L. W. An empirical test of the Howard–Sheth model of buyer behavior. *Journal of Marketing Research*, 1970, *7*, 427–438.

Feather, N. T. Valence of outcome and expectation of success in relation to task difficulty and perceived locus of control. *Journal of Personality and Social Psychology*, 1967, *7*, 372–386.

Feather, N. T., & Simon, J. G. Attribution of responsibility and valence of outcome in relation to initial confidence and success and failure of self and other. *Journal of Personality and Social Psychology*, 1971, *18*, 173–188. (a)

Feather, N. T., & Simon, J. G. Causal attributions for success and failure in relation to expectations of success based upon selective or manipulative control. *Journal of Personality*, 1971, *39*, 527–541. (b)

Feldman, J., & Newell, A. A note on a class of probability matching models. *Psychometrika*, 1961, *26*, 333–337.

Festinger, L. *A theory of cognitive dissonance*. Stanford, Calif.: Stanford University Press, 1957.

Fischhoff, B. Hindsight: Thinking backward? *ORI Research Monograph*, 1974, *14*, 1.

Fischhoff, B. Hindsight ≠ foresight: The effect of outcome knowledge on judgment under uncertainty. *Journal of Experimental Psychology: Human Perception and Performance*, 1975, *1*, 288–299.

Fischhoff, B., & Beyth, R. "I knew it would happen"–Remembering probabilities of once future things. *Organizational Behavior and Human Performance*, 1975, *13*, 1–16.

Fitts, P. M., & Posner, M. I. *Human performance*. Belmont, Calif.: Brooks/Cole, 1967.

Fontaine, G. Social comparison and some determinants of expected personal control and expected performance in a novel task situation. *Journal of Personality and Social Psychology,* 1974, *29,* 487–496.

Fontaine, G. Causal attribution in simulated versus real situations: When are people logical, and when are they not? *Journal of Personality and Social Psychology,* 1975, *32,* 1021–1029.

Foss, F. J., & Harwood, D. A. Memory for sentences: Implications for human associative memory. *Journal of Verbal Learning and Verbal Behavior,* 1975, *14,* 1–16.

Freud, S. [*Collected papers of Sigmund Freud*]. (J. Riviere, translator) London: Hogarth, 1951.

Friend, K. E. An information processing approach to small group interaction in a coalition formation game. Unpublished doctoral dissertation, Carnegie–Mellon University, 1973.

Frieze, I. Studies of information processing and the attributional process in achievement-related contexts. Unpublished doctoral dissertation, University of California at Los Angeles, 1973.

Frieze, I. Causal attributions and information seeking to explain success and failure. *Journal of Research in Personality,* in press.

Frieze, I. Sequential cue utilization for attributional judgments for success and failure. Manuscript submitted for publication, 1975a.

Frieze, I. Patterns of information utilization for attributional judgments for success and failure. Manuscript submitted for publication, 1975b.

Frieze, I., & LaVoie, A. A comparison of causal attributions for success and failure in a real and in a simulated situation. Unpublished manuscript, University of California at Los Angeles, 1972.

Frieze, I., & Weiner, B. Cue utilization and attributional judgments for success and failure. *Journal of Personality,* 1971, *39,* 591–605.

Gallup, G. Crime named more often than economic problems as top city problem. *Crime in America Series,* Part 1. Gallup poll, July 27, 1975.

Geer, J. H., & Maisel, E. Evaluating the effects of the prediction-control confound. *Journal of Personality and Social Psychology,* 1972, *23,* 314–319.

Gerristen, R., Gregg, L. W., & Simon, H. A. *Task structure and subject strategies as determinants of latencies.* (Complex Information Processing Working Paper No. 292) Pittsburgh: Carnegie–Mellon University, 1975.

Ghiselli, E. E. *Theory of psychological measurement.* New York: McGraw-Hill, 1964.

Gillette, R., & Walsh, J. San Fernando earthquake study: NRC panel sees premonitory lessons. *Science,* 1971, *172,* 140–143.

Glaser, D. *The effectiveness of a prison and parole system.* Indianapolis: Bobbs-Merrill, 1964.

Goldberg, L. R. Diagnosticians versus diagnostic signs: The diagnosis of psychosis versus neurosis from the MMPI. *Psychological Monographs,* 1965, *79*(9, Whole No. 602).

Goldberg, L. R. Simple models or simple processes? Some research on clinical judgments. *American Psychologist,* 1968, *23,* 483–496.

Goldberg, L. R. Man versus model of man: A rationale, plus some evidence, for a method of improving on clinical inferences. *Psychological Bulletin,* 1970, *73,* 422–432.

Golding, S. L., & Rorer, L. G. Illusory correlation and subjective judgment. *Journal of Abnormal Psychology,* 1972, *80,* 249–260.

Goodson, J. *An investigation of memory for interpersonal episodes.* (NIH Report CBM-TM-46) New Brunswick, N. J.: Rutgers University, Computer Science Department, 1975.

Gottesman, L. E. The institutionalized elderly: A new challenge. In G. L. Maddox (Ed.), *The future of aging and the aged.* Atlanta, Ga.: Southern Newspapers Publishers Association Foundation, 1971. Pp. 54–68.

Gottfredson, D. M., Wilkins, L. T., Hoffman, P. B., & Singer, S. *The utilization of experience in parole decision-making: A progress report.* Davis, Calif.: National Council on Crime and Delinquency Research Center, 1973.

Green, P. E., & Rao, U. R. Multidimensional scaling and individual differences. *Journal of Marketing Research,* 1971, *8,* 71–77.

Halberstam, D. *The best and the brightest.* New York: Random House, 1972.

Hamilton, D. L., & Gifford, R. K. Influence of implicit personality theories on cue utilization in interpersonal judgment. Paper presented at the annual meeting of the American Psychological Association, 1970.

Hamilton, D. L., & Gifford, R. K. Illusory correlation in interpersonal perception: A cognitive basis of stereotypic judgments. *Journal of Experimental Social Psychology,* 1976, *12,* 392–407.

Hammerton, M. A case of radical probability estimation. *Journal of Experimental Psychology,* 1973, *101,* 252–254.

Hammond, K. R. Human judgment and social policy. Unpublished manuscript, University of Colorado, Institute of Behavioral Science, Program of Research on Human Judgment and Social Interaction, Report No. 170. 1974.

Hammond, K. R. & Summers, D. A. Cognitive dependence on linear and nonlinear cues. *Psychological Review,* 1965, *72,* 215–224.

Harlow, H. F. The heterosexual affection system in monkeys. In W. G. Bennis, E. H. Schein, F. I. Steele, & D. E. Berlew (Eds.), *Interpersonal dynamics* (rev. ed.). Homewood, Ill.: Dorsey, 1968. Pp. 43–60.

Hastorf, A. H., & Cantril, H. They saw a game: A case study. *Journal of Abnormal and Social Psychology,* 1954, *49,* 129–134.

Haviland, S. E., & Clark, H. H. What's new? Acquiring new information as a process in comprehension. *Journal of Verbal Learning and Verbal Behavior,* 1974, *13,* 512–521.

Hayes, J. R. Human data processing limits in decision-making. In E. Bennett (Ed.), *Information system science and engineering. Proceedings of the First International Congress on the Information Systems Sciences.* New York: McGraw-Hill, 1964.

Heider, F. Social perception and phenomenal causality. *Psychological Review,* 1944, *51,* 358–374.

Heider, F. *The psychology of interpersonal relations.* New York: Wiley, 1958.

Hendrick, C., Mills, J., & Kiesler, C. A. Decision time as a function of the number and complexity of equally attractive alternatives. *Journal of Personality and Social Psychology,* 1968, *8,* 313–318.

Henrion, M. The limits of human stupidity. Unpublished manuscript, Carnegie–Mellon University, 1975.

Hirshleifer, J., Bergstrom, T., & Rappaport, E. Appendix 1: Applying cost-benefit concepts to projects which alter human mortality. In T. Bergstrom (Ed.), *Preference and choice in matters of life and death.* (Report No. ENG-7478) Los Angeles: University of California, School of Engineering and Applied Science, 1974.

Hoffman, P. B. *Paroling policy feedback.* (Supplemental Report 8) Davis, Calif.: National Council on Crime and Delinquency Research Center, 1973.

Hoffman, P. B., Beck, J. L., & DeGostin, L. K. *The practical application of a severity scale.* (Supplemental Report 13) Davis, California: National Council on Crime and Delinquency Research Center, 1973.

Hoffman, P. B., & Goldstein, H. M. *Do experience tables matter?* (Supplemental Report 4) Davis, Calif.: National Council on Crime and Delinquency Research Center, 1973.

Hoffman, P. J. The paramorphic representation of clinical judgment. *Psychological Bulletin,* 1960, *57,* 116–131.

Hoffman, P. J. Cue-consistency and configurality in human judgment. In B. Kleinmuntz (Ed.), *Formal representation of human judgment.* New York: John Wiley, 1968.

Hoffman, P. J., Slovic, P., & Rorer, L. G. An analysis-of-variance model for the assessment of configural cue utilization in clinical judgment. *Psychological Bulletin*, 1968, *69*, 338–349.

Hogarth, J. *Sentencing as a human process.* Toronto: University of Toronto Press, 1971.

Holmes, R. Composition and size of flood losses. In G. F. White (Ed.), *Papers on flood problems.* (Research Paper No. 70) Chicago: University of Chicago, Department of Geography, 1961.

Holmes, R. On the economic welfare of victims of automobile accidents. *American Economic Review,* 1970, *60*, 143–152.

Howard, J. A., & Sheth, J. N. *The theory of buyer behavior.* New York: Wiley, 1969.

Huston, T. L. Ambiguity of acceptance, social desirability, and dating choice. *Journal of Experimental Social Psychology,* 1973, *9*, 32–42.

Jacoby, J., Speller, D. E., & Berning, C. Brand choice behavior as a function of information load. *Journal of Marketing Research,* 1974, *11*, 63–69.

Janis, I. L., & Mann, L. *Decision making: A psychological analysis of conflict, choice, and commitment.* New York: Free Press, in press.

Jensen, G. D. Preference for bar pressing over "freeloading" as a function of number of rewarded presses. *Journal of Experimental Psychology,* 1963, *65*, 451–454.

Jervis, R. How decision-makers learn from history. In R. Jervis (Ed.), *Perception and misperception in international relations.* Princeton, N. J.: Princeton University Press, in press.

Jones, E., & Davis, K. From acts to dispositions. In L. Berkowitz (Ed.), *Advances in experimental social psychology,* Vol. 2. New York: Academic Press, 1965. Pp. 219–267.

Jones, E., & Goethals, G. R. *Order effects in impression formation: Attribution context and the nature of the entity.* Morristown, N. J.: General Learning Press, 1971.

Jones, E., & Harris, V. A. The attribution of attitudes. *Journal of Experimental Social Psychology,* 1967, *3*, 1–24.

Jones, E., Rock, L., Shaver, K. G., Goethals, G. R., & Ward, L. M. Pattern of performance and ability attribution: An unexpected primacy effect. *Journal of Personality and Social Psychology,* 1968, *10*, 317–340.

Jones, R. A., Stoll, J., Solernou, J., Noble, A., Fiala, J., & Miller, K. Availability and stereotype formation. Unpublished manuscript, University of Kentucky, 1975.

Kahneman, D., & Tversky, A. Subjective probability: A judgment of representativeness. *Cognitive Psychology,* 1972, *3*, 430–454.

Kahneman, D., & Tversky, A. On the psychology of prediction. *Psychological Review,* 1973, *80*, 237–251.

Kapla, E. J., & Brickman, P. Consistency vs. discrepancy as clues in the attribution of intelligence and motivation. *Journal of Personality and Social Psychology,* 1971, *20*, 223–229.

Kastenbaum, R., & Kastenbaum, B. S. Hope, survival, and the caring environment. In E. Palmore & F. C. Jeffers (Eds.), *Prediction of life span.* Lexington, Mass.: Heath Lexington, 1971. Pp. 249–272.

Kastenmeier, R., & Eglit, H. Parole release decision-making: Rehabilitation, expertise, and the demise of mythology. *American University Law Review,* 1973, *22*, 477–525.

Kates, R. W. *Hazard and choice perception in flood plain management.* (Research Paper No. 78) Chicago: University of Chicago, Department of Geography, 1962.

Katz, D., & Braly, K. Racial stereotypes of one hundred college students. *Journal of Abnormal and Social Psychology,* 1933, *28*, 280–290.

Katz, D., Sarnoff, I., & McClintock, C. G. Ego-defense and attitude change. *Human Relations,* 1956, *9*, 27–45.

Kaufman, M. T. *The New York Times,* October 18, 1973.

Kelley, H. Attribution theory in social psychology. In D. Levine (Ed.), *Nebraska Symposium on Motivation.* Lincoln: University of Nebraska Press, 1967. Pp. 192–241.

Kelley, H. *Attribution in social interaction.* Morristown, N. J.: General Learning Press, 1971.

Kelley, H. *Causal schemata and the attribution process.* Morristown, N. J.: General Learning Press, 1972.

Kelley, H. The processes of causal attribution. *American Psychologist,* 1973, *28,* 107–128.

Kidner, R., & Richards, K. Compensation to dependants of accident victims. *Economic Journal,* 1974, *84,* 130–142.

Kiesler, C. A., Collins, B. E., & Miller, N. *Attitude change: A critical analysis of theoretical approaches.* New York: Wiley, 1969.

Kimball, C. P. Psychological responses to the experience of open heart surgery: I. *American Journal of Psychiatry.* 1969, *126,* 348–359.

Kingsnorth, R. Decision-making in a parole bureaucracy. *Journal of Research in Crime and Delinquency,* 1969, *6,* 210–218.

Kintsch, W. *The representation of meaning in memory.* Hillsdale, N. J.: Lawrence Erlbaum Assoc., 1974.

Kleck, R. E., & Rubenstein, C. Physical attractiveness, perceived attitude similarity, and interpersonal attraction in an opposite-sex-encounter. *Journal of Personality and Social Psychology,* 1975, *31,* 107–114.

Knight, F. H. *Risk, uncertainty and profit.* Boston and New York: Houghton Mifflin, 1921.

Krantz, D. H., Luce, R. D., Suppes, P., & Tversky, A. *Foundations of measurement,* Vol. 1. New York: Academic Press, 1971.

Kubler-Ross, E. *On death and dying.* New York: Macmillan, 1969.

Kun, A., & Weiner, B. Necessary versus sufficient causal schemata for success and failure. *Journal of Research in Personality,* 1973, *7,* 197–207.

Kunreuther, H. *Recovery from natural disasters: Insurance or federal aid?* Washington, D. C.: American Enterprise Institute for Public Policy Research, 1973.

Lambert, W. W. Stimulus-response contiguity and reinforcement theory in social psychology. In G. Lindzey (Ed.), *Handbook of social psychology,* Vol. 1. Cambridge, Mass.: Addison-Wesley, 1954. Pp. 57–90.

Lampel, A. K., & Anderson, N. H. Combining visual and verbal information in an impression-formation task. *Journal of Personality and Social Psychology,* 1968, *9,* 1–6.

Langer, E. J., & Abelson, R. P. The semantics of asking a favor: How to succeed in getting help without really dying. *Journal of Personality and Social Psychology,* 1972, *24,* 26–32.

Lanzetta, J. T., & Driscoll, J. M. Preference for information about an uncertain but unavoidable outcome. *Journal of Personality and Social Psychology,* 1966, *3,* 96–102.

Lave, L. B., & Weber, W. E. A benefit-cost analysis of auto safety features. *Applied Economics,* 1970, *2,* 265–275.

Lawless, E. *Technical and social shock.* New Brunswick, N. J.: Rutgers University Press, 1975.

Lepper, M. R., Greene, D., & Nisbett, R. E. Undermining children's intrinsic interest with extrinsic reward: A test of the "overjustification" hypothesis. *Journal of Personality and Social Psychology,* 1973, *28,* 129–137.

LeShan, L. A basic psychological orientation apparently associated with malignant disease. *Psychiatric Quarterly,* 1961, *35,* 314–330.

Lewis, G., & Morrison, S. *A longitudinal study of college selection.* (Tech. Rep. 2) Pittsburgh: Carnegie–Mellon University, School of Urban and Public Affairs, 1975.

Lewis, G., Morrison, S., Penz, A., & Wicinas, B. *Unprogrammed decision making.* (Tech. Rep. 1) Pittsburgh: Carnegie–Mellon University, School of Urban and Public Affairs, 1974.

Lichtenstein, S., & Slovic, P. Reversals of performance between bids and choices in gambling decisions. *Journal of Experimental Psychology,* 1971, *89,* 46–55.

Lichtenstein, S., & Slovic, P. Response-induced reversals of preference in gambling: An extended replication in Las Vegas. *Journal of Experimental Psychology*, 1973, *101*, 16–20.

Lindzey, G. (Ed.). *Handbook of social psychology*, Vols. 1 & 2. Cambridge, Mass.: Addison-Wesley, 1954.

Lippmann, W. *Public opinion*. New York: Harcourt Brace, 1922.

Littman, D. The cognitive revolution. Unpublished manuscript, University of Oregon, 1969.

Luce, R. D. Semi-orders and a theory of utility discrimination. *Econometrica*, 1956, *24*, 178–191.

Luce, R. D., & Suppes, P. Preferences, utility, and subjective probability. In R. D. Luce, R. R. Bush, & E. Galanter (Eds.), *Handbook of mathematical psychology*, Vol. 3. New York: Wiley, 1965.

Lyon, D., & Slovic, P. On the tendency to ignore base rates when estimating probabilities. *ORI Research Bulletin*, 1975, *15*, 1.

MacCrimmon, K. R. An overview of multiple objective decision making. In J. L. Cochrane & M. Zeleny (Eds.), *Multiple criteria decision making*. Columbia: University of South Carolina Press, 1973. Pp. 18–44.

Manis, M., & Platt, M. B. Referential redundancy in the integration of verbal information. In M. F. Kaplan & S. Schwartz (Eds.), *Human judgment and decision processes*. New York: Academic Press, 1975. Pp. 173–200.

Mason, R. O. A dialectical approach to strategic planning. *Management Science*, 1969, *15*, B403–B414.

May, E. R. *"Lessons" of the past: The use and misuse of history in American foreign policy.* New York: Oxford University Press, 1973.

McArthur, L. The how and what of why: Some determinants and consequences of causal attribution. *Journal of Personality and Social Psychology*, 1972, *22*, 171–193.

McArthur, L. The lesser influence of consensus than distinctiveness information on causal attributions: A test of the person–thing hypothesis. *Journal of Personality and Social Psychology*, 1976, *33*, 733–742.

McConnell, J. D. The price-quality relationship in an experimental setting. *Journal of Marketing Research*, 1968, *5*, 300–303.

McKegney, F., & Lange, P. The decision to no longer live on chronic dialysis. *American Journal of Psychiatry*, 1971, *128*, 267.

Meehl, P. E. *Clinical versus statistical prediction: A theoretical analysis and a review of the literature.* Minneapolis: University of Minnesota Press, 1954.

Meehl, P. E. Clinical versus statistical prediction. *Journal of Experimental Research in Personality*, 1965, *63*, 81–97. (a)

Meehl, P. E. Seer over sign: The first good example. *Journal of Experimental Research in Personality*, 1965, *63*, 27–32. (b)

Meehl, P. E., & Rosen, A. Antecedent probability and the efficiency of psychometric signs, patterns, or cutting scores. *Psychological Bulletin*, 1955, *52*, 194–216.

Mehrabian, A. *Nonverbal communication*. Chicago: Aldine-Atherton, 1972.

Melges, F. T., & Bolby, J. Types of hopelessness in the psychopathological process. *Archives of General Psychiatry*, 1969, *20*, 690–699.

Mertz, W. H., & Doherty, M. E. The influence of task characteristics on strategies of cue combination. *Organizational Behavior and Human Performance*, 1974, *12*, 196–216.

Milgram, S. Behavioral studies of obedience. *Journal of Abnormal and Social Psychology*, 1963, *67*, 371–378.

Milgram, S., & Stotland, R. L. *Television and anti-social behavior: Field experiments.* New York: Academic Press, 1973.

Miller, G. A. The magical number seven, plus or minus two: Some limits on our capacity for processing information. *Psychological Review*, 1956, *63*, 81–97.

Miller, A. G., Gillen, B., Schenker, C., & Radlove, S. Perception of obedience to authority.

Proceedings of the 81st Annual Convention of the American Psychological Association, 1973, *8*, 127–128.

Miller, M. The indeterminate sentence paradigm: Resocialization or social control? *Issues in Criminology*, 1972, *7*, 101–121.

Miller, W. B. Ideology and criminal justice policy: Some current issues. *Journal of Criminal Law and Criminology*, 1973, *64*, 141–162.

Minsky, M. A framework for representing knowledge. In P. Winston (Ed.), *The psychology of computer vision*. New York: McGraw-Hill, 1975. Pp. 211–277.

Mischel, W. Toward a cognitive social learning reconceptualization of personality. *Psychological Review*, 1973, *80*, 252–283.

Mishan, E. J. Evaluation of life and limb: A theoretical approach. *Journal of Political Economy*, 1971, *79*, 687–705.

Murphy, G., & Murphy, L. B. *Experimental social psychology*. New York: Harper & Brothers, 1931.

Nagy, G. Female dating strategies as a function of physical attractiveness and other social characteristics of males. Unpublished masters thesis, Kansas State University, 1975.

Nagy, G., Jewett, R., & Shanteau, J. *Comparison of dating strategies for males and females.* (Rep. No. 76-6) Lawrence: Kansas State University, 1976.

Nagy, G., Ruggles, B., & Shanteau, J. *Influence of compatibility, probability, and physical attractiveness in dating choice.* (Rep. No. 76-7) Lawrence: Kansas State University, 1976.

National Advisory Committee on Criminal Justice Standards and Goals. *Task force report: Correction.* Washington, D. C.: U. S. Government Printing Office, 1973.

Neter, J., & Wasserman, W. *Applied linear statistical models.* Homewood, Ill.: Irwin, 1974.

Neuringer, A. J. Animals respond for food in the presence of free food. *Science*, 1969, *166*, 399–401.

Newcomb, T. M. *Social psychology.* New York: Dryden, 1950.

Newell, A., & Simon, H. A. Computer simulation of human thinking. *Science*, 1961, *134*, 2011–2017.

Newell, A., & Simon, H. A. *Human problem solving.* Englewood Cliffs, N. J.: Prentice-Hall, 1972.

Newman, J., & Staelin, R. Information sources of durable goods. *Journal of Advertising Research*, 1973, *13*(2), 19–30.

Newsweek. Cause of death: Fright. December 27, 1965, p. 62.

Newsweek. How recession can kill. November 30, 1970, p. 62.

Nicosia, F. M. *Consumer decision processes.* Englewood Cliffs, N. J.: Prentice-Hall, 1966.

Nisbett, R., & Borgida, E. Attribution and the psychology of prediction. *Journal of Personality and Social Psychology*, 1975, *32*, 932–943.

Nisbett, R., Caputo, C., Legant, P., & Marecek, J. Behavior as seen by the actor and as seen by the observer. *Journal of Personality and Social Psychology*, 1973, *27*, 154–164.

Nisbett, R., & Schachter, S. Cognitive manipulation of pain. *Journal of Experimental Social Psychology*, 1966, *2*, 227–236.

Norman, D. A., Rumelhart, D. E., & Group, L. N. R. *Explorations in cognition.* San Francisco: Freeman, 1975.

Orvis, B. R., Cunningham, J. D., & Kelley, H. A closer examination of causal inference: The role of consensus, distinctiveness and consistency information. *Journal of Personality and Social Psychology*, 1975, *32*, 605–616.

Oskamp, S. Overconfidence in case-study judgments. *Journal of Consulting Psychology*, 1965, *29*, 261–265.

Parsons, J., & Ruble, D. Attributional processes related to the development of achievement-related affect and expectancy. Paper presented at the annual meeting of the American Psychological Association, Hawaii, 1972.

Payne, J. W. Alternative approaches to decision making under risk: Moments vs. risk dimensions. *Psychological Bulletin,* 1973, *80,* 439–453.

Payne, J. W. Relation of perceived risk to preferences among gambles. *Journal of Experimental Psychology: Human Perception and Performance,* 1975, *104,* 86–94.

Payne, J. W. An information search and protocol analysis of decision making as a function of task complexity. *Organizational Behavior and Human Performance,* in press.

Petronko, M. R., & Perin, C. T. A consideration of cognitive complexity and primacy-recency effects in impression formation. *Journal of Personality and Social Psychology,* 1970, *15,* 151–157.

Pfeiffer, E. Introduction to the conference report. In E. Pfeiffer (Ed.), *Alternatives to institutional care for older Americans: Practice and planning.* Durham, N. C.: Duke University, Center for Aging and Human Development, 1973. Pp. 3–9.

Phillips, D. Dying as a form of social behavior. Paper presented at the annual meeting of the American Sociological Association, 1969.

Piliavin, I., Rodin, J., & Piliavin, J. Good samaritanism: An underground phenomenon? *Journal of Personality and Social Psychology,* 1969, *13,* 289–299.

Plato. *Five great dialogues.* New York: Black, 1942.

Posner, M. I. *Cognition: An introduction.* Glenview, Ill.: Scott, Foresman, 1973.

Rabbie, J. M., & Horwitz, M. Arousal of ingroup-outgroup bias by a chance win or loss. *Journal of Personality and Social Psychology,* 1969, *13,* 269–277.

Rappaport, E. Appendix 2: Economic analysis of life and death decision making. In T. Bergstrom (Ed.), *Preference and choice in matters of life and death.* (Rep. No. ENG-7478) Los Angeles: University of California, School of Engineering and Applied Science, 1974.

Rasmussen, N. C. *An assessment of accident risks in U. S. commercial nuclear power plans.* (WASH-1400) Washington, D. C.: U. S. Atomic Energy Commission, 1974.

Reed, J., & Reed, R. Status, images, and consequences: Once a criminal always a criminal. *Sociology and Social Research,* 1973, *57,* 460–472.

Rice, D. P., & Cooper, B. S. The economic value of a human life. *American Journal of Public Health,* 1967, *57,* 1954–1966.

Roback, H. Politics and expertise in policy making. In Committee of Public Engineering Policy, *Perspectives on benefit-risk decision making.* Washington, D. C.: National Academy of Engineering, 1972. Pp. 121–133.

Rokeach, M., & Kliejunas, P. Behavior as a function of attitude-toward-object and attitude-toward-situation. *Journal of Personality and Social Psychology,* 1972, *22,* 194–201.

Rorer, L. G. A circuitous route to bootstrapping selection procedures. *ORI Research Bulletin,* 1972, *12*(9).

Rosenbaum, R. M. Antecedents and consequences of three dimensions of causal attribution. Unpublished manuscript, University of California at Los Angeles, 1972.

Rosenberg, S., Nelson, C., & Vivekananthan, P. S. A multidimensional approach to the structure of personality impressions. *Journal of Personality and Social Psychology,* 1968, *9,* 283–294.

Rosenthal, R., & Rosnow, R. L. (Eds.). *Artifact in behavioral research.* New York: Academic Press, 1969.

Ross, L., Lepper, M., & Hubbard, M. Perseverance in self-perception and social perception: Biased attributional processes in the debriefing paradigm. *Journal of Personality and Social Psychology,* 1975, *32,* 880–892.

Ross, M. Salience of reward and intrinsic motivation. *Journal of Personality and Social Psychology,* 1975, *32,* 245–254.

Roth, S., & Kubal, L. The effects of noncontingent reinforcement on tasks of differing importance: Facilitation and learned helplessness effects. *Journal of Personality and Social Psychology,* 1975, *32,* 680–691.

Rotter, J. B. Generalized expectancies for internal versus external control of reinforcement. *Psychological Monographs*, 1966, *80*(1, Whole No. 609).

Russ, F. A. Consumer evaluation of alternative product models. Unpublished doctoral dissertation, Carnegie–Mellon University, 1974.

Russell, B. R. *Philosophy*. New York: Norton, 1927.

Russo, J. E. More information is better: A reevaluation of Jacoby, Speller and Kohn. *Journal of Consumer Research*, 1974, *1*, 68–72.

Russo, J. E., & Rosen, L. D. An eye fixation analysis of multialternative choice. *Memory and Cognition*, 1975, *3*, 267–276.

Ryen, A. H. Cognitive and behavioral consequences of group membership. Paper presented at the American Psychological Association Convention, New Orleans, 1974.

Sarbin, T. R. Contribution to the study of actuarial and individual methods of prediction. *American Journal of Sociology*, 1943, *48*, 593–602.

Sawyer, J. Measurement and prediction, clinical and statistical. *Psychological Bulletin*, 1966, *66*, 178–200.

Schachter, S., & Singer, J. E. Cognitive, social, and physiological determinants of emotional state. *Psychological Review*, 1962, *69*, 379–399.

Schank, R. C. *Conceptual information processing*. Amsterdam: North-Holland Publ., 1975. (a)

Schank, R. C. The structure of episodes in memory. In D. Bobrow & A. Collins (Eds.), *Representation and understanding: Studies in cognitive science*. New York: Academic Press, 1975. Pp. 237–272. (b)

Schank, R. C., & Abelson, R. P. Scripts, plans, and knowledge. Paper presented at the 4th International Conference on Artificial Intelligence, Tbilisi, 1975.

Scheerer, M. Cognitive theory. In G. Lindzey (Ed.), *Handbook of social psychology*, Vol. 1. Reading, Mass.: Addison-Wesley, 1954.

Schelling, T. C. The life you save may be your own. In S. B. Chase, Jr. (Ed.), *Problems in public expenditure analysis*. Washington, D. C.: Brookings Institution, 1968. Pp. 127–176.

Schleimer, J. D. The day they blew up San Onofre. *Bulletin of the Atomic Scientists*, 1974, *30*(8), 24–27.

Schmidt, C. F. Modeling of belief systems. *Second Annual Report of the Rutgers Special Research Resource on Computers in Biomedicine* (Section 3). New Brunswick, N. J.: Rutgers University, Computer Science Department, 1973.

Schmidt, C. F. Understanding human action. Paper presented at Theoretical Issues in Natural Language Processing: An Interdisciplinary Workshop in Computational Linguistics, Psychology, Linguistics, Artificial Intelligence, Cambridge, Mass., June, 1975.

Schmidt, C. F., & D'Addamio, J. A model of the common-sense theory of intention and personal causation. *Proceedings of the Third International Joint Conference on Artificial Intelligence*. Stanford, Calif.: Stanford University, 1973. Pp. 465–471.

Schmidt, F. L. & Hunter, J. E. Racial and ethnic biases in psychological tests: Diverging implications of two definitions of test bias. *American Psychologist*, 1974, *29*, 1–8.

Schneider, B. The perception of organizational climate: The customer's view. *Journal of Applied Psychology*, 1973, *57*, 248–256.

Schonfield, D. Future commitments and successful aging. I. The random sample. *Journal of Gerontology*, 1973, *28*, 189–196.

Schulz, R. The social psychology of death, dying and bereavement. Unpublished manuscript, Duke University, Department of Psychology, 1973.

Schulz, R., & Aderman, D. Effect of residential change on the temporal distance to death of terminal cancer patients. *Omega: Journal of Death and Dying*, 1973, *4*, 157–162.

Schulz, R., & Aderman, D. Clinical research and the stages of dying. *Omega: Journal of Death and Dying*, 1974, *5*, 137–143.

Schwitzgebel, R. Legal and social aspects of the concept of dangerousness. Paper presented at the Midwestern Psychological Association meeting, Chicago, May, 1974.

Scott, J. The use of discretion in determining the severity of punishment for incarcerated offenders. *Journal of Criminal Law and Criminology,* 1974, *65,* 214–224.

Sechrest, D. Comparison of inmate's and staff's judgments of the severity of offenses. *Journal of Research in Crime and Delinquency,* 1969, *6,* 41–55.

Seligman, M. E. P. *Helplessness.* San Francisco: Freeman, 1975.

Seligman, M. E. P. & Groves, D. P. Nontransient learned helplessness. *Psychonomic Science,* 1970, *19,* 191–192.

Seligman, M. E. P., Maier, S. F., & Solomon, R. L. Unpredictable and uncontrollable aversive events. In F. R. Brush (Ed.), *Aversive-conditioning and learning.* New York: Academic Press, 1971. Pp. 347–400.

Selvidge, J. A three-step procedure for assigning probabilities to rare events. In D. Wendt & C. A. J. Viek (Eds.), *Utility, subjective probability, and human decision making.* Dordrecht, Holland: Reidel, 1975. Pp. 199–216.

Shanteau, J. An additive model for sequential decision making. *Journal of Experimental Psychology,* 1970, *85,* 181–191.

Shanteau, J. Descriptive versus normative models of sequential inference judgment. *Journal of Experimental Psychology,* 1972, *93,* 63–68.

Shanteau, J. Component processes in risky decision making. *Journal of Experimental Psychology,* 1974, *103,* 680–691.

Shanteau, J. Averaging versus multiplying combination rules of inference judgment. *Acta Psychologica,* 1975, *39,* 83–89. (a)

Shanteau, J. An information integration analysis of risky decision making. In M. Kaplan & S. Schwartz (Eds.), *Human judgment and decision processes.* New York: Academic Press, 1975. (b)

Shanteau, J., & Anderson, N. H. Test of a conflict model for preference judgment. *Journal of Mathematical Psychology,* 1969, *6,* 312–325.

Shanteau, J., & Anderson N. H. Integration theory applied to judgments of the value of information. *Journal of Experimental Psychology,* 1972, *92,* 266–275.

Shanteau, J., & Nagy, G. A decision theory analysis of dating choice. Paper presented at the meeting of the Midwestern Psychological Association, Chicago, 1974.

Shanteau, J., & Phelps, R. H. Analysis of subadditivity in preferences between gambles defined by verbal phrases. Paper presented at the meeting of the Midwestern Psychological Association, Chicago, 1975.

Shepard, R. N. On subjectively optimum selection among multi-attribute alternatives. In M. W. Shelley, II & G. L. Bryan (Eds.), *Human judgments and optimality.* New York: John Wiley, 1964. Pp. 257–281.

Simon, H. A. Causal ordering and indentifiability. In W. C. Hood & T. C. Koopmans (Eds.), *Studies in econometric method.* New York: Wiley, 1953.

Simon, H. A. A behavioral model of rational choice. *Quarterly Journal of Economics,* 1955, *69,* 99–118.

Simon, H. A. *Models of man.* New York: Wiley, 1957.

Simon, H. A. The logic of heuristic decision making. In N. Rescher (Ed.), *The logic of decision and action.* Pittsburgh, Penna.: University of Pittsburgh Press, 1966. Pp. 1–20.

Simon, H. A. *The sciences of the artificial.* Cambridge, Mass.: MIT Press, 1969.

Simon, H. A. Style in design. In C. M. Eastman (Ed.), *Spatial synthesis in computer-aided building design.* London: Applied Science, 1975. Pp. 287–309.

Simon, H. A., & Chase, W. G. Skill in chess. *American Scientist,* 1973, *61,* 394–403.

Simon, H. A., & Hayes, J. R. Understanding complex task instructions. In D. Klahr (Ed.), *Cognition and instruction.* Hillsdale, N. J.: Lawrence Erlbaum Assoc., 1976.

Simon, H. A., & Newell, A. Human problem solving: The state of the theory in 1970. *American Psychologist,* 1971, *26,* 145–159.

Simon, H. A., & Rescher, N. Cause and counterfactual. *Philosophy of Science,* 1966, *33,* 323–340.

Singer, S. M., & Gottfredson, D. M. *Development of a data base for parole decision-making.* (Supplemental Report 1) Davis, Calif.: National Council on Crime and Delinquency Research Center, 1973.

Sinsheimer, R. L. The brain of Pooh: An essay on the limits of mind. *American Scientist,* 1971, *59,* 20–28.

Skeels, H. M. Adult status of children with contrasting early life experiences. *Monograph for Social Research in Child Development,* 1966, *31,* 3.

Slovic, P. Cue-consistency and cue-utilization in judgment. *American Journal of Psychology,* 1966, *79,* 427–434.

Slovic, P. From Shakespeare to Simon: Speculations–and some evidence–about man's ability to process information. *ORI Research Monograph,* 1972, *12,* 2.

Slovic, P. Limitations on the mind of man: Implications for decision making in the nuclear age. *ORI Research Bulletin,* 1974, *11*(17).

Slovic, P. Choice between equally valued alternatives. *Journal of Experimental Psychology: Human Perception and Performance,* 1975, *1,* 280–287.

Slovic, P., Kunreuther, H., & White, G. F. Decision processes, rationality, and adjustment to natural hazards. In G. F. White (Ed.), *Natural hazards: Local, national, global.* New York: Oxford University Press, 1974. Pp. 187–205.

Slovic, P., & Lichtenstein, S. Relative importance of probabilities and payoffs in risk taking. *Journal of Experimental Psychology,* 1968, *78,* 1–18.

Slovic, P., & Lichtenstein, S. Comparison of Bayesian and regression approaches to the study of information processing in judgment. *Organizational Behavior and Human Performance,* 1974, *11,* 649–744.

Slovic, P., & MacPhillamy, D. Dimensional commensurability and cue utilization in comparative judgment. *Organizational Behavior and Human Performance,* 1974, *11,* 172–194.

Smith, M. B., Bruner, J. S., & White, R. W. *Opinions and personality.* New York: Wiley, 1956.

Soelberg, P. A study of decision making: Job choice. Unpublished doctoral dissertation, Carnegie–Mellon University, 1967.

Sonquist, J. A., & Morgan, J. N. *The detection of interaction effects.* Ann Arbor: University of Michigan, Institute for Social Research, Survey Research Center, 1969.

Sosis, R. Internal-external control and the perception of responsibility of another for an accident. *Journal of Personality and Social Psychology,* 1974, *30,* 393–399.

Spiro, R. J. *Inferential reconstruction in memory for connected discourse* (Tech. Rep. No. 2). Unpublished manuscript, University of Illinois, Laboratory for Cognitive Studies in Education, 1975.

Spitz, R. A. Hospitalism: An inquiry into the genesis of psychiatric conditions in early childhood. In R. S. Eissle *et al.* (Eds.), *The psychoanalytic study of the child,* Vol. 1. New York: International Universities Press, 1945. Pp. 53–74.

Sridharan, N. S. *Architecture of believer. Part 1.* (NIH Rep. CBM-TR-46) New Brunswick, N. J.: Rutgers University, Computer Science Department, 1975.

Srinivasan, C. V. The architecture of coherent information system: A general problem solving system. *Proceedings of the Third International Joint Conference on Artificial Intelligence.* Stanford, Calif.: Stanford University, 1973. Pp. 618–628.

Srinivasan, C. V. *The meta description system.* (NIH Rep. CBM-TR-50) New Brunswick, N. J.: Rutgers University, Computer Science Department, 1975.

St. Augustine. *The confessions of St. Augustine.* (V. J. Bourke, translator) New York: Fathers of the Church, Inc., 1953.

Staelin, R. Another look at A.I.D. *Journal of Advertising Research,* 1971, *11*(5), 23–28.

Starbuck, W. H. Level of aspiration. *Psychological Review,* 1963, *70,* 51–60.

Starr, B. J., & Katkin, E. S. The clinician as an aberrant actuary: Illusory correlation and the Incomplete Sentences Blank. *Journal of Abnormal Psychology,* 1969, *74,* 670–675.

Starr, C. Social benefit versus technological risk. *Science,* 1969, *165,* 1232–1238.

Sternberg, S. High speed scanning in human memory. *Science,* 1966, *153,* 652–654.

Storms, M. D. Videotape and the attribution process: Reversing actors' and observers' points of view. *Journal of Personality and Social Psychology,* 1973, *27,* 165–175.

Storms, M. D., & Nisbett, R. E. Insomnia and the attribution process. *Journal of Personality and Social Psychology,* 1970, *16,* 319–328.

Stotland, E. *The psychology of hope.* San Francisco: Jossey-Bass, 1969.

Stotland, E., & Canon, L. K. *Social psychology: A cognitive approach.* Philadelphia: Saunders, 1972.

Streib, G. F. New roles and activities for retirement. In G. L. Maddox (Ed.), *The future of aging and the aged.* Atlanta, Ga.: Southern Newspapers Publishers Association Foundation, 1971. Pp. 18–53.

Streufert, S., & Streufert, S. C. Effects of conceptual structure, failure, and success on attribution of causality and interpersonal attitudes. *Journal of Personality and Social Psychology,* 1969, *11,* 138–147.

Suls, J. M., & Gutkin, D. C. Children's reactions to an actor as a function of his expectations and of the consequences he receives. Unpublished manuscript, Georgetown University, 1973.

Tajfel, H. Cognitive aspects of prejudice. *Journal of Social Issues,* 1969, *25*(4), 79–97.

Tajfel, H. Experiments in intergroup discrimination. *Scientific American,* 1970, *223*(5), 96–102.

Tajfel, H., & Billig, M. Familiarity and categorization in intergroup behavior. *Journal of Experimental Social Psychology,* 1974, *10,* 159–170.

Tajfel, H., Billig, M., Bundy, R. P., & Flament, C. Social categorization and intergroup behavior. *European Journal of Social Psychology,* 1971, *1,* 149–178.

Tajfel, H., Sheikh, A. A., & Gardner, R. C. Content of stereotypes and the inference of similarity between members of stereotyped groups. *Acta Psychologica,* 1964, *22,* 191–201.

Tajfel, H., & Wilkes, A. L. Classification and quantitative judgment. *British Journal of Psychology,* 1963, *54,* 101–114.

Taylor, D. W. Decision making and problem solving. In J. G. March (Ed.), *Handbook of organizations.* New York: Rand McNally, 1965. Pp. 48–86.

Taylor, S. E., & Fiske, S. T. Point of view and perceptions of causality. *Journal of Personality and Social Psychology,* 1975, *32,* 439–445.

Taylor, S. E., & Fiske, S. T. The token in the small group: Research findings and theoretical implications. In J. Sweeney (Ed.), *Psychology and politics.* New Haven, Conn.: Yale University Press, in press.

Tesser, A. Toward a theory of self-generated attitude change. Unpublished manuscript, University of Georgia, 1975.

Thaler, R., & Rosen, S. The value of saving a life: Evidence from the labor market. Unpublished manuscript, University of Rochester, Department of Economics, 1973.

Thorndike, R. L. Concepts of culture-fairness. *Journal of Educational Measurement,* 1971, *8,* 63–70.

Torrance, G. Generalized cost-effectiveness model for the evaluation of health programs. *McMaster University Faculty of Business Research Series,* 1970, *101.*

Tulving, E. Episodic and semantic memory. In E. Tulving & W. Donaldson (Eds.), *Organization of memory.* New York: Academic Press, 1972. Pp. 381–403.

Tversky, A. Intransitivity of preferences. *Psychological Review,* 1969, *76,* 31–48.

Tversky, A. Choice by elimination. *Journal of Mathematical Psychology,* 1972, *9,* 341–367. (a)

Tversky, A. Elimination by aspects: A theory of choice. *Psychological Review,* 1972, *79,* 281–299. (b)

Tversky, A., & Kahneman, D. The belief in the "law of small numbers." *Psychological Bulletin,* 1971, *76,* 105–110.

Tversky, A., & Kahneman, D. Availability: A heuristic for judging frequency and probability. *Cognitive Psychology,* 1973, *5,* 207–232.

Tversky, A., & Kahneman, D. Judgment under uncertainty: Heuristics and biases. *Science,* 1974, *185,* 1124–1131.

Valle, V., & Frieze, I. The stability of causal attributions as a mediator in changing expectations for success. *Journal of Personality and Social Psychology,* 1976, *33,* 579–587.

Verwoerdt, A., & Elmore, J. Psychological reactions in fatal illness. I: The prospect of impending death. *Journal of the American Geriatric Society,* 1967, *15,* 9–19.

von Hirsch, A. Prediction of criminal conduct and preventive confinement of convicted persons. *Buffalo Law Review,* 1972, *21,* 717–758.

Vonnegut, K. *Slaughterhouse five.* New York: Delacorte, 1969.

Wainer, H. Estimating coefficients in linear models: It don't make no nevermind. *Psychological Bulletin,* 1976, *83,* 213–217.

Walster, E., Aronson, V., Abrahams, D., & Rottmann, L. Importance of physical attractiveness in dating behavior. *Journal of Personality and Social Psychology,* 1966, *6,* 508–516.

Waterman, D., & Newell, A. Protocol analysis as a task for artificial intelligence. *Artificial Intelligence,* 1971, *2,* 285–318.

Waterman, D., & Newell, A. PAS-II: An interactive task-free version of an automatic protocol analysis system. *Proceedings of the International Joint Conference on Artificial Intelligence.* London: British Computer Society, 1973.

Watson, J. S. Smiling, cooing, and the 'game.' Paper presented at the American Psychological Association Meeting, Miami Beach, Florida, 1970.

Weigel, R. H., Vernon, D. T. A., & Tognacci, L. N. Specificity of the attitude as a determinant of attitude-behavioral congruence. *Journal of Personality and Social Psychology,* 1974, *30,* 724–728.

Weiner, B. (Ed.). *Achievement motivation and attribution theory.* Morristown, N. J.: General Learning Press, 1974. (a)

Weiner, B. Achievement motivation as conceptualized by an attribution theorist. In B. Weiner (Ed.), *Achievement motivation and attribution theory.* Morristown, N. J.: General Learning Press, 1974. (b)

Weiner, B., Frieze, I., Kukla, A., Reed, L., Rest, S., & Rosenbaum, R. *Perceiving the causes of success and failure.* Morristown, N. J.: General Learning Press, 1971.

Weiner, B., Heckhausen, H., Meyer, W., & Cook, R. E. Causal ascriptions and achievement behavior: Conceptual analysis of effort and reanalysis of locus of control. *Journal of Personality and Social Psychology,* 1972, *21,* 239–248.

Weiner, B., & Kukla, A. An attributional analysis of achievement motivation. *Journal of Personality and Social Psychology,* 1970, *15,* 1–20.

Weisman, A. D., & Hackett, T. P. Predilection to death. *Psychosomatic Medicine,* 1961, *23,* 232–256.

Wessman, A. E., & Ricks, D. F. *Mood and personality.* New York: Holt, Rinehart & Winston, 1966.

White, G. F. *Choice of adjustment to floods.* (Department of Geography Research Paper No. 93) Chicago: University of Chicago Press, 1964.

White, R. W. Motivation reconsidered: The concept of competence. *Psychological Review,* 1959, *66,* 297–333.

Whiteley, R. H. Internal–external locus of control, subjective probability of success, decision consequence and other selected variables as factors in predecisional information and acquisition. Unpublished doctoral dissertation, University of California at Berkeley, 1968.

Wicker, A. W. An examination of the "other variables" explanation of attitude-behavior inconsistency. *Journal of Personality and Social Psychology,* 1971, *19,* 18–30.

Wiggins, J. H. Earthquake safety in the city of Long Beach based on the concept of balanced risk. In Committee of Public Engineering Policy (Eds.), *Perspectives on benefit-risk decision making.* Washington, D.C.: National Academy of Engineering, 1972. Pp. 87–95.

Wiggins, J. H. Toward a coherent natural hazards policy. *Civil Engineering–ASCE,* 1974, 74–76.

Wiggins, N., Hoffman, P. J., & Taber, T. Types of judges and cue utilization in judgments of intelligence. *Journal of Personality and Social Psychology,* 1969, *12,* 52–59.

Wiggins, N., & Kohen, E. S. Man versus model of man revisited: The forecasting of graduate school success. *Journal of Personality and Social Psychology,* 1971, *19,* 100–106.

Wilkie, W. L. Analysis of effects of information load. *Journal of Marketing Research,* 1974, *11,* 462–466.

Wilkins, L. T. *Social deviance.* Englewood Cliffs, N. J.: Prentice-Hall, 1965.

Wilkins, L. T. Information overload: Peace or war with the computer? *Journal of Criminal Law and Criminology,* 1973, *64,* 190–197.

Wilkins, L. T., Gottfredson, D. M., Robison, J. O., & Sadowsky, A. *Information selection and use in parole decision making.* (Supplemental Rep. 5) Davis, Calif.: National Council on Crime and Delinquency Research Center, 1973.

Wilks, S. S. Weighing systems for linear functions of correlated variables when there is no dependent variable. *Psychometrika,* 1938, *3,* 23–40.

Wohlford, P. Extension of personal time, affective states, and expectation of personal death. *Journal of Personality and Social Psychology,* 1966, *3,* 297–333.

Wortman, C. B. Some determinants of perceived control. *Journal of Personality and Social Psychology,* 1975, *31,* 282–294.

Wright, P. Consumer choice strategies: Simplifying vs. optimizing. *Journal of Marketing Research,* 1975, *12,* 60–67.

Yntema, D. B., & Torgerson, W. S. Man-computer cooperation in decisions requiring common sense. *IRE Transactions of the Group on Human Factors in Electronics,* 1961, *HFE-2,* 20–26.

Zajonc, R. B. Cognitive theories in social psychology. In G. Lindzey & E. Aronson (Eds.), *Handbook of social psychology,* Vol. 1 (2nd ed.) Reading, Mass.: Addison-Wesley, 1968.

Subject Index

A

Additive model, 203–204, 208, 212–216, 219, *see also* Linear decision rules
Aging, *see* Control and predictability, in old age
Analytic tools, 246–247, *see also* Information-processing approach
Assessment of human potential, 5–8, *see also* Additive models; Prediction
  bootstrapping, 5–6
  linear composites, use of, 6–8
  statistical versus clinical judgment, 5
Attention, 87–88, 159
  to distinctive stimuli, 87–88
  focus of, 159
Attitudes, 40–42, 127–133, *see also* Scripts, attitudes, relation to; Stereotypes
Attribution theory, 16–21, 26–31, 47–66, 73–74, 95–127
  achievement (success/failure) events, 95–112
  consensus information, use of, 114–127
  experimental paradigm, validity of, 101–103, *see also* Experimental paradigm in social psychology, comparison to; Information-processing approach
  heuristics, relation to, 26–28
  individual differences, 20–21, 28–31, 49–50, 108–112
  information utilization, 26–28, 73–74, 96–112

Attribution theory
  information utilization (*cont.*)
    information-processing framework, 96–99
    sequential versus simultaneous, 103–108
  parole decision, application to, 18–21, 28–31
  plans and motives, 47–66

B

Base-rate information, use of, 159, 161, *see also* Concrete versus abstract information; Prediction; Probabilistic information processing
Bounded rationality, 168–169, 183, 255–256, *see also* Cognitive limitations

C

Categorization, 83–88
  and similarity, 85–87
Causation, 256–257
Cognitive dysfunction, 3, 11
  and cognitive conceit, 7
  motivation explanations, 4, 9
  philosophical background, 3
Cognitive limitations, 3–4, 10, 23–24, 75–76, 88–91, 168–173, *see also* Bounded rationality; Heuristics; Stereotypes
  illusory correlation, 23–24, 88–91
  in social psychological theories, 75–76

287

Information-processing approach, (contd.) 261–262, see also Cognitive limitations; Heuristics
computer simulation, 47–66
of attributions of plans and motives, 47–66
experimental paradigm in social psychology, comparison to, 70–74, 76
methodological requisites, 261–262
to parole decisions, 16–17, 21–32
process-tracing techniques, 28–31
Information seeking, 157–160, 187–202, see also Consumer behavior
individual differences in, 194–202
amount of information sought, 196
education, and, 201
final choice, and, 200
number of brands considered, 198
previous experience, effects of, 199
price effects, 200
sources of information used, 195–196
quantity of information effects, 186–189, 193
search strategies, 192–194
Information theory, 3

L

Lexicographic model, 205, 210–211, 213–216
Linear decision rules, 262–265, see also Additive model

M

Memory, 34–36, 52–54, 156, see also Heuristics, availability
for human action, 52–54
long-term, 156
for scripts, 34–36

P

Plans and motives, see Attribution theory, plans and motives
Prediction, 15–16, 19–20, 22–23, 28–31, 37–40, 98–99, 124–127, see also Control and predictability; Probabilistic information processing; Stereotypes
actuarial devices, 22–23, 38–40
consensus information, use of, 22–23, 124–127

Prediction, (contd.)
of parole risk, 15–16, 22–23, 28–31, 40
stability of attributions and, 19–20, 98–99
using scripts, 37–40
Probabilistic information processing, 169–172, see also Cognitive limitations; Heuristics; Prediction
anchoring and adjustment, 172
errors of prediction, 170
hindsight biases, 172
and misjudging sample implications, 169
Problem representation, 246–247
Problem solving, 10, 155–161, see also General problem solver
barriers to, 10
ill-structured problems, 155–156, 158
means–ends analysis, 158

R

Redundant information, 10, 159–160
preference for, 10, 24–25
Regression analysis, 226–227, 238
Risk-benefit analysis, 174–183, see also Probabilistic information processing
evaluating low-probability, high-consequence events, 174–178
evaluating scenarios, 177
fault-tree analysis, 175–177
justification, concept of, 181
perceived risk, 180
value of life and, 180–181

S

Satisficing, 156–158, 190, 205, 211, 213–216, see also Bounded rationality
Scripts, 33–45, 256
attitudes, relation to, 40–42
behavior, mediation of, 42–45
decision making, use in, 37–40
propositional networks, relation to, 36–37
types, 34–35
Self-perceptions, 116–123
attitudes, 122–123
emotions, 116–121
Social perception, 157–160
Societal risk taking, 165–168
and natural hazards, 166–167
and nuclear power, 167
policy issues in, 166